Good Quality

Good Quality

THE ROUTINIZATION OF SPERM BANKING IN CHINA

Ayo Wahlberg

UNIVERSITY OF CALIFORNIA PRESS

University of California Press, one of the most distinguished university presses in the United States, enriches lives around the world by advancing scholarship in the humanities, social sciences, and natural sciences. Its activities are supported by the UC Press Foundation and by philanthropic contributions from individuals and institutions. For more information, visit www.ucpress.edu.

University of California Press
Oakland, California

Library of Congress Cataloging-in-Publication Data

Names: Wahlberg, Ayo, author.
Title: Good quality : the routinization of sperm banking in China / Ayo Wahlberg.
Description: Oakland, California : University of California Press, [2018] | Includes bibliographical references and index. |
Identifiers: LCCN 2018006229 (print) | LCCN 2018006743 (ebook) | ISBN 9780520969995 (ebook) | ISBN 9780520297777 (cloth : alk. paper) | ISBN 9780520297784 (pbk. : alk. paper)
Subjects: LCSH: Sperm banks—China. | Sperm donors—China. | Artificial insemination—China. | China—Social life and customs.
Classification: LCC QP255 (ebook) | LCC QP255 .w28 2018 (print) | DDC 362.17/830951—dc23
LC record available at https://lccn.loc.gov/2018006229

26 25 24 23 22 21 20 19 18 17
10 9 8 7 6 5 4 3 2 1

For Helle, Mathias, and Jonas

Contents

Illustrations

TABLES

Acknowledgments

As is so often the case, serendipity played its part in the making of this book. Had I not met Lu Guangxiu through my position as a research fellow on the European Commission–funded BIONET project in 2007, I would not have had the opportunity to visit her fertility clinic in Changsha and eventually to carry out ethnographic research at China's oldest and largest sperm bank. Ever since my first visit to Changsha, capital of Hunan Province, in the fall of 2007, I have had my sights set on accounting for the astounding rise of a reproductive technology like sperm banking in China. I could not have done so without the help of a vast group of informants, colleagues, collaborators, assistants, friends, and family.

In Changsha, I owe special thanks to Professor Lu Guangxiu not only for her committed support of my research but also for her insistence that anthropological insights have value in medical settings like those found at the CITIC-Xiangya Reproductive and Genetic Hospital and the Hunan Sperm Bank. Changsha is my home away from home when I am in China thanks in large part to the hospitality of Lu Guangxiu and her family. A particular thanks to Lin Ge who has been supportive of my research during and in between my visits. Throughout the many years of research that went into the pages that follow, I have had the pleasure and benefit of working closely with He Jing (Ginny), who has been a vital support. Without Ginny's generous and expert assistance in all manner of research and not-so-research-related matters, this book would not have been possible. I am so very grateful to her and her family.

The Hunan Sperm Bank in Changsha was my primary field site and I have consequently spent many hours with the team there over the last many years. I owe Professor Fan Liqing and Director Zhu Wenbing as well as all of their staff members huge thanks for their patience and willingness to answer countless questions. I would in particular like to thank Dr. Nie Hongchuan, whose support has been invaluable during fieldwork, through WeChat, weekend bike rides, and over meals with his wonderful family. I would also like to thank Hu Jing for her kind assistance during my stays in Changsha. Each of the following staff members deserve thanks for allowing me to participate in their daily work at the sperm bank: Li Baishun, Xin Niu, Huang Xiuhai, Yang Yang, Liu Wen, Wu Huilan, Jiang Hongwei, Long Xingyu, Luo Qing, Zhou Haibin, Guo Zhijie, Dai Haibo, Zou Min, Zhang Jie, Wu Jian, Tan Zhilin, Zhou Gaojian, Ou Lingzhi, Sun Zheng, Liu Hao, Guo Huihua, Yang Jinhua, and Tang Ruilin. Moreover, I am especially grateful to the many donors and infertile couples who agreed to share their stories with me.

For help elsewhere in China I would like to thank Li Zheng, director of the Shanghai Sperm Bank, as well as Tang Lixin, the late director of the Guangdong Sperm Bank, for hosting me and facilitating interviews with donors during my visits to their respective facilities in 2013. In Beijing I would like to thank the director of the fertility clinic at the Third Hospital, Professor Qiao Jie, and Li Rong, as well as Professor Cong Yali of the Medical Ethics Unit at the Peking University Health Science Center, where I spent a semester as a visiting fellow in the fall of 2007.

In carrying out the research for this book I have relied on and received the assistance of a great number of persons to whom I owe a debt of gratitude for helping in the collecting of documents, transcription of interviews, and translation. For translation help during interviews my thanks to He Jing, Long Xingyu, Nie Hongchuan, Hu Jing, and Tang Ruilin. For help in transcription and translation of interviews and various documents my thanks to Vicky Wang, Katherine Tchemerinsky, Yang Jiani, He Jing, Nie Hongchuan, Long Xingyu, Wang Xingming, Tang Wuilin, Lu Haiyuan, Xu Fang, and

Aelred Doyle. The research for this book was made possible, in part, by a generous *Sapere Aude* Young Researcher Grant (no. 10–094341) from the Danish Council for Independent Research, which I would like to sincerely thank. Independent research funding is an increasingly endangered species and I hope this book can play its part in attesting to the importance of long-term, independent research.

Over the last decade, while working on this book, I have had the great fortune of working in a number of conceptually fertile research environments. From 2003 to 2009 I was based at the BIOS Centre, London School of Economics. I can safely say that I would not be the scholar that I am today had I not had the opportunity to work with Nikolas Rose, Sarah Franklin, Ilina Singh, Filippa Lentzos, Carlos Novas, Linsey McGoey, Scott Vrecko, David Reubi, Chris Hamilton, John Macartney, Megan Clinch, Joy Zhang, Michael Barr, Amy Hinterberger, Des Fitzgerald, and many, many more who spent time at the BIOS Centre in the noughts.

In 2009, I was once again fortunate when securing a position at the Department of Anthropology, University of Copenhagen, yet another vibrant research community. My thanks go to all of my colleagues at the department, especially members of the Health and Life Conditions and the Technology and Political Economy researcher groups who have shared their thoughts on various chapter drafts over the past years. A special thanks to Tine Gammeltoft, with whom I have had the privilege of working very closely ever since I arrived at the department and who patiently read through every chapter of this book, providing important feedback.

Housed in a building just fifty meters from our department (what luck!) is the University of Copenhagen's innovative Center for Medical Science and Technology Studies (MeSTS), where I enjoyed a semester as a visiting scholar in early 2009. My thanks to Lene Koch, Klaus Høyer, Mette Nordahl Svendsen, Anja Bornø Jensen, Maria Olejaz Tellerup, Sebastian Mohr, Zainab Afshan Sheikh, and Stine Willum Adrian (based at Aalborg University) for their insights and feedback on various chapter drafts. At the Copenhagen University Hospital's (Rigshospitalet) fertility clinic I would like to thank Anders Nyboe Andersen and Søren Ziebe as well as Lone Schmidt from the University of Copenhagen for supporting my research project through the years and for their hospitality during exchange visits from Changsha.

At the University of Cambridge, I have benefited greatly from spending time with the Reproductive Sociology Research Group during the writing of the book. My thanks to Sarah Franklin, Janelle Lamoreaux, Katie Dow, Noémie Merleau-Ponty, Zeynep Gürtin, Karen Jent, Robert Pralat, Marcin Smietana, Mwenza Blell, and Lucy van de Wiel. Likewise, participating in the IVF Global Histories conference at Yale University in April 2015 was a huge inspiration. My thanks to the organizers Marcia Inhorn and Sarah Franklin as well as participants Aditya Bharadwaj, Bob Simpson, Andrea Whittaker, Daphna Birenbaum-Carmeli, Soraya Tremayne, Elizabeth Roberts, Viola Hörbst, Charis Thompson, Sandra Gonzalez-Santos, Michal Nahman, Sebastian Mohr, and Trudie Gerrits. Learning about national IVF histories from around the world has shaped many aspects of this book. Also in the United States I would like to thank Lisa Handwerker for sharing her fieldwork experiences in Beijing in the early years of reproductive technologies in 1990s China and for her comments on my historical account of the development of reproductive technologies in China. Thanks are also due to Reed Malcolm and two anonymous reviewers from the University of California Press for comments that have greatly improved this book. For guiding me through the production process special thanks are due to Zuha Kahn, Tom Sullivan, Nicholle Robertson, and Kate Warne.

Parts of chapter 1 appeared in *Reproductive Biomedicine & Society Online* as "The Birth and Routinization of IVF in China" (2016); parts of chapter 2 appeared in *The Right to Life and the Value of Life*, edited by Jon Yorke (2010), as "Assessing Vitality: Infertility and 'Good Life' in Urban China"; and parts of chapter 3 appeared in *Anthropology and Nature*, edited by Kirsten Hastrup (2013), as "Human Activity between Nature and Society: The Negotiation of Infertility in China," as well as in *Science, Technology & Society* as "Exposed biologies and the banking of reproductive vitality in China." (2018) My thanks to Routledge, Ashgate, Sage, and Elsevier for permissions to reproduce sections from these publications.

And finally, long-term research endeavors such as the one that lies behind this book would simply not be possible without the love and support of family and friends. A special thanks to my parents, who showed my brothers and me the world before we realized there was anything else. And last, but most importantly, thank you Helle, Mathias, and Jonas for always reminding me how good life is.

Abbreviations

AID	artificial insemination by donor
AID	artificial insemination by donor
AIH	artificial insemination by husband
ART	assisted reproductive technology
CCTV	China Central Television
ED	endocrine disruptor
GLP	good laboratory practices
GMP	good manufacturing practices
ICSI	intra cytoplasmic sperm injection
IVF	in vitro fertilization
MCS	multiple chemical sensitivity
PGD	preimplantation genetic diagnosis
RMB	renminbi (Chinese yuan)
SOP	standard operating procedure
SRT	selective reproductive technology
TDS	testicular dysgenesis syndrome
TILT	toxicant-induced loss of tolerance

Introduction

SPERM CRISIS

In the early months of 1981, Lu Huilin received a letter at his office in the bustling, river-laced city of Changsha, capital of China's Hunan Province. The letter was from a patient who said he suffered from azoospermia, the severest form of male infertility. He had read somewhere that farmers were creating sperm banks for cows and pigs, prompting him to write to Lu, a prominent medical geneticist at Xiangya Medical College: "Why can't you build one for humans? I could be your first experiment!"

Lu had developed a keen interest in reproductive technologies ever since news of Louise Brown, the world's first so-called "test tube baby" had filtered through to Changsha, some months after her birth in England in 1978. Conditions were harsh for scientists in the years following the Cultural Revolution; clinical and laboratory facilities were dilapidated and access to equipment and the latest scientific findings all but nonexistent. Nonetheless, moved and perhaps also intrigued by the man's plea, Lu had an idea. He placed the letter into a new envelope together with a cover note and posted it to his daughter, Lu Guangxiu, in Beijing, who recounts:

> My father forwarded this letter to me in Beijing. At that time, I had just finished three months of study in Beijing, so I thought about it and asked my teachers at the Chinese Academy whether there is a sperm bank in Beijing.

1

They said there is a sperm bank for cows in the countryside, so I rode two hours by bicycle [laughter] to the countryside to have a look at the sperm bank. Only one whole afternoon, I got to know how to freeze the sperm, how to use yolk and glycerol to freeze the cow sperm, only in this afternoon. I learned quickly! After that I came back to Changsha. I figured that we can get oocytes through our clinical work, but if there is no sperm, we still won't be able to do any research on in vitro culturing. So if we establish a sperm bank, this is one way we can treat the patients with this kind of disease while at the same time also being good for our research. So that's how we started our first human sperm bank in 1981.

Fast-forward to 2011. It's a sunny day in May, the relentless kind that sees people scurrying for the shade of roadside trees and the borrowed air-conditioning of corner shops. I jump off bus 405 as it stops along Furong Road, a congested six-lane thoroughfare, which, much like the Xiangjiang River, splits Changsha north to south. Just off Furong, Xiangya Road is its usual bustling self as cars honk and pedestrians push past pharmacies, food stalls, clothes shops, vegetable stands, shoe-shiners, and fortune tellers. It is my first day of fieldwork on a project about sperm banking in China, although not my first time on Xiangya Road. Indeed, I know what to expect as I approach 84 Xiangya Road where the fifteen-story CITIC-Xiangya Reproductive and Genetic Hospital lies, home to one of the world's largest sperm banks and fertility clinics. Even so, I'm astounded. Hordes of people are milling around the entrance, a much larger crowd than I had seen on previous visits. Most of them are there to seek fertility treatment, clutching their queuing tickets as they wait their turn to be called to the triage desk that manages inquiries from new patients. I squeeze my way through the crowds outside and enter the hospital lobby. The cacophony is thunderous. Patients are impatiently asking when their turn might come while white-coated doctors and pink-coated nurses somehow go about their daily routines, weaving through the throngs as they do. Two men are wheeling a large tank of liquid nitrogen toward the elevator, pleading for headway as they inch forward. Nothing stands still as I ponder how best to make my way to the sperm bank on the fourth floor. Let one of my sperm donor informants take it from here:

You know this hospital . . . it is full of infertile couples . . . actually they are ten times more than we donors. We could also see their faces and that would

Figure 1. Crowds congregate outside the CITIC-Xiangya Reproductive and Genetic Hospital.

make us feel anxious. Ehh, usually I get upstairs by foot not elevator because the elevator is always full and cannot hold me. . . . When I arrived here [on the fourth floor], I thought this place is not exactly what I thought the donor room would be. First of all, this is too small, too crowded and full of people. I thought there would only be a few boys who would want to be a donor but I . . . what I found was a room especially for donors but I couldn't find a seat, it was too full! (twenty-one-year-old student, Changsha)

From crude and uneasy beginnings sperm banking has become a routine part of China's pervasive and restrictive reproductive complex within the space of thirty years. Today, there are twenty-three sperm banks spread out across China's twenty-two provinces, the biggest of which screen some two thousand to four thousand potential donors each year.[1] Those who qualify donate ten to fifteen times over a six-month period in return for the satisfaction of being able to help involuntarily childless couples as well as monetary compensation for their inconvenience. The first baby conceived from frozen donor sperm in China was born in 1983 in Changsha, but the provincial government in Hunan prohibited the practice of artificial insemination in 1989. This ban has since been overturned, and in 2003 it was superseded by national legislation, which, for the first time, legalized and regulated the provision of assisted reproductive technologies (ARTs), including sperm banking and assisted insemination by donor (AID). It is thus especially in the last ten years that sperm banking has become routinized in China with the closure of "rogue" banks and the establishing of strict licensing requirements and operating procedures. Routinization notwithstanding, with an estimated one to two million azoospermic men in China (men who are unable to produce their own sperm), the demand for donor sperm remains insatiable. China's twenty-three sperm banks simply cannot keep up, spurring the directors to publicly lament chronic shortages and even warn of a national "sperm crisis" (*jingzi weiji*). As we will learn, this crisis is related firstly to an apparent national decline in sperm quality. The possible causes—lifestyle changes and the toxic effects of environmental pollution—have become matters of concern and objects of scientific research in China and elsewhere. And secondly, the crisis is related to chronic national shortages of donor sperm (amounting to a "state of emergency") despite the efforts of sperm banks to mobilize potential donors on university campuses throughout the country. Faced with such a crisis, sperm banks in China have their work cut out for them.

The routinization of sperm banking in China has by no means been inevitable, fraught as it has been with paradoxes, hurdles, setbacks, crises, injunctions, taboos, limits, and reservations. To begin with, the condition for which sperm banking and AID were being developed to address in the 1980s, namely infertility, was and remains contested in China. As Judith Farquhar has argued, in many Chinese *fu ke* (women's medicine) clinics in the early 1980s, infertility was not seen to result "from a permanent structural abnormality of the body but rather from an (often subtle) deficiency of normal physiological functions" (Farquhar, 1991, p. 374). An inability to conceive children was of course nothing new in China in the 1980s and various treatments aimed at redressing such diagnosed deficiencies were available from practitioners of traditional Chinese medicine. And so, when the likes of Lu Guangxiu in Changsha and Zhang Lizhu in Beijing began developing reproductive technologies in the early 1980s, biomedical interpretations of infertility had to contend with deficiency interpretations treated by practitioners of Chinese medicine in *fu ke* clinics. Some doctors resisted "the hegemonic medical models" (Handwerker, 1998, pp. 193–97) and encouraged patients to visit traditional Chinese practitioners.[2] To this day, couples' quests for conception often include visits to both Chinese and biomedical clinics, just as practices in these clinics often combine diagnostics and/or therapies from both versions. Moreover, while the subspecialty of *fu ke* within Chinese medicine has an ancient history and a normative focus on the reproductive body, Everett Zhang has shown that the first *nan ke* (men's medicine) clinic did not emerge in China until 1983, thanks not so much to a biomedical concern with male infertility, as with the newly biomedicalized problem of impotence (Zhang, 2007; 2015). Notwithstanding the availability of microscope-aided sperm count tests since the early 1980s, childlessness was (and remains) exceptionally gendered with women more often than not bearing its burdens even when male factor infertility is the more likely culprit.

Secondly, Zhang Lizhu and Lu Guangxiu began experimenting with reproductive technologies at exactly the same time that an unprecedented effort to engineer national fertility was being rolled out across China. Over the course of the late 1970s and 1980s, China's reproductive complex was configured to resolutely restrict fertility (Greenhalgh, 2008; Greenhalgh & Winckler, 2005). Indeed, China's so-called "one-child policy" is one of its most internationally recognizable features today, even if it has since been tweaked into a "two-child policy."[3] Launched in the late 1970s by late chairman of the Communist Party, Deng Xiaoping, China's family planning policies enforced birth control through a series of targets set at regional and local levels aimed at lowering China's high fertility rate, which was considered a hindrance to economic development. Family planning authorities were charged with meeting such targets through the provision of contraception, sterilization, and abortion services as well as through the fining of couples who exceeded their quota of children—targets that have at times been forcibly realized. Attempts to develop reproductive technologies in order to *promote* fertility in the 1980s were predictably seen by some state officials and scientists as conflicting with ongoing efforts to stringently prevent births (see Handwerker, 2002; chapter 1). In the chapters that follow, we will learn how assisted reproductive technologies, including sperm banking, eventually settled alongside ligation operations, abortions, and maternal and infant health care as technologies of *birth control* within China's restrictive reproductive complex. Indeed, the perceived contradiction between the one-child policy and ARTs is so great that I shared my sperm donor informant's sense of astonishment at the vast numbers of infertile couples and potential donors upon visiting the sperm bank in Changsha for the first time in 2007.

Thirdly, as already noted, the decade-long Cultural Revolution (1966–1976) had had a destructive impact on scientific research in China, with scientists and teachers among those elite groups that were persecuted by the Red Guards (see Dikötter, 1998). Conditions for carrying out laboratory research in the early 1980s were crude, just as access to national or international research findings was sparse. And, as if these challenges weren't enough, the fact that requisite research experiments required the soliciting and collection of sperm and eggs made matters more complicated. While eggs would eventually be medically procured in connection with certain forms of surgical procedures carried out in hospitals, "manual" sperm collection was surrounded by taboo, considered "dirty," immoral, and harmful. Indeed, the one proverb I would hear repeated most often during my fieldwork was "one drop of sperm is the same as ten drops of blood" (*yi di jing shi di xue*), albeit more often than not by donors laughing at the "old-fashioned" views of their parents and grandparents. The proverb has its origins in Chinese medical texts, which conceptualize semen (*jing*) as a vital essence that should be preserved to maintain health (Shapiro, 1998). In the early years of sperm banking, finding voluntary donors was a constant struggle and scientists had to delicately negotiate already scarce laboratory access from skeptical and disapproving colleagues in order to carry out all but clandestine research on gamete fertilization and embryo development. The 1980s were truly trying years for experimentation with reproductive technologies in China.

And finally, during the 1990s, improvement of population quality became an equally important demographic goal for the Communist Party in China (Greenhalgh, 2010). Family planning slogans, commonly seen displayed on billboards throughout the country, were adjusted accordingly to proclaim "Control population growth, raise the quality of the population" or "In raising the quality of the population, family planning is of vital importance." This time it was medical doctors in charge of genetic counseling and prenatal care who were given the task of "improving the quality of the newborn population" (P. R. China 1994, Article 1) through premarital health checks as well as prenatal screening and testing as means to prevent the birth of children "suffering from a genetic disease of a serious nature" or "a defect of a serious nature" (ibid., Articles 18 and 19; see also Sleeboom-Faulkner, 2010a & b; Zhu 2013; chapter 2). With this law, family planning in China expanded its responsibility beyond limiting the number of children being born to assuring the quality and health of newborns. When ARTs were legalized in 2003, regulations stipulated that fertility clinics "must obey national population and family planning legislation and policies," which included "promot[ing] population quality" (MoH, 2003a, pp. B1, E1). As a result, sperm banking in China is today an ART and an SRT (selective reproductive technology), by which I mean a technology used not only to assist involuntarily childless couples to conceive, but also to prevent or promote the birth of certain kinds of children (Gammeltoft & Wahlberg, 2014). In the face of a looming national "sperm crisis," sperm banking has been seen as a way to achieve better population quality through the selective recruitment of "high-quality" (*suzhi gao*) donors.

At the same time, however, fears about the detrimental impact of consanguineous marriage on population quality have emerged as a hindrance to the business model of Chinese sperm banks. Chinese regulations strictly limit the number of women who can give birth to a child with sperm from a single donor to five. The most common explanation I heard for this "restrictive" limit is that it reduces the risk of unwitting consanguineous marriage (which in turn is seen to increase the risk of birth defects) while also reducing the risk of unwittingly spreading a genetic disease (should a sperm donor turn out to have a late-onset genetic disorder that was not caught through standard screening procedures). China's five-women's-pregnancies limit coupled with the sheer demographic and epidemiological scale of male infertility has generated unique and arduous daily routines in Chinese sperm banks, which need to recruit and screen substantially more (potential) donors than Western sperm banks do to serve similar numbers of families.[4] At the same time, infertile couples will often have to wait two to three years before being able to access donor sperm because of a chronic "state of emergency" at sperm banks.

And so, to get to grips with how a medical technology like sperm banking came to be an established practice in China over the past three decades or so, we need to understand how this practice has been shaped by (among many other conditions) the crude laboratory conditions available in China throughout the 1980s (and indeed into the 1990s), the co-circulation of deficiency and biomedicalized interpretations of infertility in clinics and among infertile couples, a family planning program designed to prevent rather than promote birth, taboos around sex and masturbation, and anxieties about possible unwitting consanguineous marriages between donor siblings. Only then can we account for the unique form of sperm banking that we find in China today.

SPERM BANKING IN CHINA

In what follows, I will show how sperm banking came to be a routinized part of China's restrictive reproductive complex. It is the making of sperm banking rather than the experience of donors or couples undergoing AID that is the object of my ethnography. As such, *Good Quality* is what I would call an assemblage ethnography, combining not so much multisited (Marcus, 1995) as a site-multiplied tracking strategy with a cartographic partiality toward, again not so much "the world system" that multisited ethnography was originally proposed as a methodological response to,[5] as the *configurations* found within infrastructures, assemblages, complexes, or *dispositifs* on the part of the ethnographer. These interrelated concepts have been proposed by social scientists in recent decades to try to capture the ways in which particular juridical, medical, social, economic, cultural, and institutional configurations are consolidated over time and in particular places. Michel Foucault spoke of what he called a *dispositif* or apparatus: "a thoroughly heterogeneous ensemble consisting of discourses, institutions, architectural forms, regulatory decisions, laws, administrative measures, scientific statements, philosophical, moral, and philanthropic propositions. . . . Such are the elements of the apparatus. The apparatus itself is the system of relations that can be established between these elements" (Foucault, 1977). As examples, we have, a decade later in 1989, and invoking American president Dwight Eisenhower's notion of a "military-industrial complex" from 1961, historian of science David Turnbull arguing that the development of a malaria vaccine through an Australia–Papua New Guinea collaboration in the 1980s could only take place as a "consequence of a complex of technical, social, economic, and political factors" (Turnbull, 1989, p. 283). Within the field of contemporary American health care, anthropologist Sharon Kaufman has likewise mobilized Arnold Relman's (1980) writings on America's "new medical-industrial complex" to examine the "increasing encroachment of the private sector into research, technology development, therapeutics, and insurance reimbursement" (Kaufman, 2015, p. 54). Similarly, in her analysis of the development of a repro-tech sector in Israel, Sigrid Vertommen has charted the "emergence of a reproductive-embryonic industrial complex in which the interests of a pronatalist Jewish state and a biomedical establishment—consisting of academic entrepreneurs, venture capitalists, biotech companies, and pharmaceutical giants—have coalesced" (2016, p. 5).

On a global scale, Brian Larkin has recently reignited anthropological interest in infrastructures that he defines as "built networks that facilitate the flow of goods, people, or ideas and allow for their exchange over space. . . . They comprise the architecture for circulation, literally providing the undergirding of modern societies" (Larkin, 2013, p. 328). In a similar vein, Stephen Collier and Aihwa Ong proposed the term *global assemblages*, which they see as "specific technical infrastructures, administrative apparatuses, or value regimes," which facilitate the transportation of global phenomena that "have a distinctive capacity for decontextualization and recontextualization, abstractability, and movement, across diverse social and cultural situations and spheres of life" (Collier & Ong, 2007, p. 11). Building on their work, Marcia Inhorn has described a global reproductive assemblage as "involving the global diffusion of IVF and its underlying technoscience; international circuits of travelling people and, increasingly, their body parts (gametes, frozen embryos, and other biological substances); systems of administration involving both medical and tourism industries; increasing regulatory governance, on the part of both nations and professional bodies; and growing ethical concerns about various forms of licit and illicit exchange, including unprecedented evasion across national and international borders" (Inhorn, 2015, p. 22).

Although their terminology differs, each of these scholars has worked to articulate some kind of a whole comprised of an ensemble of interconnected parts that, when configured in specific ways, allow for the deployment, circulation, movement, and organization of specific forms of goods, people, capital, and/or ideas in specific ways. As such, these concepts allow us to think about and analyze historically and ethnographically situated governmental configurations (cf. Foucault 1991). A complex, then, as I define it, is a domain—systems of relations—within which we can discern heavy accumulations of patterned knowledges and practices around a distinct "aggregate problem" such as infertility, overpopulation, or low fertility. What I am calling a reproductive complex is thus in no way transient. Rather, reproductive complexes are very often nationally circumscribed (albeit with regional, if not global, overlaps), emerging over decades and involving scientists, doctors, nurses, hospitals, policy makers, laws, media, laboratories, techniques, secretaries, janitors, drivers, and more. Consequently they are rarely reconfigured overnight. Moreover, as Barbara Prainsack and I argued in "Situated Bio-Regulation," "certain regulatory configurations [are] tied to what [i]s thinkable and sayable" (Prainsack & Wahlberg, 2013, p. 341) in a given place, at a given time. In China, over the course of the last three or four decades, a reproductive complex has coalesced around the dual objectives of controlling population growth and improving population quality. It comprises a total set of laws, regulations, family planning institutions, quotas, information campaigns, experts, hospitals, clinics, pharmaceutical companies, premarital counseling sessions, prenatal screening services, and more. Medical procedures and techniques related to birth control (population quantity) include contraception, sterilization, and abortion as well as ARTs, while those related to the health of newborns (population quality) include genetic counseling, fetal education, prenatal screening, and abortion as well as SRTs. It is within such reproductive complexes that what anthropologists Lynn Morgan and Elizabeth Roberts have called *reproductive governance* takes place as "legislative controls, economic inducements, moral injunctions, direct coercion, and ethical incitements ... produce, monitor, and control reproductive behaviours and practices" (Morgan & Roberts, 2012, p. 241).

Empirically attending to how sperm banking came to fit within China's reproductive complex has required what I have called a site-multiplied assemblage ethnography,[6] which is to say a site-specific, in-depth ethnographic study of the Hunan Sperm Bank in Changsha from where I nonetheless followed and participated in national and global flows and exchanges of knowledge, people, equipment, and regulations related to sperm banking. The siting of this assemblage ethnography was essential, as it is in particular sites that we see how the knowledge-practice configurations that characterize China's reproductive complex are manifest in the daily routines and practices that make up sperm banking. While by no means mutually exclusive, it can be helpful to contrast assemblage ethnographies with ethnographies of lived experience on the one hand and laboratory ethnographies on the other. If ethnographies of lived experience generate insight into the ways in which individuals and communities experience, navigate, negotiate, or relate (for example, to infertility and insemination with donor sperm) and laboratory ethnographies examine how specific forms of knowledge, truth, or fact are produced through practice, assemblage ethnographies generate insight into the ways in which certain problems, or better yet problematizations, take form.[7] This is not to say that I have been uninterested in the experiences of sperm donors and couples undergoing AID or in the laboratory practices that generate knowledge about sperm, but rather it is to point out that the task of my ethnography has been to provide an account of *the making of sperm banking in China* through a heavy accumulation of patterned knowledges and practices, enmeshed within a very particular reproductive complex.[8] As a result, readers will note that I have not set myself the task of explaining what is particularly *Chinese* about sperm banking or male infertility in Hunan;[9] instead, I have been concerned with how *sperm banking* is practiced on a daily, routine basis *in China*. Mine is an assemblage ethnography of sperm banking in China rather than an ethnography of Chinese sperm donors or infertile couples. As such, throughout the book I will attend to the central questions of: How has routinized sperm banking become possible in China? What forms of problematization have allowed sperm banks a legitimate place within China's restrictive reproductive complex? What style of sperm banking has emerged in China as a result? How has AID become an acceptable reproductive technology in China?

When it comes to medical technologies I define "routinization" as a socio-historical process through which habituated regimes of daily micropractices coalesce, thereby shaping a medical technology and its uses. Routinization indexes the transformation of a technology from frontier to

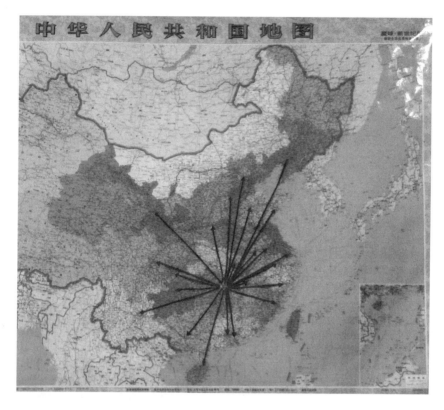

Figure 2. Site-multiplied, Hunan Sperm Bank provides donor sperm to fertility clinics around China.

mundane, as "new technologies must traverse this continuum, changing from a status of pure experiment to the standard of care" (Koenig, 1988, p. 466). Barbara Katz Rothman (1993), Marcia Inhorn (1994; 2003), Lisa Handwerker (1995a; 2002), Sarah Franklin (1997), Rayna Rapp (2000), and Gay Becker (2000) have been pioneers in the social and ethnographic study of new reproductive technologies, showing us how the development and routinization of technologies such as in vitro fertilization (IVF), amniocentesis, or prenatal genetic diagnosis (PGD), on the one hand, resulted from complex intersections within and between biomedical research, healthcare services, social policy, social movements, popular media, and more in a particular country; and on the other, turned them into an important part of the daily lives of providers, donors, patients, and family members alike. Hence, building on their work, with the term routinization I point firstly to socio-historical processes whereby certain forms of medical technology come to be (re-)produced and entrenched within particular juridical, medical, social, economic, cultural, and institutional configurations. Not only were there technical, cultural, and logistical obstacles to sperm banking in a post–Cultural Revolution China, but sperm banking also had to mold into a suitable form to fit within a reproductive complex that was otherwise configured to strictly restrict fertility. Following initial resistance, sperm banking (together with other forms of reproductive technology) has gone on to be championed by scientists, doctors, and administrators as a national project that can help not only infertile couples, but also the nation itself. Also at stake have been the multiple ways of knowing infertility that continue to circulate in China today, often leading to pluralist medical practices and therapeutic itineraries.

Secondly, I refer to all those daily practices through which certain medical technologies become an established and habituated part of health delivery, which is to say a standard of care for a given condition provided in a fixed setting. As Barbara Koenig has argued, "perhaps the most important change during routinization is the change in who actually *performs* the [. . .] procedure" (1988, p. 476) once its novelty has worn off and standardized protocols have enabled a hierarchized division of laborious and repetitive tasks in hospitals and clinics. There is what I would call a "daily grind" to the emergence of any medical technology, and in the case of sperm banking in China this has involved donors, doctors, andrologists, laboratories, egg yolks, chemicals, cryotanks, regulations, paperwork, computers, medical files, money, recruiters, leaflets, patients, university campus dormitories, social media, and more. Buildings have to be maintained, cryotanks need to be procured, liquid nitrogen stocks have to be replenished, staff must commute to work, rosters have to be planned and monitored, workflows developed and managed, students recruited and screened, telephone calls made, accreditations maintained, straws of sperm shipped to clinics, activities assessed, and so forth. While this is true of any sperm bank, the particular ways in which these daily practices play out in different sperm banks are never the same, not least because of the reproductive complexes within which they operate. In

TECH + PROCEDURE

China, a five-woman's-pregnancies limit coupled with family planning policies have resulted in a unique style of sperm banking, which requires mass recruitment and appropriate logistics to achieve that. The largest sperm banks in China assess the sperm quality of up to 100 men per day, which profoundly shapes workflows, socialities, and donation processes.

Thirdly, and finally, for a medical technology to become routine it must also be a normalized part of daily life, in the sense that it is available to and used by its (un)intended users in a routine manner. As Gay Becker observed, "When a specific medical technology is no longer viewed by medicine as experimental, that technological innovation may be increasingly accepted by the public and may eventually be viewed as commonplace" (Becker, 2000, p. 13). New reproductive technologies have tended to go through variegated patterns of "acceptance": starting from pioneering "breakthroughs," surrounded or followed by a period of concern and resistance, then by normalization through regulation and eventually by routinization as particular procedures are scaled up and made available (Wahlberg & Gammeltoft, 2017). Today in China, artificial insemination with donor sperm (AID) from a sperm bank has become a realistic and accepted option, albeit for those involuntarily childless couples (where the man is azoospermic) who are able to afford it and who are willing to accept a wait of up to three years. As the cases that will be discussed in chapter 6 attest, engagement with donor sperm is not somehow restricted to a middle-class elite; rather, knowledge of it has become commonplace and a shadow black market exists not least because of China's chronic donor sperm shortage. And although use of AID continues to be shrouded in secrecy—sperm banks operate according to strict "double-blind" principles that keep donor identity secret from both doctor and patients and vice versa, just as many patients insist on keeping their use of AID a secret from all but their most trusted relations—donor recruitment is an open practice on university campuses, sperm bank directors are regularly in local and national media appealing for more donors, and clinics have lengthy waiting lists for donor sperm. In short, as we will see, the pursuit of conception through ARTs including AID has become a "way of life" (Franklin, 1997) for the increasing numbers of couples in China who look to and can afford medical technology in their quests to overcome infertility (cf. Inhorn, 1994).

I propose to insist that sperm banking practices cannot be detached from the reproductive complexes within which routinization is unfolding. Sperm banking and AID are medical technologies that, like others, are constantly in the making, and as such we must, as scholars, relentlessly attend to the productive and often unintended effects of their making. Through my assemblage ethnography I have set out to identify the contours of the configurations that allow for sperm banking in China today (chapters 1, 2, and 3), to track the "daily grind" practices that constitute it (chapters 4 and 5), and to examine how sperm banking comes to be used in the treatment of infertility (chapter 6). This requires attendance to the styles of knowing and rationalities of governing that shape and are shaped by regimes of reproductive practice on the ground, in the clinics and laboratories currently developing and scaling up individual techniques, from IVF to AID. Hence, akin to the analytical work that has been done around the emergence of particular "styles of thought" in biomedical science (Fleck, 1979), my central argument in this book is that—as the cryopreservation and insemination of third-party sperm have come to be translated into routinized medical practice over the last thirty years—a certain *style* of sperm banking has emerged in China that is unique because of the ways in which it has been shaped by the particular cultural, juridical, economic, and social configurations that make up China's restrictive reproductive complex.

In making this argument, I want to mobilize Ludwik Fleck's insights into how thought collectives can form in biomedical research settings. However, the sciences of sperm cryopreservation and artificial insemination have long since been translated into the medical technology of sperm banking–AID in China and elsewhere. Sperm banking is a routinized medical technology and as such the primary task of the sperm bank is to deliver quality-assured donor sperm to fertility clinics that provide regular AID treatment to couples living with male-factor infertility. And so rather than a thought collective, I will show how the sperm bank in Changsha (and in other cities) is better conceived of as a *practice collective* within which we find routinized and protocolled daily procedures as well as socialities of lab workers, nurses, recruiters, doctors, donors, and administrators. Fleck argued that "like any style, the thought style also consists of a certain mood and of the performance by which it is realised" (1979, p. 99), and indeed in what follows we will gain insights into the mood and performance within the practice collectives that make up sperm banking in China today.[10] For, while each sperm bank in China can be analyzed as a practice collective in its own right, I will show that there are commonalities linking each of these practice collectives in China together to the extent that it makes sense to talk about a specific cyclic and high throughput *style* of sperm banking. This style of sperm banking manifests itself in the ways in which daily routines are organized around tasks of recruitment, screening, semen analysis, record-keeping, cryopreservation, and distribution, which, in turn, shape the ways in which donor sperm is made available to and accessed by certain bureaucratically circumscribed infertile couples who can afford AID cycles in China.

In carrying out the research for this book, I have been guided by two overarching analytical and methodological objectives. Firstly, I have wanted to broaden the empirical scope of social studies of sperm banking beyond America and Europe. Research from this part of the world has often pointed to and been critical of an ongoing commodification of the body and its substances. In a global reproductive bioeconomy, gamete procurement, fertilization, implantation, gestation, termination, and birth have each become specialized fields of laboratory-clinic practice. Rene Almeling and others have shown how "the practice of clinically transferring eggs and sperm from body to body is now part of a multi-billion-dollar market" in countries like the United States and Denmark (Almeling, 2011, p. 2; see also Adrian, 2010; Kroløkke, 2009; Mamo, 2005; Martin, 2017; Mohr, 2016; Moore, 2008; Tober, 2001; Waldby et al., 2013), a market that is but one subfield within ever expanding exchanges of human biological material—from organs to blood, bone, and cadavers—across the globe (Hoeyer, 2013; Scheper-Hughes, 2000). Sperm banks, egg agencies, and commercial fertility clinics recruit and screen donors, pay for their eggs and sperm, and market extended profiles of "super donors" to infertile couples, single women, as well as gay and lesbian couples who can "click-a-donor" as they shop around. What we have yet to see, however, are social studies focusing on the development and routinization of sperm banking outside of a Western setting.

In the following chapters, I will argue that while ARTs in general and sperm banking in particular are certainly being commercialized in China today (they are seriously big business); alongside health care in general, the analytical traction that commodification provides in accounting for the daily routines of sperm banking in China is limited (cf. Hoeyer, 2007). First of all, Ministry of Health guidelines in China specify that "it is prohibited to market sperm [which] shall not be treated as a commodity in market transaction" (MoH, 2003b, p. F3), even if a case can be made that it to some extent is, not least in the form of a shadow black market for sperm. Moreover, in accordance with family planning regulations, only married couples in China with "qualification of pregnancy" certificates can access donor sperm. Single women and lesbian couples (the only real "growth segment" in America and Europe these days, I was told by one sperm bank director from Europe) are barred from using sperm banks, even as sperm banks have their work cut out for them just to meet demand from infertile couples. Chinese regulations prohibit the import and export of sperm, thus restricting the operation of sperm banks. On their part, infertile couples in China have little choice when it comes to sperm donors in the face of chronic shortages. There are no websites that would allow them to click through extended donor profiles. Instead, couples most often wait two to three years before donor sperm becomes available and are then advised by doctors when looking at a list of perhaps four to six different anonymous donors on an Excel sheet with fifteen columns of basic information. And finally, restricting the number of women's pregnancies per donor to five, as I have pointed out, has resulted in an arduous and costly high throughput style of sperm banking, which bank administrators see as "constraining" for their operations, however much they might agree with the reasons for it. Costs per donor are much higher in China because one qualified donor can be used by only five couples, compared to as many as 30 to 100 offspring from a single donor in Europe or America.

My second overarching objective has been to shift analytical attention away from globalization, exportation, importation, and technology transfer, toward routinization and making when studying reproductive technologies in non-Western parts of the world. Lisa Handwerker (1995), Marcia Inhorn (2003), Aditya Bharadwaj (2003; 2016), Viola Hörbst (2012), and Elizabeth Roberts (2012) have been among the first ethnographers to study the burgeoning use of ARTs outside Europe and

America—in China, Egypt, India, Mali, and Ecuador respectively. Common to their studies has been an analytical emphasis on "rapidly globalizing technologies" (Bharadwaj, 2003, p. 1868) through the "wholesale exportation of Western-generated new reproductive technologies into . . . pronatalist developing societies" (Inhorn, 2003, p. 1837). As such, their ethnographies have examined "the importation of Western reproductive technologies" (Handwerker, 2002, p. 310); the "arrival of assisted-reproductive technologies in a developing nation" (Roberts, 2012, p. 39); or the "dissemination of ARTs to Mali" (Hörbst, 2012, p. 194). Although each of these scholars meticulously demonstrates the complex ways in which such a global form as ART becomes recontextualised and reshaped in their specific countries of study, globalization has nevertheless been one of the key ethnographic tropes in studies of reproductive technologies in the so-called Global South. In the case of China (and beyond), I argue that we need to (re-)orient our analyses toward routinization processes, regardless of where sperm banking and insemination treatments were invented.

As will become clear, while global flows and interactions have figured throughout the making of ARTs in China, it would be misleading at best to suggest that they have been imported into, arrived in, or disseminated into the country.[11] ARTs are not products; rather, they are assemblages of skills, petri dishes, needles, microscopes, protocols, regulations, patients, donors, clinics, recruitment flyers, advertisements, and more. Hence, accounting for the birth and routinization of ARTs like sperm banking or IVF in China requires a recentering of our analyses. Ethnographic and historical attention is shifted to the ways in which these technologies have followed routes of experimentation, development, and routinization *within* the nation, in the same way that, for example, Sarah Franklin (1997) and Rayna Rapp (2000) have tracked the routinization of IVF in the United Kingdom or amniocentesis in the United States respectively. It is by focusing on routinization that we can get a sense of how a particular style of sperm banking has emerged in China. As I will show, to the extent that there have been global connections, these have been components rather than drivers of the making of sperm banking in China, just as we know that the development of reproductive technologies in Europe and America have also been facilitated by global connections.

ASSEMBLAGE ETHNOGRAPHY

What follows, then, is not an account of the commodification of bodily substances in China as an inevitable effect of globalization, standardization, and commercialization. Instead, we will ethnographically follow how the "daily grind" of sperm banking is currently unfolding in China. If we are to understand how a medical technology like sperm banking could become routine in China, we must attend to the ways in which sperm banks are used by infertile couples who pursue artificial insemination with donor sperm, the daily micro-practices of sperm banking (from recruitment to quality assessment, storage, and distribution), and the socio-historical processes that mold it. The book is based on eight years (2007–2014) of episodic fieldwork (Whyte, 2013)[12] primarily in Changsha but also in Beijing, Shanghai, and Guangzhou, consisting of ten trips lasting between three months and a couple of weeks. Through this fieldwork I have amassed a rich dataset consisting of field notes, interview transcripts, medical journal articles, media reports, regulations, guidelines, conference reports, "gray literature" in the form of brochures and leaflets, informed consent forms, donor screening criteria, standard operating procedures, and more. My research has involved participant observation, interviews, and the collecting of documents in equal measure and I consider the resulting materials as of equal importance for the task I have set myself, that is, accounting for the routinization of sperm banking in China. Let me describe how I was able to carry out the research for this book.

In January 2007 I was lucky enough to be awarded a research fellowship on a European Commission–funded project called BIONET (2006–2009) based at the BIOS Centre on the tenth floor of Tower 2 at the London School of Economics. The project was a Sino-European collaboration on the ethical governance of biomedical research, which aimed to explore some of the challenges that increasing cross-continental research collaboration in the life sciences had brought in its wake: In which country should ethical review take place in collaborative research? What were some of the differences in how informed consent procedures were carried out and understood? Can researchers from two countries collaborate if their laws conflict? and so on (see Wahlberg et al., 2013). One of the

partners in the project was Lu Guangxiu, who guided our work on reproductive technologies and stem cell science through a series of workshops
and conferences held in Beijing, Shanghai, and Changsha. It was through
this project that I began the research that has culminated in this book.
Having developed a productive working relationship with Lu and her
team in Changsha, I asked toward the end of the BIONET project whether
she would support an ethnographic project that focused specifically on
sperm banking carried out by me based at her hospital in Changsha. She
agreed enthusiastically and I then prepared a research grant application,
which, having failed first time around (my proposed methods were not
sufficiently aligned with my research questions) in 2009, was eventually
successful in 2010, when I received generous funding from the Danish
Council of Independent Research to carry out a three-year ethnographic
project on sperm banking in China. The research project was designed
as a Sino-Danish collaboration from the outset, and further to my own
research costs we had also agreed to budget for two conferences (one in
China and one in Denmark)[13] as well as researcher exchanges between
China and Denmark.

Fieldwork

How then does one carry out an assemblage ethnography of the routinization of sperm banking in China? As site-multiplied research I have carried
out in-depth ethnographic fieldwork in China's largest and oldest sperm
bank in Changsha as my primary site while also following connections to
sperm banks and fertility clinics in Beijing, Shanghai, Guangzhou, and
indeed Denmark. Fieldwork has comprised observations and participation
during recruitment visits to university campuses, reception of potential
and qualified donors at the sperm banks, medical screening of potential
donors, analysis of sperm quality in the laboratories, cryopreservation of
qualified donor sperm, the filing of donor and sperm sample information
as well as consultations with infertile couples. My main sites of observation
were the donor reception and waiting rooms on the one hand, and on the
other, sperm bank laboratories where analysis of sperm samples is carried
out and qualified sperm is prepared for cryopreservation. I also joined a
mobile sperm bank crew on three of their weekly visits to collect donor

sperm in cities outside of Hunan Province's capital, Changsha. This field-work, recorded in my field notes, was essential to get a sense of the "daily grind" at the sperm bank, how the routines, rosters, and workflows shaped practices and socialities. I have used pseudonyms for all the persons referred to in those chapters that use material from my observations.

Interviews

Interviews were carried out with some of the pioneers of ART in China as well as around twenty staff members at the different sperm banks and fertility clinics I visited (many of them repeatedly). Over a period of eight years (2007–2014) I had the opportunity to speak to and interview Lu Guangxiu on numerous occasions in Changsha. Four of these interviews were recorded and transcribed. My requests for interviews with Zhang Lizhu in Beijing were gently declined because of her advanced age. I was, however, able to spend time at, and speak to staff members of the Third Hospital in Beijing where she had worked. Moreover, a series of TV, radio, and journal interviews with Zhang, publicly available online, were transcribed and translated. I have numbered these interviews; the websites where they can be found are included in the reference list. For further insights into the daily workings of sperm banks I interviewed sperm bank managers, doctors, laboratory technicians, nurses, and recruiters. Finally, I interviewed over fifty (potential) sperm donors as well as ten involuntar-ily childless couples to get a sense of how donors and recipient couples reasoned about sperm donation and the processes of donation and insem-ination respectively. Interviews provided me with a chance to follow up on some of the impressions that I got through fieldwork, while also at times functioning as expert interviews that helped me in my own reproductive science education. Most interviews were carried out in Mandarin, and despite my best efforts to improve my Chinese over these eight years I relied on help from a group of dedicated research assistants (see the acknowledgments) throughout when interviewing informants and for translation and transcription of interviews.[14] Interviews were transcribed into Mandarin first and then translated into English. When full names are used in the chapters that follow these are the real names of interviewees; whereas when only a first name is used this is an anonymized pseudonym, just as I at times attribute a quote to a "donor," "doctor," or "administrator" generically.

Scientific Articles and Reports

Scientific articles and reports were collected with a focus on infertility, andrology, and epidemiology in China. I have in particular collected studies that were designed to assess infertility rates, aggregate sperm quality, and the toxic effects of pollution on sperm quality. As a supplement to these studies, I participated in a total of seven workshops and conferences on assisted reproduction in China held in Beijing, Shanghai, Guangzhou, and Changsha, which gave insights into some of the challenges facing fertility clinics and sperm banks in China as ARTs are scaled up on hitherto unimaginable numbers. I listened to talks, participated in discussions, and collected PowerPoint presentations at these events while also organizing site visits with contacts that I met. Thanks to my research grant, together with the Hunan Sperm Bank, we were able to organize the first ever national conference on social and ethical challenges in sperm banking in China in 2012, at which representatives from all of China's (at the time) fifteen sperm banks as well as from Europe attended and presented. These conferences and workshops have been important fieldwork activities for me as well, since the discussions and debates that I participated in provided further insights into the daily workings of sperm banking. Finally, thanks to my grant I have been able to organize a series of researcher exchanges with Chinese sperm bank staff visiting Europe and vice versa, allowing me to spend more time with them than is often possible within the constraints of hectic daily life in a sperm bank or fertility clinic.

Laws, Regulations, and Guidelines

As became clear to me from the very outset of my study, ARTs are inextricable from the laws, regulations, and guidelines that have shaped reproduction in China in so many fundamental ways. China's Marriage Law, Law on Maternal and Infant Health Care, Regulation on Assisted Reproductive Technologies, to name a few, have each played a pivotal role in the molding of sperm banking into the particular form it has in China. At the level of the clinic or sperm bank, guidelines, regulations, standard operating procedures (SOPs), and protocols shape work practices and daily routines. I therefore spent a considerable amount of time collecting a complete set of repro-regulations in China, as these provided crucial information on how certain practices are permissible while others are prohibited.

Newspaper Articles and Media Stories

Finally, I also put together a database of newspaper articles and media stories specifically on sperm banking, sperm donation, and infertility in China. While not systematic, I have nonetheless amassed a comprehensive collection of news stories from both Chinese-language and English-language news outlets. News reports can help us understand how certain issues emerge as matters of concern in a given setting. I have read these media reports not to gain some kind of "accurate" picture of sperm banking in China, but rather to see which kinds of issues have surrounded routinized sperm banking and donation in China today. I use the full names of reproductive scientists who are cited in media reports while also attributing the quote to the appropriate news story. Thanks to my grant I was able to enlist my research assistants to help with the task of translating some of the central scientific, legislative, and media documents that I have amassed.

The resulting dataset of field notes, interview transcriptions, scientific articles, media reports, laws, regulations, as well as laboratory protocols forms the basis of the analysis that follows in this book. It is this data that has allowed me to piece together the routes of routinization that sperm banking has followed in China. All of this has been necessary for me to get to grips with the socio-historical processes, the daily micro-practices, and the uses of donor sperm that have shaped the routinization of sperm banking in China (and vice versa), which is to say the emergence of a certain style of sperm banking in China. What I have learned over the last years is the importance of mapping out and analyzing country-specific (indeed at times clinic-specific) routes of routinization when it comes to medical technologies. As I have already underscored, sperm banking is not a medical technology that was imported into China through processes of globalization; rather, it was developed and routinized *in* China through the work of scientists, laboratory technicians, infertile men, donors, doctors, nurses, and many others, just as it has been in other countries around the world. To be sure, this routinization has of course engendered and worked through global flows of expertise, equipment, standardized protocols, and people (my own research included). However, in China, it is as components of such routinization that global flows must be accounted for rather than the other way around. Regardless of where sperm banking was "invented" or how much technology is "transferred" across borders, the processes by which it became routinized have been far from inevitable, highly localized, very experimental to begin with, and fraught with specific obstacles, constraints, and challenges. Even in countries where the building up of ART sectors has relied extensively on international expertise (see Hörbst, 2012; Inhorn, 2015), I maintain that further analytical traction can be gained from asking how ARTs are routinized within as opposed to imported into a particular country. In China, sperm banking, AID, and other forms of ART have traversed the continuum from experiment to standard care practice as arduously as they have in any other place.

GOOD QUALITY

Very early on in the research process it became apparent to me that the concept of quality—in various guises—would be central to my study (see Wahlberg 2008; 2010; 2014a). Sperm banking is saturated with vital assessment, a task that would not be possible without the concept of quality. In China, sperm banks must promote population quality (*renkou suzhi*); they recruit high-quality (*suzhi gao*) donors from university campuses; assess the sperm quality (*jingzi zhiliang*) of up to four thousand individuals per year; adhere to good laboratory practices (GLPs) and standard operating procedures (SOPs) in order to assure a good quality (*zhiliang hao*) supply of sperm; and provide donor sperm to infertile couples with the aim of improving their quality of life (*shenghuo zhiliang*) and happiness. As my research wore on, it also became clear that it was not only the vitality of men and their sperm cells that were on trial, so too was the vitality of the nation, not least against a backdrop of national crises and perceived anthropogenic threats to this vitality (see also Dow, 2016). I have tracked these various notions of quality as ethnographic tropes in my efforts to understand and map out the style of sperm banking that has emerged in China over the course of the last three decades. Vital quality is that which makes good life possible in China today, yet it is this same vital quality that is considered to be under constant threat in a time of compressed modernization (cf. Kyung-Sup, 1999) and "sperm crisis."

Each of the chapters that follow addresses some aspect of the vital assessments that organize sperm banking in China today. In some respects, my assemblage ethnography was guided by attempts to follow the concept of "quality" around as it circulated in different forms—as imaginary, technical specification, interpellation form, regulatory requirement, or marker of vitality. What the concept of quality does is allow for classifications along good–bad continuums, which in turn are stabilized through the guidelines, procedures, and practices that keep sperm banks operating. Yet these same classifications are open to contestation and query, for example, when donor screening criteria are debated; when negotiations about sperm quality standards are initiated; when quality assurances are questioned; or when quality assessments rely on the judgment of individual laboratory staff working at the bench (see also Mohr & Hoeyer, 2012).

The first chapter chronicles the difficult birth of ARTs in China through the 1980s and 1990s, showing how ideas of improving population quality acted as a persuasive "alibi" for those pioneers working to develop fertility technologies at a time when contraception rather than conception was at the top of the political agenda. From difficult beginnings in the 1980s, ARTs have now settled firmly *within* China's restrictive reproductive complex, which in turn has allowed it to grow into a thriving sector. China is now home to some of the world's largest fertility clinics and sperm banks. Since 2003, it has also been one of the most strictly regulated ART sectors in the world, as it has had to conform to national family planning regulations. As always in China, the sheer scale of operations is astounding. When keeping in mind that an estimated 10 percent of couples have trouble conceiving "naturally" in China, the potential demand for ART is hardly matched anywhere else in the world.

In the second chapter, I examine how sperm banking has been shaped by one of the defining governmental objectives found within China's reproductive complex today, namely the improvement of population quality (*renkou suzhi*). Further to the treatment of infertility, albeit in far fewer cases, donor sperm is also made available to couples where the male is considered to suffer from a genetic disease that is deemed "not suitable for reproduction" because of a risk that the disease will be transmitted to future offspring, thereby negatively affecting the quality of the newborn population. In chapter 2, we learn how AID both purports to contribute to the improvement of national population quality while at the same time introducing a potential threat to this quality in the form of possible unwitting consanguineous marriage of donor siblings. As we will learn, sperm banking in China is inextricably bound to national family planning objectives to improve the quality of newborns.

The looming images of smog-choked cities, cancer villages, and contaminated food have become iconic of a modernizing China, the tragic, perhaps unavoidable, side effects of a voracious economy. In contemporary China, urban living has become toxic living in many ways. In the third chapter, I examine how the sperm bank—*jingzi ku*—in China has emerged quite literally as a sanctuary of vitality amid concerns around food safety, air and water pollution, rising infertility, and declining population quality. As a twist on Margaret Lock's concept of "local biologies," I suggest *exposed biologies* have become a matter of concern in China in ways that have created a place for hi-tech sperm banks within China's restrictive reproductive complex. Exposed biologies are a side effect of modernization processes, as industrially manufactured chemicals are increasingly held culpable for a range of pathologies, from cancers to metabolic diseases, disorders of sex development and infertility. Amid concerns that pollution and modern lifestyles are deteriorating sperm quality in China, the sperm bank stands out as a repository of screened, purified, and quality-controlled vitality and consequently sperm banking can be seen as a form of reproductive insurance, not only for individuals but also for the nation.

In the fourth chapter, I turn my attention toward the mobilization of sperm donors on university campuses. As I have already noted, a limit of five women's pregnancies per donor in China has spawned "high throughput" sperm banking, which requires getting great numbers of potential donors to show up at the sperm bank for screening. Sperm banks will usually only accept between 10 and 30 percent of those who come in for screening in a given year. For this reason, sperm banks in China are dependent on the efforts of their young recruiters (often former donors themselves) to bring potential donors into the bank. Chapter 4 shows how novel strategies of recruitment have been devised and adjusted to address the chronic shortage of donors in China. Such strategies involve recruiters who seek out male university students through university web message boards and social networking platforms as well as through direct dialogue, especially in men's dormitories on university campuses. In particular I show how recruitment strategies are designed to appeal to the national and personal pride of university students while also highlighting the financial compensation and free health checks that donors are entitled to. The chapter also shows how daily life in a Chinese sperm bank stands in stark contrast to that in a European or American sperm bank. It is not uncommon for larger sperm banks to receive and assess the samples of up to 100 university students in a single afternoon session, which in turn has great bearing on the donation process for donors.

Donor screening in sperm banks has become increasingly medicalized through the last few decades. Potential donors must submit to physical examinations and blood tests as well as provide detailed medical histories in order to minimize the risk of transmitting infectious or hereditary diseases. In line with international guidelines, sperm samples must be assessed, and those considered suitable for banking quarantined for six months, at which point the donor must be retested for HIV before his "straws" are made available to prospective recipient couples. In chapter 5, I suggest that practices which take place within the sperm bank's facilities and laboratories can helpfully be analyzed as technologies of assurance (*que bao*). To "assure" means to render safe or secure, but it also means to ensure. For a sperm bank to be licensed in China it must adhere to family planning laws as well as medical technology regulations, which require it to ensure the safety and quality of its sperm.. Sperm is a vital yet potentially dangerous substance. To improve its quality, sperm banks advise potential donors on how best to prepare themselves prior to donating. To mitigate the dangers sperm poses, sperm banks screen potential donors as a way to prevent transmission of genetic and infectious disease from donor to recipient. They comply with auditable good laboratory and manufacturing practices in order to prevent transmission of bacterial infections between qualified donor samples as well as from qualified donor to recipient. Essential to such practices of assurance are numbers: sperm cells per milliliter, motility grades, percentage of normal morphology, milligrams of fructose per milliliter, and chromosome counts. Such numbers are what make sperm quality auditable and thereby amenable to assurance.

Once quality controlled, donor sperm is "released" to the thousands of couples who are involuntarily childless. In the final chapter, I examine how donor sperm is made available to these couples. For those infertile couples who "borrow" sperm in China, secrecy is vital because male infertility is stigmatized. Indeed, sperm donation operates through a double-blind system where recipients consult with doctors who make their requests to sperm banks, which anonymize donors. When making a decision about which donor to use, doctors and infertile couples cannot know the identity of the donor. Through fertility clinics, AID emerges as an opportunity to achieve a visible pregnancy, a pregnancy that couples are in pursuit of and expected to achieve by family and friends. The chapter examines how in one-child policy China, recipient couples and donors mobilize strategies of "hearth" management and trouble-avoidance even as third-party conception has become acceptable for increasing numbers of involuntarily childless couples who are living with male infertility.

Good Quality is a book about the routinization of sperm banking in China. It is at the same time an exploration of how vitality, which is to say both life (*shengming*) and living (*shenghuo*), is assessed and valued in China today. In a country currently beset by enormous transformations, it is little wonder that questions of what good life is abound (see Kleinman et al., 2011; Zhang, Kleinman, & Tu, 2011). In the pages that follow, we will see how an assemblage ethnography of sperm banking in China can provide insight into the ways in which good life emerges out of a heavy accumulation of patterned knowledges and practices around the problem of male infertility, which are calibrated to constantly assess and intervene into that very vitality.

1 The Birth of Assisted Reproductive Technology in China

It's about 1978, and the first IVF baby was born in the United Kingdom, but during that time, you know, China had had ten years of Cultural Revolution, so we didn't hear any news from foreign countries and we couldn't read any materials from foreign countries. So during that time, we didn't know this great news until 1979, when my father was able to read some newspapers and magazines from foreign countries. That way he learned that a test-tube baby was born in the U.K. in 1978. So he thought that in China, because of the Qing dynasty Chinese people have suffered a lot not only from the war, but also from drugs, because some of them became addicted to drugs. He said that if you want to change the whole country, you must have a healthy body, so it is also important to have a healthy baby for every Chinese family. At that time, my team was doing prenatal diagnosis for genetic diseases and we found many couples with such diseases, but they could only choose to do an abortion; this was the only option for them. My father thought that maybe if we can find a good way to have a sperm and oocyte cultured in vitro, then we can identify not-good genes and choose the good ones. So his first thought for doing IVF technology was not for infertile couples, but for couples with genetic diseases. But this was a long way off and we also found that it was not easy to do this work. After all our research we decided, then, to also do the treatment for infertile couples. (Lu Guangxiu)

There is an almost precise coincidence of timing in the births of Louise Brown in July 1978 and China's restrictive family planning policy a few months after in 1979. These two landmark events stand at odds with each other in many ways. For Robert Edwards and Patrick Steptoe, the two doctors who helped Lesley and John Brown give birth to Louise using the technique of in vitro fertilization (IVF), infertility was the problem that needed to be overcome. In contrast, for systems engineer Song Jian, mathematician Li Guangyuan, and other architects of the so-called "one-child-policy," fertility was the problem that needed to be addressed (Greenhalgh, 2008). The technique of IVF alone has brought an estimated 5 million babies into the world globally (in China, some 200,000),[1] while it is said that the one-child policy has prevented some 140 million births in China.

It is worth remembering that, as Martin Johnson and colleagues (2010; see also Johnson, 2011) have shown, Edwards and Steptoe faced numerous setbacks during the early days of their research on IVF in the United Kingdom. They were refused funding by the Medical Research Council in the early 1970s in a scientific climate where research into infertility "was accorded a low priority" (Johnson et al., 2010, p. 2158) when compared to contraception and abortion. Similarly, beginning in the early 1980s, reproductive scientists Lu Guangxiu, Zhang Lizhu, and He Cuihua also faced many setbacks (albeit eventually securing government funding for their research in 1986) in a country where concerns about overpopulation were immediately national rather than global.

What, then, were the conditions that allowed assisted reproductive technologies (ARTs) to be developed in China during the exact same period that one of the world's most comprehensive family planning policies aimed at *preventing* birth was being rolled out? First of all, in what follows, we will see how ARTs would have be molded into a suitable form to fit within China's restrictive reproductive complex before they could gain formal authorization through national law as late as 2003. In doing so, these technologies eventually settled alongside contraception, sterilization, and abortion as just another technology of *birth control*. This might seem counterintuitive, seeing as birth control is most often defined as fertile couples' active efforts to *prevent* unwanted pregnancies as a matter of (in China, state-stipulated) family planning. Nonetheless, as we will see, for ARTs to be legalized, infertile couples would have to be subject to the same kinds of family planning restrictions as fertile couples. We can say that for increasing numbers of infertile couples in China, birth control can be defined as an active effort to achieve *wanted* pregnancies using ARTs in order to have one child in strict accordance with family planning policies. Moreover, since China's reproductive complex came to be configured around the dual objectives of controlling population growth and improving population quality, the medical genetic potentials of reproductive technologies were actively mobilized from the outset in China, as highlighted by Lu Guangxiu in this chapter's opening quotation.

Secondly, I will show how even if ARTs such as sperm banking or IVF were invented in the United States and United Kingdom, this did not relieve scientists of a need for experimentation in China, and hence we should not view their development and routinization as an "importation of Western reproductive technologies" (Handwerker, 2002, p. 310; cf. Inhorn, 2003). Instead, we need to trace the transformation of such technologies from pioneering to mundane within China (rather than across borders). By tracing the ways in which ARTs came to be accepted in China we gain insights into the particular form—what we might think of as "one-child ART"[2]—they have taken (cf. Knecht, Beck, and Klotz, 2012).

I begin by looking at how two of the pioneers of reproductive science in China—Lu Guangxiu in Changsha and Zhang Lizhu in Beijing—began experimenting with assisted reproduction, eventually embarking on a collegial yet competitive race to achieve the country's first test tube baby, culminating in the birth of Zheng Mengzu in March 1988 in Beijing, closely followed by a baby girl in Changhsa three months later. Their recollections, recorded in interviews, are interwoven to capture a sense of the pioneering spirit that carried their efforts forward. I will use Zhang and Lu as narrators of the story of the difficult birth of ARTs in China. As we will see, there is a certain style to nostalgic remembering when legacies have already been consolidated, allowing for playful self-deprecation as a means of emphasizing the hurdles and challenges that had to be overcome. Zhang and Lu's personal recollections are balanced against additional interviews with some of the other scientists as well as Ministry of Health officials who were active in reproductive research and policy through the 1980s and 1990s; participation in a series of workshops and conferences on assisted reproduction in China held in Beijing, Shanghai, and Changsha, which gave insights into the history of ART in these cities; as well as on secondary archival sources. Accounting for the birth and routinization of sperm banking in China requires accounting for the development of IVF since, as we saw in the introduction, China's first sperm bank was established by Lu Guangxiu in Changsha to facilitate lab research on in vitro fertilization. Therefore this chapter chronicles the rise of both forms of reproductive technology.

ORIGIN STORIES

Helping You Have a Healthy Little Angel

Our hospital is the first modern large-scale reproductive and genetics hospital in China, and a model for putting technological developments to practical use. . . . From 1980 it was under the direction of Professor Lu Huilin, the founder of the study of medical genetics in China. Professor Lu Guangxiu was the first to begin developing human-assisted reproduction research and clinical medical work in China. In 1980, the Human Reproductive Engineering Research Department, a platform for human-assisted reproductive technology, was founded. . . . [T]his was the first center in China to begin studying human ovum development, external maturation of ovum, and in vitro fertilization. Projects became national key scientific projects of the Seventh Five-Year Plan. There are world-class equipment and a very talented team. The center has made great achievements in the area of assisted reproduction and preimplantation diagnosis in the past twenty years. . . . Founded in 1981, the technological instruction center of the National Sperm Bank of the Ministry of Health was China's first sperm bank, with a very talented team, advanced quality control equipment, computer-based data management, and the ability to preserve 120,000 frozen sperm samples. (Hospital presentation flyer, CITIC-Xiangya Reproductive and Genetic Hospital)

Scientific teams, clinics, and indeed countries often engage in a race to be the first when it comes to "new" or "frontier" technologies; whether in the United Kingdom or in India there is prestige to be won from achieving a first in the ever-growing field of reproductive technologies (Bharadwaj, 2002; Franklin & Roberts, 2006). Global firsts (such as Louise Brown or Dolly the sheep) are perhaps the most prestigious, but by no means at the cost of national firsts. In China, as already noted, two scientists have in particular been recognized, not least through national awards and prizes, as the pioneers of ART—Zhang Lizhu of Beijing's Medical University Third Hospital and Lu Guangxiu of the CITIC-Xiangya Reproductive and Genetic Hospital in Changsha. If ARTs are completely routinized today in China, they were very much experimental technologies in 1980, which was a pivotal post–Cultural Revolution year for reproductive science in China. It was in 1980 that the Human Reproductive Engineering Research Department was founded at the Xiangya Medical College in Changsha by Lu Huilin, father of Lu Guangxiu. It was also in that year that Zhang Lizhu, a trained gynecologist, returned to prominence as invited speaker on China's one-child policy and related public health issues at the United Nation's Second World Conference on Women held in Copenhagen.

Yet, Zhang and Lu arrived at assisted reproduction along very different paths, as endocrinologist and geneticist respectively. Having studied gynecology in Shanghai, New York, and Baltimore through the 1940s, Zhang took up her first position as resident gynecological physician at the Marie Curie Hospital in London in 1949.[3] She returned to China in 1951, eventually becoming the director of Gynecology and Obstetrics at the Peking University Third Hospital in 1958. During the 1960s, her endocrinological research was focused on the increasing numbers of patients reporting menstrual irregularity. By 1965, as the Cultural Revolution began, Zhang's international background was turned against her. She was demoted from her position as director and sent to work in the countryside for a year where she trained so-called "barefoot doctors," followed by a job as hospital janitor at the Third Hospital back in Beijing.[4] Zhang was able to resume her work as clinician and researcher only once the Cultural Revolution had ended in 1978, in a newly established endocrinology laboratory at the Third Hospital. This change in fortune was directly linked to the Four Modernizations program that Deng Xiaoping had launched that year to repair some of the many setbacks that agriculture, industry, defense, and science and technology had suffered during the Cultural Revolution. Zhang picked up where she had left off, concentrating on her patients' menstrual irregularities, a specialization that would inevitably draw her into the field of infertility, as she recalled in an interview with the Chinese Obstetrics and Gynecology forum:

My expertise was in reproductive endocrinology. When I treated patients with period issues in the 1980s, I found that many of them not only wanted to cure their period problems, but also mainly wanted to get pregnant. A lot of them had been married for over two years but still couldn't get pregnant. Therefore I began to look into what was causing their infertility. After research and analysis I found out it was due to blocked fallopian tubes. In most cases this was the major problem. Blocked fallopian tubes were mainly an issue in China, which was completely different from other counties. In China 31.3 percent of female infertility was caused by tuberculosis. We proved that they had tuberculosis through research and biopsy. So this cause was not necessarily the same as in other counties. The main clinical manifestation was pelvic adhesions, and the surface of the ovary couldn't even be seen. (Zhang, Interview 1)

Lu, on the other hand, was introduced to the field of ART by her father Lu Huilin, one of the founders of medical genetics in China. Lu Huilin had traveled to the United States in 1924 to further his education at Columbia University, studying under Thomas Hunt Morgan and Edmund Beecher Wilson for a master's degree in genetics. Armed with a number of Morgan's works, such as *Human Inheritance* (1924) and *Evolution and Genetics* (1925), Lu returned to China in 1929. Disrupted by illness and the Japan-China war (1937–1945), Lu eventually set about translating Morgan's texts in the late 1940s with a view to spreading his theories to a Chinese audience. In 1950, he published a book on the theory of the gene and Mendelian inheritance and began teaching this theory at the medical college in Changsha. He was widely criticized in a newly communist China, which officially favored the now discredited ideas of Russian scientist Trofim Lysenko on the heritability of acquired characteristics (see Lamoreaux, 2016). Lu's studies and teaching were interrupted as the Cultural Revolution took hold in the 1960s. As a result, he shifted his attention to medical genetics in the 1970s, forming a research group in Changsha that would develop prenatal diagnosis and genetic counseling techniques. It was this group that would be formally institutionalized in 1980 as the Human Reproductive Engineering Research Department of the Xiangya Medical College. And thus Lu Huilin's interest in reproductive technologies began to take shape. His initial excitement upon hearing news of Louise Brown some months after her birth in 1979 was sparked by the possibilities of utilizing IVF not so much to overcome infertility as to

Figure 3. Lu Guangxiu and her father, medical geneticist Professor Lu Huilin. (Photo courtesy of Lu Guangxiu.)

avoid transmission of genetic diseases.[5] It was at this time, in the late 1970s, that Lu Huilin's daughter, Lu Guangxiu, would unknowingly be enlisted in China's efforts to develop reproductive technologies. As she explained in an interview in her office surrounded by a forest of indoor plants one late afternoon in May 2011:

> I was a surgeon in Guangdong in 1979, and at that time, because my father's health was not very good, I came back to Changsha to take care of him. During that time, he posed a question to me, asking: "Do you know how we can get an oocyte?" I was astonished to get this question! Because I had never observed any oocytes during ultrasound and the technical equipment was also very poor at that time. So, as a surgeon, I answered, "Maybe you have to open the abdomen to get this oocyte." I also wondered why he would ask this question. When I came back to Changsha, I had become a teacher of anatomy. In those days, I could teach for half of the year and have my own time for the other half of the year. Being a surgeon was hectic every day, so I was used to the old busy days. I felt I had too much free time in Changsha and I hadn't many things to do. So I asked my father why he asked this question and he said that he would like to try for an IVF baby. I then said, "Why

don't you let me have a try?" But my father said that I am a surgeon and so I lack basic knowledge of this research and he would think about it. After several days, he gave me some examples of what preparations I would make if I was going to be engaged in this research, such as the equipment, technology, and knowledge; so all these things, I had to begin from scratch. "You will encounter many difficulties and you have to overcome them," he told me. I thought about it and accepted it and began the research.

Lu Huilin sent his daughter to Beijing on a three-month study trip in 1980 to learn how to fertilize eggs and culture embryos from cows, rats, and mice. Lu Guangxiu's sister was studying at Beijing University at the time and had many friends and classmates working at the Chinese Academy of Sciences in the field of genetics. So, whereas Zhang Lizhu's attention had been drawn to infertility by the patients she encountered as a clinical gynecologist, Lu Guangxiu was introduced to reproductive science by her medical geneticist father whose initial interests focused on the use of reproductive technologies to engineer and improve the strength of China's population. This intersection of clinical infertility and medical genetics, as we will see, turned out to be propitious for the development of ART in China. As they set out to develop reproductive technologies in the early 1980s, one of the first hurdles faced by Zhang and Lu (much like all other early reproductive science pioneers) was how to get a hold of human gametes.

GETTING GAMETES

While artificial insemination (AI) using donor sperm has a long history, it was not until the first techniques for viable cryopreservation of sperm were developed in the 1950s that sperm banks —repositories of frozen sperm samples—became feasible (see Swanson, 2012). Working with animal sperm in 1949, a group of British researchers led by Chris Polge "made the discovery that glycerol had the remarkable property of protecting living cells from damage during freezing and thawing" (Polge, 2007, p. 513). A few years later, Polge and his team had engineered the birth of Frosty, the first calf born from frozen sperm with "millions more to follow . . . [as] the technique spread rapidly round the world until nearly all the cows bred by AI were with frozen semen" (ibid., p. 514). Encouraged by Polge's work, Jerome Sherman and Raymond Bunge from the University of Iowa in America were the first to apply these findings to human sperm in the early 1950s (see Swanson, 2012). By 1953, they reported that "clinical application of practical storage banks for human spermatozoa in infertility problems is now in progress" (Sherman & Bunge, 1953, p. 688) and (following three successful pregnancies using frozen sperm) that "the ability of glycerol-treated, frozen, and thawed human spermatozoon to fertilize and actuate the human ovum has been observed" (ibid., p. 768).

Notwithstanding this early work on the use of cryopreserved human sperm for insemination in the 1950s, historian Kara Swanson has shown that doctors in America continued to prefer using fresh semen for insemination in the ensuing decades and as a result "frozen sperm would not become a significant part of reproductive medicine until the 1980s" (2012, p. 272). This was also the case in China. As we saw in the introduction, by 1980 Chinese breeders had established a sperm bank for bulls in Beijing, which Lu Guangxiu had visited during her three-month study trip to learn how to freeze sperm with liquid nitrogen. It was on the basis of this visit that she would establish China's first human sperm bank upon her return to Changsha toward the end of that year, ensuring a significant place for sperm banking in Chinese reproductive medicine during the 1980s, as we will see.

If the main challenge for Sherman and Bunge and for Lu was to transfer techniques for storing bovine sperm to storing human sperm, scientists working with human oocytes in the same period had to tackle the problem of how to retrieve oocytes in a medically and ethically responsible manner. In a 1968 letter to the editor in *The Lancet*, Patrick Steptoe had reported that "all aspects of the ovaries . . . can be inspected in minute detail through the modern laparoscope" (Steptoe, 1968, p. 913). This microscopic technique, which allowed surgeons to see inside the abdomen through a small incision using a viewing instrument attached to a tube, had initially been developed in France for purposes of sterilization, but upon reading Steptoe's letter, Robert Edwards saw its potential as a technique for obtaining oocytes, prompting him to initiate what would become a famous collaboration with Steptoe. It was through the retooling of laparoscopic techniques for purposes of egg retrieval that Edwards and Steptoe would go on to develop IVF in the United Kingdom during the 1970s.

Not only did the carrying out of early research on fertilization and embryo development require gametes, it also required having access to them in highly coordinated and controlled ways. This was among the reasons Lu Guangxiu gave for learning how to freeze sperm using egg yolk and glycerol in 1980, that is, to have access to sperm in the laboratory for in vitro research purposes. However, it was one thing to know how to cryopreserve sperm; when it came to human sperm, getting the sperm proved to be quite a challenge in Changsha. The director of the sperm bank in Changsha today, Fan Liqing, worked closely with Lu in the 1980s and he explained to me what they saw as their primary obstacle in the early days:

> At that time, the technical conditions were not the biggest problem. The problem was how to overcome the ideas of ordinary people, because during that time, all the people were still conservative and they were very sensitive when talking about sex. So it was very hard to collect semen to establish our sperm bank. We tried to find people with a good educational background in the university. But everyone declined. I remember we talked with an old professor, and because during that time, we still lived in quite poor life conditions, we said that if you can donate sperm, we can provide some compensation for you. The guy said, "I'd rather beg than donate sperm!" So it was very hard for people to accept it.

Lu concurs: "China had just undergone the Cultural Revolution, so collecting sperm was like a dirty thing. So when I built the sperm bank [in 1980] we did everything covertly and it was very difficult to collect sperm." Initially, Lu and Fan tried to collect "leftover sperm" from outpatients, but quickly found that there were no such leftovers. Consequently, Lu discussed her quandary with her husband and asked whether he would be willing to provide sperm for research purposes. "He agreed immediately!" and indeed one day in early 1981, when Lu wanted to do some research, she brought sperm samples from her husband and put them on her desk:

> When one of the vice directors [of the Xiangya Medical College] had a look at the sperm samples and asked where I got them from I replied that they were from the outpatients, but the vice director responded that they can't be from outpatients because they are of good quality! [laughter] So I said: "This is from my husband; you are male teachers, but you can't donate any sperm for research purposes?" So from that time on, our male teachers also donated their sperm for research, like volunteers.

Once they had mastered the art of freezing and thawing sperm (on which more in a later section), the next step was to secure donors who would be willing to donate their sperm for reproductive purposes rather than solely for research. One of Lu's colleagues, who had worked in the countryside like so many others during the Cultural Revolution, suggested that they pay a visit to a steel factory to ask whether workers there would be willing to donate. When this did not pan out (the workers refused to provide sperm samples), they moved on to a mine in a mountainous region of Hunan. "We had to take a bus first and then change to a train and we had to bring the liquid nitrogen . . . carrying it by hand, it was very hard at that time." This time they succeeded in convincing workers to participate in a physical examination that included the provision of a sperm sample for analysis and possible donation in return for a small compensation fee. "We collected like forty people's, more than forty people's sperm samples and brought them back to Changsha." This group of men became in effect China's first frozen sperm donors.

Then, in early 1982, with donor sperm in their bank's tanks, Lu Huilin contacted the man who had originally written to him asking about sperm banks for humans (see the introduction). The man arrived in Changsha with his wife and after two attempts at insemination—"we didn't know when the best time for ovulation was so I had to read in a book about contraception, which described at what time in a cycle contraception was needed, so I guessed this is the ovulation time [laughter] because there is no information in other books"—in January 1983 Lu Guangxiu and her team succeeded in using frozen donor sperm to secure the birth of a healthy baby boy for the first time in China. Bearing in mind the moral disapproval they met from many of their medical colleagues, Lu Huilin decided to keep news of this achievement a secret.

Meanwhile, in Beijing Zhang Lizhu was busy trying to develop a method for retrieving eggs. As noted earlier, Zhang had traveled to Copenhagen in 1980 to speak at the UN Women's Conference. Upon being asked whether she had learned about in vitro fertilization on this trip, she responded: "I went abroad in 1980 with some women's groups to visit many places. However, our visit at the time didn't consider test tube baby technology at all. What we looked at was how to do female health care, how to do family planning—meaning abortions and birth control—as well as learning about condoms and intrauterine devices; therefore we didn't really keep up with the trends at the time" (Zhang, Interview 2). Instead, once she did begin focusing her attention on the infertility problems of her patients, she embarked on her own forms of experimentation. Lu had been astonished when her father had asked her "Do you know how to get an oocyte?" since she had worked as a surgeon rather than an obstetrician or gynecologist. Zhang, on the other hand, had experience from working with her patients. She recalls how she began working to locate and retrieve oocytes:

> There were test tube babies elsewhere in the world at this time. The first test tube baby was born in 1978 in the U.K. At that time they were all using laparoscopic surgery to retrieve eggs. Once the laparoscope was put in, the surface of the ovary could be seen, and the ovary follicle could be seen too, which was the place the needle needed to penetrate. However, in China we couldn't do the same because the surface of the ovary couldn't be seen at all using a laparoscope [due to tissue damage from tuberculosis in some cases, or difficulties in manipulating the laparoscope]. So the only method we had at the time was retrieving ova by hand while treating pelvic cavity disease. Manually reaching the ovary follicle and judging by instinct where to insert the needle, sucking the ovarian follicular fluid out, and then finding the ova in the ovarian follicular fluid. Therefore we used a different strategy by finding ova in the ovarian follicular fluid we retrieved, and learned more about the ova. (Zhang, Interview 2)

Jiang has argued that we should take this account of an "indigenous method" with a grain of salt, since the fact was that laparoscopy was a difficult technique for anyone to learn, let alone in China where clinical and laboratory conditions were so poor in the early 1980s (Jiang, 2015, pp. 46-47). There were not many patients who were willing to undergo experimental procedures solely for egg retrieval.[6] Instead, patients were asked if they would agree to egg retrieval for research purposes once open pelvic surgery for a medical indication had been safely completed.

Lu Guangxiu's initial attempts to secure oocytes during this time were also through surgery, because as she told me "we didn't know how to do laparoscopy." Zhang has recounted how in these early years "we [started] from not being able to identify ova" just as Lu has recalled, "I didn't know what the eggs looked like at that time." As a result, there was a lot of trial and error involved. For Lu, this involved countless trips throughout Changsha to hospitals that carried out surgery for the treatment of gynecological disease to ask for assistance in getting oocytes:

> Egg retrieval had been done in Xiangya hospital; however, as they didn't support our work, and I was refused permission to go into the surgery room I had to go to other hospitals for eggs. I sometimes rode a bicycle and carried a bucket as I visited many hospitals in Changsha. But I had little chance to get eggs, since sometimes we couldn't find follicles in ovarian tissues. Besides, it was also very hard for me to recognize eggs, as human eggs were different from mouse eggs. That's why I set up a sperm bank at that time, because I couldn't tell whether the eggs were mature or immature when I got eggs, so I had to fertilize all the eggs [and see which were mature enough]. So I set up a sperm bank in order to fertilize the eggs once I got them. Without ovulation induction, it was very difficult at that time.

Zhang, on the other hand, was familiar with and had direct access to the departments at the Third Hospital that carried out routine open pelvic surgery for a variety of conditions. Yet, she would also have trouble finding willing patients, and when she did there were numerous practical challenges related to timing operations such that they coincided with ovulation. Without a sperm bank of her own in Beijing, Zhang relied on the husbands of her infertile patients to provide sperm samples, not all of whom agreed to do so. Moreover, Zhang was initially hampered by not having seen a human egg before, having only microscopically observed pig and mouse eggs.

The early 1980s were truly experimental years for assisted reproduction in China. Those scientists who became interested in reproductive technologies had to devise ways of getting gametes in China, and were faced with at least as many (if not more) challenges in this as their colleagues anywhere else in the world.

EXPERIMENTING

Let us now take a closer look at how Zhang and Lu were able to lead their respective teams to achieve China's first IVF births in 1988. Lu and her team had already secured the birth of the first baby using frozen donor sperm, but Lu and her father continued to pursue IVF research with the hopes of securing yet another first. Both Zhang and Lu were working under incredibly crude conditions and with meager resources, just as both had to negotiate the disapproval they were met with by some colleagues and officials, whether for moral or demographic reasons. Not surprisingly, both would enlist the help of others, nationally and internationally. And it was in partnership (together with He Cuihua from the Peking Union Medical College) that they would secure funding for their research from the National Natural Science Foundation in 1986.

When it came to both sperm and eggs, much of the first half of the 1980s was spent not just experimenting with cryopreservation and retrieval techniques, but also grappling with the harsh aftermath of the Cultural Revolution. This was a motif that ran through many of the interviews and discussions I had with those researchers who had been active in reproductive science during the 1980s and 1990s. Visiting China's grid-locked metropolises today it can be easy to forget just how much cities like Beijing and Changsha have transformed over the last twenty-five years. Following the Cultural Revolution, which ended in 1976, many laboratories had become almost derelict and there were no reliable suppliers of laboratory equipment or chemical agents. The bicycle was still the most common form of urban transportation.

In recollections of the many difficulties they had faced, both Zhang and Lu convey a sense of pride and perhaps also nostalgia for the excitement of the times. When it came to freezing sperm for the first time in Changsha, Lu recalls:

> We did not have any equipment to do this research. I also needed a protective agent for freezing the sperm and we knew that we could use egg to do that, but you have to pasteurize the egg at a temperature of about 56 degrees Celsius. But without any equipment—we only had an oven, which was in poor condition [laughter], so when I put the egg inside the oven to pasteurize it, after half an hour, the egg became a cake [laughter]. All the people laughed! And there was no freezing agent or liquid nitrogen either. During that time, we didn't have any equipment; we hadn't even seen a fridge before. But at the Dermatology Department in our hospital, they had a new laboratory and certain equipment to freeze the skin from the pig. The director was also very kind and offered that I could use his laboratory to do this research, so we went to the laboratory, myself and a male colleague. . . . They

Figure 4. China's first frozen sperm bank for humans, 1983. (Photo courtesy of Lu Guangxiu.)

brought some liquid nitrogen into the laboratory to have the sperm frozen. But it was the first time for them to see the steam, they were afraid that maybe it will explode! [laughter]. . . . So they measured the temperature through the whole night, they just observed the temperature and they dared not to cover the tank with a lid, because they were afraid that if you cover it with the lid, it will explode. So for the whole night, they were just sitting there and observing all the things, also through the next day until the evening. They succeeded in freezing the sperm and were very happy at that time!

Similarly, Zhang recalled how equipment shortages were a constant problem when she and her colleagues were trying to develop egg retrieval techniques:

We described the difficulties we faced as "poor and blank" (*yiqiong erbai*). Conditions were really poor. All equipment had to be used repeatedly. For example, there were only a few ova-retrieving needles, which were brought back from overseas. They had to be washed and high-pressure sanitized. Vessels had to be used again and again too, and then washed and high-pressure sanitized. At that time we had a lot of cases but there were no infections. This was very impressive and staff in our laboratory worked really hard. There were whorls at the very top of the needles . . . which made it easy to know where to penetrate. The whorls got worn down. We took the needles to watchmaker shops to sharpen them. After being sharpened and reused so many times, we had to throw them away, since the whorls could barely be seen anymore. The conditions really were poor at the time. (Zhang, Interview 3)

Since Zhang had not had experience with identifying oocytes, she allied herself with embryologist Liu Bin who had studied mammalian developmental biology in the 1970s in Belgium. It was in collaboration with Liu that Zhang would learn how to identify human eggs by watching and discussing one of the films Liu had brought back from Belgium showing how animal embryos developed, as well as by studying images of human oocytes published in international scientific journals, which were slowly becoming available in Beijing (Jiang, 2015, p. 15).

YOUSHENG — SUPERIOR BIRTHS

By 1984, Zhang had developed her own technique of egg retrieval, just as Lu had established China's first sperm bank. Up to that point, the two had worked without much knowledge of each other's work. That would change in late 1983 when an exhibition on "superior births" (*yousheng*)[7] was organized by the Family Planning Department of the provincial government in Hunan Province. Participants at the exhibition discussed prenatal screening and both "negative" (abortion) and "positive" ways of improving population quality. Since preimplantation genetic diagnosis was a long way off at that stage, sperm banking was discussed as one possible method of improving population quality. A group of journalists who were attending the exhibition got wind that a sperm bank had in fact been established in Changsha:

> They came here for an interview and then they sent out a report saying that in Hunan there is a sperm bank. This was kind of explosive news in China, because every newspaper carried this information and they kept reporting it. And suddenly we got very famous around China! [laughter] And we got hundreds of letters from patients and from other institutes. Although many people praised us, some people criticized us[;] . . . they thought we were treating people like animals, since we are just collecting sperm.

Shortly after news of Changsha's sperm bank had broken nationally, Zhang Lizhu and Lu Guangxiu began communicating. Together with one of Zhang's peers in Beijing, He Cuihua from the Peking Union Medical College (who had been introduced to assisted reproduction during a study trip to Singapore), the trio agreed to prepare an application for research funding, which would be sent to the Ministry of Health. After some discussion between them, they agreed to title their application "*Yousheng*: The Protection, Preservation, and Development of Early Embryos," a decision that cannot be detached from the restrictive family planning measures that were being rolled out across China in this exact same period, as well as the growing interest in population quality on the part of family planning officials. As Zhang put it: "There were other voices at the time. Some people said: China already has such a huge population, why do you still want to work on test tube babies? They said this went against the national family planning policy" (Interview 3). Similarly, when I asked Lu about the apparent contradictions of carrying out IVF research in China in the 1980s, she replied, "There were many doctors and researchers who asked the same question as you did just now. Under this population policy we are doing this kind of technology, something that is contradictory." As we saw earlier, Lu Guangxiu's route to reproductive science had been through medical genetics. Her team at the Human Reproductive Engineering Research Department was as engaged in prenatal genetic testing as it was in IVF research. The medical genetic potentials of reproductive technologies had been at the very core of Lu Huilin's and Lu Guangxiu's early engagements with reproductive science. In the way that their research application was framed, reproductive technologies emerged as techniques that could contribute to the improvement of population quality in China (rather than infertility treatment as such), a demographic aim that was beginning to emerge alongside the controlling of population growth as a primary family planning objective (see Greenhalgh, 2008; Jiang, 2015).

Having witnessed the great difficulties that his daughter was facing in trying to get gametes and equipment for fertilization research, Lu Huilin decided in 1984 that she needed to travel outside China for more training. She recalls, "My father said that we can't go on like this, so he told the university that I need to have some training in foreign countries."

Arrangements were made for Lu Guangxiu and her colleague Xu Lili to travel to Yale University, a long-time partner of the Xiangya Medical College, in 1985. Lu was charged with learning laboratory procedures such as sperm washing, determination of the level of maturity of an egg, culture medium preparation, and embryo morphology assessment, while Xu received training in clinical procedures such as control ovarian hyperstimulation and egg retrieval. Six months later, the pair returned to Changsha, bringing back with them as much equipment as they could carry, including electronic scales, an osmotic pressure tester, and even a bottle of ultrapure water. "I came back in 1986 and established a laboratory immediately with all the equipment. . . . Doctor Xu did egg retrieval here in Changsha. I had learned how to recognize eggs, but Doctor Xu was responsible for the surgery on egg retrieval while another group who were at the Xiangya Hospital did laparoscopy for egg retrieval, so we began the work in 1986."

Now, one might be tempted to argue that clearly Lu Guangxiu, Zhang Lizhu, and He Cuihua received training and inspiration outside of China; hence perhaps this is after all a story of importing Western technologies into China. However, we know that, for example, Robert Edwards and Patrick Steptoe interacted with numerous international colleagues, and Steptoe traveled to France to learn laparoscopy from Raoul Palmer (Litynski, 1998), yet it is the United Kingdom that is most often credited as the "birthplace" of IVF. My point is that regardless of where they received training and where IVF was invented, Lu and Zhang had to experiment in order to develop it in China; they were not able to "skip" experimentation and merely set about routinizing IVF. Moreover, in setting out to develop reproductive technologies in China they were responding to local concerns arising out of the clinic (in Zhang's case) as well as out of a growing interest in population quality on the part of government officials (in Lu's case). As was the case with Edwards and Steptoe, Zhang and Lu built upon a range of already established procedures, technologies, and lab equipment that were circulating through global flows of technology and knowledge as they developed IVF in China.

It was also in 1986 that the "*yousheng*" research project received funding from the National Natural Science Foundation of China, which had been established under the auspices of the Four Modernizations program.

The foundation awarded RMB 100,000 to be split between the three researchers and their laboratories. The amount was therefore hardly sufficient, although the recognition that came with being awarded such a grant was perhaps of even more importance, as theirs became a so-called key research project of the Seventh Five-Year Plan. Reproductive science had become a part of China's overall modernization program, just as the race to produce China's first IVF child was in effect on.

This time, Zhang won. After thirteen attempted cycles with different women, thirty-nine-year-old Zheng Guizhen from Gansu became pregnant and gave birth to Zheng Mengzu on March 10, 1988, in Beijing. "There were three hospitals at the time working on this. . . . We were the first to produce test tube babies" (Zhang, Interview 3). In a television program called *Fendou* aired on China's CCTV network in August 2011, Zhang tells of her nerves on the scheduled day of Zheng Mengzu's birth by caesarean section with the nation's eyes fixed on her:

> When the first test tube baby was born, there were a lot of reporters waiting outside the operating room. So when I was on the way to the operating room I didn't really want to face them. I passed by with a blank face without even nodding at them, without a word, because I was worried. I was not worried about the operation. What I was worried about was the baby's being born with some kind of malformation, such as a harelip. So this is what I was worrying about when I performed the surgery. Then I saw the baby and checked her whole body and she was totally fine, crying really loudly. I felt I could relax afterward. They said at this point I looked happy, with a little smile. So I really didn't know how to cope with the media at the time. I should have talked to them a little bit, which I didn't do at all. (Zhang, Interview 4)

It is telling that the health of Zheng Mengzu was foremost on Zhang's mind. Since Zhang, Lu, and He had claimed that IVF was a technique that would contribute to "superior births," it would have been a major setback had the child not been healthy.

Meanwhile, in Changsha, yet another race was playing out: Lu recalls, "We didn't succeed for more than one year [after 1986], so I worried much about that. The country had spent so much money on my training and there were a lot of expectations on me from others, especially from my father. He was eighty-eight years old at that time, so I also hoped to succeed as soon as possible. However, I failed for over one year so that I felt a lot of pressure." Changsha's first IVF babies were finally born exactly three months after Zheng Mengzu in June of 1988. As it happened, two patients had had their eggs retrieved and fertilized around the same time in the second half of 1987. Once their eggs had been fertilized with their respective husbands' sperm, one of the patients ended up with very poor quality embryos while the other patient ended up with leftover good-quality embryos. Since "there was no freezing equipment and technology, we usually had to abandon the spare embryos. Instead, we asked her [the woman who only had poor-quality embryos] if she would like to accept the other couple's embryo, and she said yes. Actually she was the first one who got pregnant in our center. . . . We don't know how we succeeded in the first one, maybe it's because we had done this work for a certain time and had gained some experience. However, the success rate at that time was still very low and it was probably less than 5 percent." And so, Zhang Minxing, Changsha's first IVF baby (China's second) was born on June 5, 1988, closely followed by Luo Youqun, China's first embryo donation baby, on June 7, 1988. In all, a flurry of four IVF babies were born in 1988, two in Beijing and two in Changsha. Both Zhang and Lu had used open pelvic surgery to retrieve eggs in their first successful IVF cases. He Cuihua had used laparoscopic methods to try to obtain eggs and never did succeed in her quest for a "first" IVF baby at the Peking Union Medical College in the late 1980s.

LEGALIZATION—THE BIRTH OF "ONE CHILD" ART

Although the births of the first IVF babies in China were widely celebrated in the media as examples of China's national scientific capabilities (Jiang, 2015), it would take a further fifteen years before ARTs would formally be legalized and thereby authorized in China. Indeed, the 1990s turned out to be very different for Zhang and Lu. In Changsha, provincial Ministry of Health officials had made it clear to Lu and her team that they were not in favor of assisted reproduction. They did have an interest in the potential of selective reproductive technologies (SRTs) for improving population quality, but when it came to helping couples have babies, they felt that this conflicted with their systematic efforts to bring down fertility rates. As the director of the sperm bank in Hunan, Fan Liqing, explained, some government officials "had opinions that if we have this kind of technology, then we will increase the population and because of this, Hunan Province issued a regulation to prohibit artificial insemination technology." Indeed, on December 3, 1989, reproductive technologies were targeted for the first time in Hunan's provincial Family Planning Regulations, which were issued at the twelfth meeting of the Seventh People's Congress Standing Committee of Hunan in Changsha. The preamble of these regulations states that the overall objective of family planning in Hunan is "to control population growth and improve population quality [through] late marriage and childbearing with *yousheng* births" (Hunan Province, 1989, §1.1, 1.3). Article 25 specifically prohibits "fetal sex identification for pregnant women" and "artificial insemination," the latter of which was included as a direct consequence of the national media notoriety that Changsha had attained for having China's first sperm bank as well as delivering two IVF babies. No other provinces would legally ban assisted reproduction.

The impact of this regulation was immediate. The Xiangya Medical College forbade Lu and her team from continuing to work with patients, and so for most of the 1990s, reproductive research and experimentation in Changsha was confined to animals and basic research:

> In 1989, there was a government official from the national government who came to Hunan Province and also met with me. He suggested to me that because China has such a large population, "why don't you try this kind of technology on pandas instead of human beings?" So I worked in Sichuan Province in Wolong, from 1989 to 1991. Every April and May, I would go to this place and participate in the project with them to do research on insemination of pandas. . . . And also because we could not do any treatment from the sperm bank for [infertile] human beings, another local government official from the Ministry of Public Health suggested that I go to this village in Hunan Province, in the western part of Hunan, because in that village people were born with low intelligence. The official suggested that maybe I could offer the sperm in our sperm bank to them. He said, "If it's a genetic disease, then you can help them to have a healthy baby." But if it is not a genetic disease, then it wouldn't help. So from 1989 to 1992, for four years, I carried out a project there to study whether it was a genetic disease and

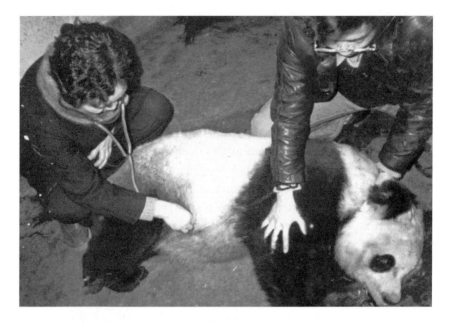

Figure 5. In March 1990, Professor Lu Guangxiu (left) successfully applied artificial insemination technology in Sichuan province where giant panda Wolong gave birth to a pair of twins. (Photo courtesy of Lu Guangxiu.)

after four years, we got the results. . . . They lacked iodine, so we gave some suggestions to remedy this.

In stark contrast, Zhang was able to continue developing ART treatments in Beijing. Her stature had grown immensely following the birth of Zheng Mengzu and she continued to receive support from the central government. As I learned from Qiao Jie, director of the Medical Center for Human Reproduction at the Third Hospital who worked under Zhang in the 1990s, in the first half of that decade Zhang went on to deliver China's first frozen embryo baby as well as China's first baby through gestational surrogacy.

It was in these early 1990s years that anthropologist Lisa Handwerker carried out her pioneering fieldwork on infertility in Beijing, charting what she saw as a growing "high-tech baby-making industry," which somewhat ironically was being fueled by the one-child policy. Through her many interviews with infertile women in Beijing, Handwerker docu-

BENEFITS OF IVF

mented the devastating stigmatization that especially women in Beijing were facing who were popularly referred to as "the hen that can't lay an egg" (Handwerker, 1998, p. 192). The one-child policy, she found, was in fact intensifying this stigmatization. As one of her woman informants put it, "The one child policy is really the 'you must have one child policy'" (Handwerker, 2002, p. 302; see also chapter 6).

While she observed growing consumer demand when more people learned about ARTs through media reporting, Handwerker also vividly saw the resistance that such technologies met in the early years. As she put it, "Some government officials, doctors, and citizens are ambivalent at best and even largely unsympathetic to infertility research and clinical medicine. State doctors often have to justify their work and need for resources" (Handwerker, 2002, p. 304). By 1993, some fifty IVF babies had been born in China, mostly in Beijing. Yet Zhang would still have to defend her work to those colleagues, government officials, and journalists who

> asked how the country benefited from test tube babies. Of course it was hard to say what benefit it brought to the country. However, people are part of this country. There is no country if there are no people. Test tube babies brought happiness to many people. If people have a need like this, then we should fulfill it for them. People did have this need, and some of them needed it urgently. We received 6,300 letters from people who were infertile [in the years following Zheng Mengzu's widely publicized birth]. We analyzed these letters and a lot of them had really hard lives: lots of people had extremely low self-esteem; the relationship between husband and wife was really bad; some divorced; some had family conflicts and didn't work anymore. This affected society's harmony, and this is in the end related to the country. (Zhang, Interview 3)

Since ARTs were neither legal nor illegal in most provinces at this point, numerous sperm banks and fertility clinics began cropping up throughout China. In one of many discussions with Fan Liqing, he suggested that "some experts think that 1997 was a Chinese IVF year, because in that year there were many centers appearing at the same time." Yet these many centers were not regulated. A number of "rogue" sperm banks in places like Qingdao and Chongqing had begun offering donor sperm without any systematized screening practices and without maintaining any records for traceability should anything go wrong. As Lu put it,

"Suddenly sperm banks were getting out of control and a lot of people were providing this service; some were even operating out of a hotel!" In 1999, the Xinhua News Agency reported that "China's 1st notables' sperm bank" had opened in Sichuan Province, "which only accepts donors with academic degrees equal to associate professor and above" (Xinhua, 1999). In 2001, Wang Yixing from Renji Hospital in Shanghai told a *Shanghai Star* reporter that "sperm banks seemed to be popping up all around the country overnight, and some of them can't ensure the sperm source and quality" (Hu, 2001).

Back In Changsha, Lu Guangxiu had not given up her hopes of establishing a fertility clinic. While numerous clinics and sperm banks were being established throughout China in the 1990s, Lu and her team continued to lobby provincial government officials in Hunan to get them to change their position on assisted reproduction. Meetings and workshops were organized in Changsha with the participation of local family planning officials, Ministry of Public Health representatives, bioethicists, and legal advisers. Lu explained her tactics at these meetings:

> I told them that my opinion is that the population policy requires that every family have only one child, but this is for fertile couples. But for infertile couples we should help them to have one healthy baby. So this is the real population policy. I told the Family Planning Bureau in Hunan that our population policy should be based on this idea that every family should have one healthy baby, not only fertile, but also infertile couples, so this is fair to every family.

On August 3, 1999, Hunan's Family Planning regulations were amended. This time Article 23 stated that "artificial insemination is prohibited, with the exception of institutions approved by the nation for scientific research, and those approved by family planning administration departments of the provincial people's government" (Hunan Province, 1999).

But it was not only Family Planning and Ministry of Health authorities in Hunan that had taken note of the growing yet unregulated ART sector in China, and the need to establish controls. During one of my stays in Beijing in 2007 as a visiting scholar at the Peking University Health Science Center, just opposite the fertility clinic at the Third Hospital, I met with one of the Ministry of Health officials in Beijing who coordinated the drafting of national regulations for assisted reproductive technologies. I was told, "We carried out a survey in 1999 where we found out that about two hundred centers were offering assisted reproductive technologies, but the standards were not good and they were not regulated. This was not acceptable. That's why we decided to put an expert group together to prepare regulations for these technologies, so that these clinics would require a license to provide assisted reproductive technologies." Similarly, Lu Guangxiu had been appalled that:

> Before 2001 . . . at that time sperm banks were out of control, no one really managed them or gave any regulations. So there were no regulations that you should be licensed to run a human sperm bank; anyone could do that. And for the sperm donors, they were not doing any selection of donors; everyone can be a donor and they are also not doing any examinations of the donors. And if they were supplying any sperm to other institutes, they also weren't required to provide any information and they were not keeping track of success ratios. They just gave the sperm not knowing what happened to the sperm afterward.

And so it was that, between 2001 and 2003, the Ministry of Health issued a set of laws, regulations, and technical specifications that finally legalized ARTs nationally (just as Hunan Province had legalized them provincially in 1999). These included the Regulation on Assisted Reproductive Technology and Ethical Principles for Human Assisted Reproductive Technology and Sperm Banks, both of which were issued in 2001 and revised in 2003. With these regulations, assisted reproduction finally settled into a form that suited the country's restrictive reproductive complex. Henceforth, clinics providing ARTs would have to live up to a series of strict requirements in order to be licensed.

Apart from a number of technical requirements concerning the equipment, procedures, and personnel that clinics must have, what made these regulations distinctive to China was the following passage:

> Organizations operating IVF-ET [embryo transfer] and related technologies, must obey national population and family-planning legislation and policies. . . . Organizations must first carefully inspect a couple's ID, marriage certificate, and original copy of their qualification of pregnancy certificate issued under national population and family planning legislation and policies. Photocopies of the mentioned documents should be saved for the records. (MoH, 2003a, pp. B1, B2)

As a result, ARTs are now only available to couples who have both a marriage certificate and a pregnancy certificate.

The impact of the 2003 revised regulations on ARTs was immediate. Only 90 of the 200 or so clinics that were providing ARTs at the time were able to live up to the licensing requirements stipulated in the regulations. The regulations served to routinize the practice of ART. This routinization was vividly on display in the lobby of one of the provincial family planning hospitals that I visited. The hospital's directory was displayed on a large billboard, which confirmed that among the services on offer in the same building on different floors were IVF, a human sperm bank, prenatal screening, ligation operations, ligation reversal operations, and pregnancy terminations. ARTs have become but one among many other techniques of birth *control* that aim to regulate population growth and improve population quality in China. For Lu, this alignment of ARTs with China's population improvement aims has been an important compromise: "Under these new regulations and also management guidelines, we incorporated a lot of experiences from foreign countries, but we combined these with the Chinese situation. We are required to inform our patients who should sign informed consent forms, but because of our population policy, we require that every couple should have pregnancy certificate to ensure that they only have one baby, and in this way we also obey the population policy."

SCALED-UP ART

Since 2003, the number of clinics providing ARTs under license has steadily climbed back to and surpassed the 200 that the Ministry of Health had identified in its 1999 survey. By 2014, an estimated 400 centers offer ART services and there are a total of twenty-three provincial sperm banks. In Beijing, the number of IVF babies has skyrocketed from the 50 reported by Handwerker in the early 1990s to more than 10,000 in 2011 and somewhere around the 200,000 mark nationally in 2017. In Changsha, it was in 2002 that Lu and a group of investors formed the CITIC-Xiangya Reproductive Genetic Hospital, which has exponentially increased the number of IVF cycles annually from 700 in 2002 to some 40,000 in 2016 (see table 1.1). Scaled-up IVF is now a reality in China, with profound

Table 1.1 Annual IVF and insemination cycles carried out at the CITIC-Xiangya Reproductive and Genetic Hospital in Changsha

	2002	2007	2010	2011	2012	2013	2014	2015	2016
No. of IVF cycles/clinical pregnancy rate (cpr)[a]	700	6,192	13,160	18,235	22,161	27,587	31,677	35,273	40,733
	30.5%	44.9%	51.5%	53.6%	59.1%	59.6%	59.1%	60.1%	59.1%
No. of IVF cycles with donor sperm/cpr	23	529	997	1,189	1,894	2,248	2,344	2,688	2,398
	40.9%	56.2%	63.59%	65.9%	71.1%	71.0%	72.9%	70.8%	68.8%
No. of IUI-ICI cycles with donor sperm/cpr[b]	1,403	3,440	3,392	3,470	3,631	2,771	2,038	1,809	1,597
	22.3%	22.2%	24.5%	26.3%	25.1%	25.3%	26.1%	24.7%	26.5%

SOURCE: CITIC-Xiangya Reproductive and Genetic Hospital.

NOTE: Frozen embryo transfers are not included in the breakdown.
a. Clinical pregnancy rates in table 1.1 are self-reported and cannot be used to compare the CITIC-Xiangya Reproductive and Genetic Hospital with other fertility clinics, because there are many factors affecting clinical pregnancy rates (e.g., age of couple undergoing IVF or insemination, severity of their condition, number and quality of eggs retrieved following ovarian stimulation, number and quality of embryos resulting from IVF, and more). There are also varying methodologies for calculating clinical pregnancy rates.
b. The decline in numbers of insemination cycles (both intrauterine and intracervical) with donor sperm does not reflect falling demand, but rather reflects a strategic (commercial) reprioritization at the CITIC-Xiangya Reproductive and Genetic Hospital away from insemination and toward IVF, as can be seen in their self-reported statistics.

implications for the ways in which the logistics of IVF are organized and patients experience their treatments. Growth continues to be driven both by insatiable demand (in Beijing and Changsha, huge crowds congregate every morning hoping to register as patient-customers) and because ART has become a very lucrative sector with private investors providing much of the capital required to get started or expand.

According to Ministry of Health statistics, in 2013 there were a total of 609,009 ART cycles carried out in China (including AIH: 91,725; AID: 30,229; IVF: 221,025; ICSI: 98,935; and frozen embryo: 167,095). These cycles resulted in 193,863 pregnancies in 2013 and 145,108 live ART births. The estimated cost per AID cycle is 3,000 RMB; for an IVF cycle it is 20–30,000 RMB; while for ICSI it is 25–35,000 RMB per cycle. Fertility treatment is not covered by public or private insurance, which means that for many infertile couples in China, ARTs remain financially out of reach.

The newest purpose-built IVF laboratory that I visited in Changsha was surrounded by no fewer than four egg retrieval/embryo transfer theaters, each with a hatch into the central laboratory. The walls of the laboratory were stacked with IVF incubators, some of which were equipped with time-lapse embryoscopes. On my tour of these facilities one of the embryologists exclaimed that "our tanks are bursting!" when I asked what couples did with any so-called "spare" or "leftover" embryos if they succeeded in having a child, given the then one-child policy. As it happens, many couples had been (cryo-)banking on a change in family planning regulations, as indeed did happen in early 2016 when all couples were given permission to have two children. This policy change made these frozen embryos bureaucratically viable for the first time. While the scale of ART in China may appear enormous to most, it does not seem out of keeping with other forms of health delivery and hospital care in China. If we accept estimates that some 10 percent of couples of childbearing age are having trouble conceiving without assistance in China, the math speaks for itself.

CONCLUSION

In the space of three decades, ARTs like sperm banking and IVF have gone from technological frontier to routinized on an astounding scale in China as they have traversed the continuum from experimental to standard of care within the country. As we have seen, the birth of sperm banking in China was inextricably bound to the development of IVF, which is the biggest and most lucrative form of ART in China today. It is absolutely the case that Zhang, Lu, and others had received training and inspiration internationally when experimenting with reproductive technologies during the 1980s, but this training did in no way allow them to "merely" introduce and adapt an already existing technology to fit China's social, cultural, legal, and socioeconomic conditions. Even though sperm banking had been developed in the United States in the 1950s and IVF had been invented in the United Kingdom in 1978, this was not a case of simply importing preexisting ARTs into China; rather, bound up in global flows of knowledge and technology (much like all other scientists in the world), Zhang, Lu, and others experimented in conditions that were extremely crude in comparison to those found in Europe in the 1970s. Following this experimentation in the 1980s, it would take almost two decades before ARTs were officially accepted and sanctioned through legislation amid much resistance and skepticism on the part of some government officials and fellow scientists. Since 2003 regulations requiring couples to present clinics with their "qualification of pregnancy certificate," making the procedure acceptable as national policy, we have seen a globally unprecedented scaling up of ART in China. Notwithstanding this growth, sperm banks and clinics simply cannot keep up with demand.

Yet, as I have shown in this chapter, the routinization of ART has by no means been self-evident or an unavoidable consequence of globalization. Instead, ARTs emerged in China in response to local concerns (not least tuberculosis-induced infertility and a governmental push to improve population quality) and within the framework of the so-called "one-child policy" in a way that makes them best understood as technologies of birth control. It is in this way that routinization must be understood firstly as a socio-historical process whereby ARTs came to be (re-)produced and entrenched within a particular reproductive complex. And, as I will show in the chapters that follow, it is within this reproductive complex that a unique style of sperm banking has emerged over the last fifteen years in China.

2 Improving Population Quality

During an interview carried out under the shade of a tree next to a newly landscaped brook on the sprawling campus of Changsha's University of Science and Technology, twenty-year-old Xueyu, a first-time sperm donor who had yet to qualify, was asked whether he thought that anyone should be allowed to donate sperm. After thinking about the question he replied:

XUEYU: The ones who have genetic diseases shouldn't be admitted to come. Otherwise the bad genes will be transmitted to offspring. We need to make sure that the outstanding genes will be transmitted.

AW: Do you think donors should be recruited only from universities?

XUEYU: No. You can also do that in offices. Their excellent work performance shows their perfect genes, so they also can provide good genes to the couples.

Although this was not the only view I met, as other interviewed donors emphasized physical health and a kind heart rather than profession or intelligence, there is no question that ideas about genetic transmission of traits and diseases has played an important part in the fashioning of sperm banking in China. Some sperm banks explicitly connect their fertility services to national goals of improving population quality when recruiting new donors. University students are considered to be of "high quality" (*suzhi gao*) and, all things being equal, it is assumed that their donations will help assure the stock of sperm stored in sperm banks will contribute to the strengthening of the Chinese population.

There is nothing particularly Chinese about more or less explicit links between gamete banking and the goal of improving population genetics. Cynthia Daniels and Janet Golden have traced the role of populist eugenics in shaping the American sperm cryobanking industry through the twentieth century, concluding that "the attributes used to market 'high quality sperm'—attributes of racial purity, physical prowess, and intelligence—also become (or remain) idealized. Sperm banking and the popular eugenics of its clients combine to perpetuate the myth that desirable human traits are transmitted genetically, not socially, and that the traits most characteristic of certain races and social classes are the most desirable universal human traits" (2004, p. 20). Similarly, Charlotte Kr=løkke has shown how a Danish sperm bank "cleverly connects Scandinavian genes with quality" when marketing its sperm online to customers around the world (2009, p. 13). And, in the field of egg donation, Lauren Jade Martin has argued that "third-party egg transfer reinforces genetic determinist ideas about the production of children with desirable and superior qualities while screening out less than desirable traits. The recruiting, screening, marketing, and matching process used by brokers is based on their ideas about what constitutes fitness, desirability, and marketability" (2017, p. 167). Sperm banking and artificial insemination by donor (AID) are as much selective reproductive technologies (SRTs) used to prevent or promote the birth of certain kinds of children (Gammeltoft & Wahlberg, 2014) as they are assisted reproductive technologies (ARTs), even if one has every reason to be skeptical about any claims concerning the possibility of selecting traits. As Rayna Rapp has pointed out, "Many potential consumers of selective repro-technologies increasingly believe that complex traits such as intelligence, height, beauty, musicality, and more have become the objects of gamete selection. This is hardly the case: scientific technique works most effectively at selecting out undesirable traits" (2017, p. vii).

Notwithstanding similar connections between sperm banking and eugenics throughout the world, I will in this chapter examine how the

Chinese state's explicit commitment to improve the quality of the population has shaped the particular style of sperm banking we find in China today, especially as regards a state-set limit of five women's pregnancies per donor. To begin with, as many scholars have pointed out, efforts to improve the quality or stock of a national population in East Asia should not be equated with those efforts found in the United States or Europe (see Dikötter, 1998; Gammeltoft, 2014; Greenhalgh, 2010; Ivry, 2009; Sleeboom-Faulkner, 2010b). Regions and countries have their historical and cultural specificities that have profoundly shaped the ways in which population quality improvement is conceived. We saw in the previous chapter that when it comes to reproductive politics in China, if "during the long 1980s [1979–1993], the dominant norm promoted by the state was one of quantity . . . in the 1990s and early 2000s . . . the enhancement of population 'quality,' has become increasingly central to the politics of population" (Greenhalgh & Winckler, 2005, pp. 215, 217). It was also during this time that the term *rénkǒu zhìliàng* was gradually replaced by *rénkǒu sùzhì* in official and popular discussions about "population quality," as the meaning of *sùzhì* ("inner quality") was transferred from things to persons (Bakken, 1999, p. 60; Fong, 2007; Kipnis, 2006). Scholars have long pointed to the contemporary pervasiveness of the *sùzhì* concept in China as a kind of spontaneous ideology; it permeates not just official population strategies and policies but also everyday practice through popular media, consumer goods, pharmacies, pregnancy advice, and more (Anagnost, 2004; Kipnis, 2007; R. Murphy, 2004; Zhu, 2013). This is not to say that questions of quantity have become any less pressing (as attested to by the easing of the one-child policy into a two-child policy in 2015); rather, the point is that in the last two decades or so questions of quality have become equally important at the bio-political level of managing the population.

In sperm banking, individualized norms of quality are used to assess the reproductive vitality of donors and their sperm.[1] How do these individualized quality norms differ from this notion of "population quality" (*rénkǒu sùzhì*)? Most importantly, as always in matters of population, *rénkǒu sùzhì* concerns an aggregated collective, which is to say "population" as an entity, object, or body in its own right that can be mapped out in terms of fertility, mortality, morbidity, literacy, and productivity rates and measured against norms of wealth, health, and quality (Greenhalgh &

Winckler, 2005; Wahlberg & Rose, 2015). With *rénkǒu sùzhì*, it is the inner quality of such an aggregated collective rather than an individual person or biological sample that is at stake.[2] At the same time, however, just as one can distinguish between a subjective form of quality of life of individuals and the biological quality of their gametes or embryos in the treatment of infertility, so too can one at the collective level distinguish between "superior childrearing" (*yōuyù*) and "superior education" (*yōujiāo*) on the one hand, and "superior birth" (*yōushēng*) on the other. The former two concern pedagogical and educational efforts to improve "spiritual civilization" (*jīngshén wénmíng*) through the "raising of people's political consciousness and moral standards . . . as well as raising the level of the general knowledge of the people" (Hu Yaobang quoted in Bakken, 1999, p. 55). That is to say, improving the quality of the population in this sense requires *postnatal* cultivation of the physical, intellectual, and moral qualities of the people through education and training programs such as the "education for quality" (*sùzhì jiàoyù*) campaign introduced by the national government in the 1990s (Bregnbæk, 2016; Kipnis, 2007; R. Murphy, 2004).[3] *Sùzhì*, in this sense, is therefore something to be acquired, cultivated, and improved through education, training, awareness raising, and other forms of spiritual advancement.

Yōushēng (superior birth), on the other hand, concerns *preconception* and *prenatal* biomedical and educational efforts aimed at ensuring healthy births by preventing the transmission of "serious hereditary diseases" and congenital malformations through general medical advice, genetic counseling, prenatal screening and testing, as well as by encouraging healthy pregnancies through fetal education (*tāijiāo*) programs (Dikötter, 1998; Sleeboom-Faulkner, 2010a; Zhu, 2013). It is these forms of improving biological population quality by promoting *yōushēng* that will be the focus of this chapter.

IMPROVING THE QUALITY OF THE NEWBORN POPULATION

In December 1993, the Chinese government proposed a draft bill on "Superior Birth and Health Protection" (*yōushēng bǎojiàn*). In part as a response to international reactions, which dubbed it China's "eugenics law" (*Nature*, 1994), the law was revised, renamed "Law on Maternal and Infant Health Care," and subsequently passed in October 1994 with primary aims of "ensuring the health of mothers and infants and improving the quality of the newborn population" (P. R. China, 1994, Article 1).

This raises questions of just how the quality of the newborn population can improve (or deteriorate) as well as for what reasons it should be improved. What is it that is "better" in this context after *rénkǒu sùzhì* has been improved? And for the purposes of this chapter, how does male infertility treatment (which must "obey national population and family-planning legislation and policies" [MoH, 2003a, p. B.1]) contribute (or detract) from this objective? We find part of an answer to this question in the 1994 Law on Maternal and Infant Health Care, which made it obligatory for all couples to undergo a premarital medical examination "to see whether [the male or female] suffer from any disease that may have an adverse effect on marriage and childbearing" (P. R. China, 1994, Articles 7 and 10), keeping also in mind that China's Marriage Law from 1980 had prohibited marriage "if either the man or the woman is suffering from any disease that is regarded by medical science as rendering a person unfit for marriage" (P. R. China, 2001, Article 7). Also internationally controversial have been Articles 16 and 18, which concern genetic counseling for married couples of childbearing age and prenatal screening of fetuses for pregnant women respectively.

What links Articles 10, 16, and 18 in the Maternal and Infant Healthcare Law (1994) is an objective to prevent the transmission of defects and genetic diseases "of a serious nature" to future offspring with the help of premarital, preconception, and prenatal medical examinations and related counseling. Unmarried couples found to be suffering from "certain genetic diseases of a serious nature which are considered to be inappropriate for childbearing from a medical point of view" were given permission to marry only if they consent to "long-term contraceptive measures or performance of ligation operations" rendering them "unable to bear children" (P. R. China, 1994, Article 10). Married couples of childbearing age found to be suffering from a genetic disease of a serious nature were to be given "medical advice, according to which the said couple shall take corresponding measures" (Article 16). And finally, pregnant women who, following prenatal diagnosis, were found to be carrying a fetus "suffering from a genetic disease of a serious nature" or "a defect of a serious nature" were to be given "medical advice on a termination of gestation ... subject to the consent and signing of the person per se" (Articles 18 and 19).[4]

In 2003, premarital medical examinations were made voluntary in connection with an adjustment of China's marriage laws. Moreover, couples would have to pay for such examinations. As a direct result, the proportion of couples who underwent premarital examination reportedly "plummeted from 68 percent in 2002 to 3 percent in 2005" (*China Daily*, 2007a). This prompted Zhao Shaohua of the All-China Women's Federation to warn that "if the rate of premarital medical examinations continues to decrease so sharply ... the quality of the population will be seriously affected" (quoted in Chen, 2005). Two years later, at a conference held in Chengdu, capital of Sichuan Province, in October 2007, the deputy head of the National Population and Family Planning Commission, Fan Jiang, joined what had become a growing chorus of critics when he argued that: "a baby with defects is born every thirty seconds in China, and this situation has worsened year by year ... [which] directly affects China's comprehensive national strength, its international competitiveness, sustainable socioeconomic development, as well as the realization of our strategic vision to construct a full-scale well-off society" (quoted in *China Daily*, 2007b).

What this suggests is that to understand the biological norms contained within the concept of *rénkǒu sùzhì* that allow for assessments of population quality, it is necessary to unpack what is meant by defects and genetic diseases of a "serious nature." For it is these diseases and defects that are considered to negatively impact or lower population quality if biologically transmitted to offspring through reproduction, and, conversely, preventing their transmission is seen by some as a way of improving the quality of the newborn population because it helps to sequester "the unhealthy genes of our country's gene pool" (Zhu Hong, quoted in Dikötter, 1998, p. 140).

It is important to note that there is currently no consensus in China (or any other country for that matter) on what constitutes a "serious disease."[5] Before the national Law on Maternal and Infant Health Care came into force in 1995, a number of individual provinces in China had especially emphasized "mental diseases" (*jīngshénbìng*) in their definitions of "serious hereditary disease," thus listing psychosis, cognitive deficiency, and mental retardation as inappropriate for childbearing on the grounds that persons suffering from such conditions were likely to transmit these conditions through reproduction and were not able to look after themselves, let alone any children (Dikötter, 1998; Kristof, 1991). According to the 1995 law, the criteria for determining which diseases and defects are serious are that they "may totally or partially deprive the victim of the ability to live independently" and are "medically considered inappropriate for reproduction" (Article 38).

When it comes to *rénkǒu sùzhì* in a biological sense, "good life" animates a healthy, vibrant, and strong aggregate population[6] free of persons suffering from genetic diseases of a serious nature, congenital defects of a serious nature, infectious diseases, as well as so-called "relevant mental diseases." And although *rénkǒu sùzhì* is often used to refer to China's population as a whole, it can also be used to parcel out and break down this national aggregation into sub-populations that can subsequently be ranked according to their *sùzhì*. Those born with a "serious disease," "congenital defect," or "relevant mental disease" are considered of "low quality" compared to *yōushēng* newborns (see also Kohrman, 2005).[7]

Debates and regulations concerning population quality are relevant to ART clinics and sperm banks since they are required by Ministry of Health regulations to obey national population and family-planning legislation and policies. That is to say, there are instances where clinics are forbidden from providing fertility treatment to a couple. Some of these instances are administrative, that is, if a couple is unable to provide the hospital with a copy of their ID documents, marriage certificate, and an original copy of their pregnancy qualification certificate that confirms they are allowed to have a child in accordance with family planning laws.[8] And since premarital check-ups have become voluntary, the Regulation on Assisted Reproductive Technology stipulates that treatment cannot be provided in situations where the "wife or husband has a severe mental disease, genitourinary system inflammation, or sexually transmitted diseases" and/or where "in accordance with the Law on Maternal and Infant Healthcare, the couple have serious diseases considered inappropriate for conception and PGD" (P. R. China, 2003b, 1.C.2). In situations concerning the former, fertility treatment may be offered once the wife or husband has overcome the illness, whereas in the latter, treatment cannot be offered at all to the couple in question. Treatment can only be offered to those persons who are "qualified under national population regulations" (P. R. China, 2003b, D.1). And so, in the context of ART, "raising population quality" (*tígāo rénkǒu sùzhì*) refers to practices that promote "superior birth" (*yōushēng*) by screening involuntarily childless couples and gamete donors in order to prevent the transmission of certain "serious hereditary diseases" and to minimize the risk of "serious congenital defects."

Yet, there are also instances where ART itself is seen to negatively impact population quality, for example, by those who suggest that using a husband's "inferior quality" (*lièzhì*) sperm to fertilize eggs through ICSI (intra cytoplasmic sperm injection) technology[9] may perpetuate "genetic flaws": "harmful sperm development can adversely affect the quality of the population: fetal deformities, premature births, stillbirths, and birth defects may all be related to sperm" (Zhao, 2008). In China, as elsewhere, there are some who argue that using low-quality sperm for ICSI treatment will have a deleterious effect on the future child: "sperm injection technology is likely to use low-quality sperm. . . . This 'inferior quality' (*lièzhì*) sperm carries large amounts of bad genes and when it combines with the egg it is difficult to ensure that future generations do not inherit their genetic flaws" (Jia, 2001). At the fertility clinic in Changsha, despite the rise in use of ICSI, doctors continue to have similar reservations. In an interview with Li, a doctor specialized in male fertility, I learned of a case where a few single motile sperm cells were found in a semen sample much to the joy of the patient, who spontaneously embraced Li upon being told. Yet Li hesitated before offering him ICSI:

> With this patient I had a deep talk and he told me that during his childhood his mother said he had had many, many bouts of high fever so we thought that what caused this situation [low-quality sperm] maybe has a strong relation with these repeated high fevers; therefore it's not a genetic disease. So we say that we can do ICSI; this was our evaluation. . . . So we did ICSI one time and success! And one boy and one girl were born. I just called them two weeks ago and they are doing very fine, they are very healthy. . . . But for another patient, if he has a severe sperm quality problem but has no other medical history, generally we tell him his risk [of transmitting male infertility to his offspring] is very high.

In such latter cases, doctors will advise a couple to use a sperm donor instead as such a diagnosis falls under the category of serious genetic disease considered "medically inappropriate for reproduction."

Finally, when it comes to improving the quality of the newborn population, it should be noted that for those involuntarily childless couples who are lucky enough to achieve a viable pregnancy with the help of an ART like AID (around 25 percent of AID cycles result in pregnancy), the quest not only concerns having a successful birth, but also a superior birth (*yōushēng*) with the help of pregnancy nutrition advice, fetal education (*tāijiāo*) practices aimed at nurturing fetuses throughout pregnancy, as well as standard prenatal screening and health care (Sleeboom-Faulkner, 2010a; Zhu, 2013). Indeed, prenatal diagnoses of a "serious disease" or malformation in assisted pregnancies can be among the most devastating, since getting pregnant in the first place has most likely been an arduous, perhaps unrepeatable, task. While no statistics are available, in all of the fertility clinics I visited in Changsha, Beijing, Guangzhou, and Shanghai, doctors noted that although some patients choose to avoid prenatal screening (because of worries about possible post-screening abortion), most do not, and if prenatal screening does result in a diagnosis of, for example, Down's syndrome or a congenital malformation, couples will "usually choose to have an abortion" (see also Shih, 2017; Zhu, 2013). In Changsha, I was told of only a single case in which an AID cycle resulted in a child born with a congenital malformation (sperm banks are required by law to gather and record information about birth outcomes), albeit not medically attributable to the donor sperm.

LINEAGE ENHANCEMENT

Although there are far fewer cases compared to when male infertility is the issue,[10] donor sperm is also made available to couples where "the husband and his family have a severe heritable disease unsuitable for reproduction" (MoH, 2003a, p. C.2). Indeed, in such cases, fertility clinics are obliged by law to insist on the use of donor sperm, although as I have already noted, it is not always clear just what a "severe heritable disease" is (see also Wahlberg, 2009). Compare the views of the donor at the beginning of this chapter who insisted that sperm banks should ensure that excellent genes be passed on to a case handled by the ethics committee of one of the fertility clinics that I visited. The case, which was prepared for a workshop on informed consent in reproductive medicine held in Beijing in April 2007, was as follows:

> Chen who was twenty-two years old and unemployed and Xie who was thirty years old and likewise unemployed had been married for three years but had failed in having a baby during this time. When Xie's parents had heard about assisted reproductive technology (ART), they brought the couple to a reproductive hospital for consultation. Doctors noted that Xie lacked comprehension and communication abilities, and he was accompanied by his mother throughout the process of consultation. They learned that he was the only child in the family, and that his parents were longing to have a grandchild. Both Xie and Chen underwent a series of diagnostic tests that confirmed that Chen's indexes of physical growth and reproductive endocrine levels were normal. In their physical examinations of Xie, who had a height of 1.5 meters, doctors observed that he was slow in response and action, while his sperm quality met the standards recommended for AIH (artificial insemination by husband). Nonetheless, doctors were told that, since the wife considered her husband bad-looking and not intelligent and her mother-in-law also worried that his mental retardation might affect her grandchild, both Xie's mother and wife strongly asked for AID (artificial insemination by donor). During the examinations, doctors noted that although Xie once expressed his unwillingness to employ AID, he eventually yielded under his mother's demand. (BIONET, 2007a)

Anthropologist Margaret Sleeboom-Faulkner has shown how a commitment to continuing family lineages in rural households is sometimes at odds with the state's explicit aims to improve the quality of the Chinese population through premarital and prenatal medical checks. She argues that rural households are often driven by traditions to preserve lineage, and that can lead to various efforts to bypass state family planning policies. For example, since a serious diagnosis delivered during a premarital checkup is potentially devastating to efforts to ensure a son's or daughter's marriage, some families would knowingly seek to avoid such check-ups (which, as noted, have been voluntary in China since 2003) as well as to withhold medical history from future in-laws. Sleeboom-Faulkner wants to "emphasize . . . how national discourses are adapted to the expectations of rural families" (2010a, p. 124) as they seek to ensure that their lineages are continued through marriage and childbirth. What makes Xie and Chen's case interesting, however, is exactly how a rationale of lineage enhancement converges with state family planning policies of population quality improvement. It was Xie's mother who had taken the initiative to seek AID as she feared that his cognitive deficiencies would otherwise be transmitted to a future offspring. A similar case was discussed at a workshop on ethics in sperm banking held in Guangzhou in May 2012, where the parents of a man with cognitive difficulties had accompanied their son and his wife for a consultation at a fertility clinic. In this case, it was the doctors who were unsure of whether they should insist on AID or not provide any form of fertility treatment to the couple.

These two cases were brought to the respective clinics' ethics committees to decide whether the men suffered from conditions that were inappropriate for childbearing as well as whether they were likely to transmit these conditions through reproduction. As we saw earlier, the Law on Maternal and Infant Health Care defined "genetic diseases of a serious nature" as those "that are caused by genetic factors congenitally, that may totally or partially deprive the victim of the ability to live independently, that are highly possible to recur in generations to come, and that are medically considered inappropriate for reproduction" (Article 38). It was therefore often a fertility clinic's ethics committee (if it had one) that was asked to decide whether a man's cognitive difficulties ruled him out of a right to parenthood or whether his condition was likely to be genetic and thereby "inappropriate for reproduction." In these kinds of cases, which are far fewer than those where male infertility is at stake, there is an explicit link between sperm banking and the state's aims of improving the quality of the population.

RECRUITING HIGH-QUALITY DONORS

Some sperm banks also make explicit reference to the national goal of improving population quality when recruiting for sperm donors on university campuses, appealing to the personal and national pride of students.

This text is from one of the over twenty recruitment flyers I collected from five different sperm banks in China:

> How are you! We are the hospital staff responsible for advising you. As is well known, recently, more and more infertile couples have not received treatment in time, bringing great sadness to many families. We call on our university friends to help in this regard. . . . Donating sperm is like donating blood; both are in the service of the people. In order to understand how you can contribute please read the following points:
>
> 1. Donating can bring happiness to many infertility patients and help scientific research. Donating sperm is not only altruistic, it can also improve the Chinese people's quality (*zhonghuá mínzú sùzhì*). Since you are university students you are of very high quality (*sùzhì gao*), so if you join this project we will reach this goal quicker.
>
> 2. Our hospital is a standard hospital . . . so it can provide those students who are considering donating free medical tests covering chromosome, blood, microorganism, and whole body examinations. In order to assure the quality of sperm, and thereby ensure superior birth (*yōushēng*), every donor should have a systematic body examination, free of charge.

While there are many other forms of appealing to potential donors that sperm banks deploy in their recruitment materials, as we will see in more detail in chapter 4, this flyer framed the act of sperm donation as an important contribution to the goal of improving national population quality.

Yet, ideas about high-quality sperm donors notwithstanding, using a sperm donor is of course no guarantee for the quality of offspring, a point made very clear in the informed consent form that must be signed by those couples who decide to pursue AID (see Box 2.2). By signing the form, couples confirm that:

> We also know that many factors can affect the pregnancy so the hospital cannot assure that every insemination will result in a pregnancy. Currently, our center's artificial insemination cycle pregnancy rate is about 20 percent. We also know that even in normal people there will be some babies born with deficiency in body or intellect (about 4 percent) so this deficiency can also happen with artificial insemination. The doctors cannot control this, thus we understand and also agree that the reproductive center's doctors have no responsibility regarding the deficiency of offspring resulting from artificial insemination.

Informed consent form for sperm donors

Sperm donation is a completely voluntary action. I voluntarily donate sperm, understand and agree to the cryopreservation of my donated sperm at the qualified sperm bank inspected by the Ministry of Health. My donated sperm can be provided to medical institutions authorized to develop assisted reproductive technology, to be used as supply for artificial insemination or in vitro fertilization, IVF-embryo transfer, or medical science research.

I will not ask for or seek out any information on the patients who receive my sperm or any offspring produced from my sperm. I understand that I have neither rights over nor responsibility for these children, and that my identity will remain strictly confidential.

I understand that the sperm I donate can be used for a fixed maximum number of pregnancies, regulated by the Ministry of Health. The doctor has informed me that in order to avoid the very remote possibility of inbreeding, the sperm bank has created a permanent computer database of sperm donation and supply, and provides free consultation for sperm donors and recipients. In order to avoid my future natural children or grandchildren from one day marrying a child born as a result of my sperm donation, the doctor suggests that they come to consult the sperm bank before they get married, which I confirm that I understand.

The point being that however much you medically screen sperm donors, there can be no guarantees (all sperm banks can do is assure the quality of their sperm) that an AID child will be born healthy, either because a genetic flaw was not detected in the screening process, because of a *de novo* genetic mutation, a congenital malformation arising at conception, or because of an unknown hereditary disease on the woman's side. Indeed, as we will see in chapter 4, while sperm bank administrators might wish to expand the five-women's-pregnancies limit in China, they nevertheless concede that this limit minimizes risks of inadvertent transmission of a genetic condition.

In these ways a concern with the quality of newborns shapes the ways in which donor sperm is made available in China today. However, concerns about population quality were not only related to infertile couples' quests for conception, sperm donors too—their perceived "high quality" notwithstanding—were also implicated.

Informed consent form for recipient couples

After serious consideration we give doctors approval to use anonymous donor sperm to do one or more cycles of artificial inseminations. Doctors will do their best to select a qualified donor according to our wishes but we may not be able to use the same donor sperm for different cycles of artificial insemination.

We also know that many factors can affect the pregnancy so the hospital cannot assure that every insemination will result in a pregnancy. Currently, our center's artificial insemination cycle pregnancy rate is about 20 percent. We also know that even in normal people there will be some babies born with deficiency in body or intellect (about 4 percent) so this deficiency can also happen with artificial insemination. The doctors cannot control this, thus we understand and also agree that the reproductive center's doctors have no responsibility regarding the deficiency of offspring resulting from artificial insemination.

We know that the donor has no duties or rights, and we will never query the donor's ID. We acknowledge that a child born from artificial insemination is ours and that we are bound by the same rights and duties as with a child born from a natural pregnancy.

"EVERY DONOR'S SPERM CAN ONLY CONTRIBUTE TO FIVE WOMEN'S PREGNANCIES AT THE MOST"

During all my years of research, no one ever was able to tell me why the Ministry of Health ended up deciding on a maximum of exactly five women's pregnancies per sperm donor. Most countries have some kind of limit, but why five in China? A country like Denmark, with a population of five million, currently allows twelve (having previously allowed twenty-five) while Belgium, with a population of eleven million, allows six. With the recent switch from a one-child to a two-child policy in China, one sperm donor can now potentially have a total of ten offspring resulting from his donations but only if all five couples decide to try for a sibling from the same donor. All of the sperm bank managers and fertility experts I met expressed some degree of frustration with what they saw as an overly restrictive limit. Lu Guangxiu, for example, has vocally argued for a change to this limit, as she did in an article from 2010 concerning the chronic shortage of sperm donors in Changsha: "It's been scientifically proven that in a country with a population of three million, the chance of intermarriage between the offspring of one sperm donor is extremely slim when sperm is provided to five women. For a country of 1.3 billion people, one man's sperm could safely be provided to at least ten women" (cited in Cui 2010). Similarly, at the first conference on the social and ethical challenges of sperm banking in China held in Changsha in 2012 (thanks to the grant that financed the research for this book), a director from one of China's other sperm banks also suggested ten:

> Qualified sperm donors are in such limited supply that infertile couples often wait for long periods before receiving donor sperm. Considering Mainland China's enormous population, the number of donor offspring should be reevaluated. Our policy is too strict. I did a survey [according to which], only 1 percent of people would like to donate their sperm, among that 1 percent, almost one-tenth or one-twentieth are not qualified for various reasons. We make so many efforts [to recruit donors] and each can only impregnate five women. In Denmark, sperm can be exported to other countries. I think we must reevaluate our policy. Ten is quite a safe number, because in China, the population is very large.

For sperm bank directors, notching up this limit to ten would be one of the most effective ways to address the chronic shortage of sperm donors in China, in effect doubling the "reach" of a single donor, not to mention increasing monetary yields per donor. Yet, it is exactly this fear of unwitting consanguineous marriages that surrounds the five-woman limit in China. In his discussion of the motivational factors behind the drafting of China's Law on Maternal and Infant Health Care in the early 1990s, bioethicist Qiu Renzong makes the following point:

> The Chinese Revolution originated in remote, mountainous areas which were called Revolutionary Old Bases. Officials who returned to their villages where they had stayed during the war against Japanese occupation or civil war were shocked by their extreme underdevelopment. They were especially appalled by so-called "idiot villages" where almost all villagers were physically deformed or mentally retarded, none of whom were capable to serve as treasurer or as head of the village, and all of whom had to be completely dependent upon support from the community and government. In the Dabie Mountains, one of these Revolutionary Bases, the source of 37.5 percent of

severe mental retardation was inbreeding. Many suffered from cretinism. (Qiu, 2003, p. 188)

We will recall from the previous chapter that in those years when Lu Guangxiu had been forbidden to offer ART treatment to infertile couples during the 1990s, she had worked on a project to investigate why in particular rural villages of Hunan "people were born with low intelligence." The assumption among government officials had been that this apparent prevalence of low intelligence was the result of inbreeding, and one Ministry of Health official had even mooted using donor sperm to eradicate this problem in the villages. However, neither the prevalence of low intelligence nor the suggestion that inbreeding was the cause had been scientifically established, Lu explained:

> We followed six groups of people during our research in this village. In one group we measured the intelligence of both children and adults, in another group we carried out chromosome examinations and in another we selected some of the food, water, soil, and grain [they used] to have them examined in order to see whether there was any radiation in the environment. But we found nothing abnormal in any of these six groups. And then one day, when we were having a rest in this village, we noticed that a lot of the villagers had big necks [from goiter] because they lacked iodine [which can lead to mental retardation in children]. ... So in 1994, we added iodine in their salt. Our findings provided proof and evidence for this new policy. You know, this condition of an enlarged thyroid was very prevalent in Gansu Province during that time, but no one knew the reason. So in Gansu Province, they even required people who have this disease to have a ligation operation. This also led to a controversial international discussion because it's a kind of a human rights issue and you can't just ask people to undergo a ligation. I had done my research in Hunan Province and so I gave my recommendations on this. It was not about the human [genetics], but about the environment. So that's why we still have this salt regulation.

My point in highlighting these two case studies from Qiu Renzong and Lu Guangxiu is to suggest that the "restrictive" five-women's-pregnancies limit per donor in China cannot be detached from the wider reproductive politics that have informed China's reproductive complex over the past decades. A concern with the negative effects of apparent inbreeding had influenced the drafting of the Law on Maternal and Infant Health Care in the early 1990s and it is clear that this concern was among the considerations of experts involved in drafting ART regulations (including Qiu Renzong and Lu Guangxiu) at the turn of the millennium. Around half of the fifty sperm donors I spoke to mentioned the possibility of inbreeding as something that concerned them, although most of them considered chances to be very remote as they made the point that "the Chinese population is so large, the probability of an encounter is very small." One of the donors I spoke to did explicitly state that he would prefer his sperm to be sent to another province even if the population of Hunan Province is 67 million, as this would minimize any risks of unknowing half-siblings falling in love. Another donor recalled a television show he had seen when asked about the risk of unwitting intermarriage of half-siblings:

> What you said reminds me of a TV series called *Home to the Nth Power* directed by Zhao Baogang, which was about the relationship between two siblings brought together following divorce. They have no blood relations, but one of them was from a sperm donor, so ethically they can't be together. I think the donor child should be able to accept this reality when he is an adult, they will know how to do their own thing and respect their parents, as he is already an adult. (thirty-year-old office worker, Guangzhou)

To be absolutely safe, sperm donors and recipient couples are advised to consult with the sperm bank when their own future "natural" children (in the case of donors) or donor offspring (in the case of recipient couples) are about to marry as part of informed consent procedures. Lu Guangxiu explained this to a worried reporter from the *People's Daily* in January of 2005:

REPORTER: Is there a possibility that one donor's sperm is provided to more than one woman? What if their offspring fall in love, which obviously violates traditional ethics? What can we do about that?

LU GUANGXIU: The regulation is that one donor's sperm can only be provided to a maximum of five women, under no circumstances to more than five. In this way the chance of inbred marriage is avoided as much as is possible. The sperm bank data is kept permanently, about seventy years [*sic*]. Once a child reaches the age of considering marriage, his parents know where the sperm donation came from and can check the files. If there is no same father/different mother relationship, the couple can get married. This is one side of it. The other aspect of assisted reproductive technology is to maintain strict control of the supply from the sperm bank. In the future, a central sperm bank will be set up to manage all sperm banks through the Internet to eliminate the possibility of inbred marriage. However, we still cannot guarantee this 100 percent; 95 percent should be no problem. (Li, 2005)

Further to the emotional and moral unease that unwitting intermarriage can generate, the impact of inbreeding as a population problem in China (and elsewhere) cannot but avoid introducing a potential threat (however remote) to the future quality of a sperm donor's grandchildren and thereby the quality of China's population. And it is this potential threat that to this day has kept China's limit at five women's pregnancies per donor.

CONCLUSION

However strictly sperm donors are screened, sperm banks will never be able to guarantee the quality of offspring born following AID. Throughout the world, eugenic legacies have shaped gamete banking practices; however, the point I have made in this chapter is that we cannot assume that understandings of what constitutes superior birth and how it might be actively pursued by couples, doctors, genetic counselors, or state agencies are the same everywhere. The style of sperm banking found in China today is inextricably bound up with state-led efforts to improve the quality of China's population. Indeed, routinized sperm banking has taken its place as yet another technology that can be harnessed in state-led efforts to control population quantity (only married couples with a pregnancy qualification certificate can access donor sperm) and improve population quality (by recruiting and screening "high-quality" donors and offering AID to couples where the male is deemed to have a genetic disease that is "medically inappropriate for reproduction").

3 Exposed Biologies

One March morning in 2013, I joined a crew from the Hunan Human Sperm Bank on one of their trips to Changde, where weekly donation sessions were held at a local women's hospital. It was a cool morning, and after a quick pit stop for breakfast noodles at a nearby restaurant, our minivan headed north along the Xiangjiang River. Traffic was rush-hour slow in Changsha, the capital of Hunan Province, as we crossed one of the Xiangjiang's tributaries on to the Longzhou peninsula. Lin leaned back and said, "Now you will see Changsha's new forest." He was right, even if there was hardly a tree in sight. Instead, a brand-new two-kilometer residential stretch came into view on our left. Seemingly endless rows of twenty-story high-rises stood like naked pine trees as far as I could see ahead. On such a cool morning, a mix of smog, mist, and low-hanging clouds created an eerie, somehow absurdly enchanting effect as the minivan drifted past this condoland for what seemed like ages. Lin laughed at how quickly the apartments, with such an attractive location close to the city center, had been snapped up by eager buyers sparking off a raucous minivan debate about the population influx, urbanization, and rising square-meter prices, which our driver insisted were beginning to rival those found in European capital cities.

In the eight years that I carried out episodic fieldwork in Changsha, Beijing, Shanghai, and Guangzhou, food safety scandals and an unfolding "environmental crisis" (*huanjing weiji*) were pervasive. From melamine-tainted milk powder to contaminated drinking water, discarded gutter oil collected for resale, fake eggs and toxic dumplings, felonious imaginations, it seemed, knew no bounds within a voracious economy. And as if such food safety scandals weren't hazard enough, residents in many of China's cities and so-called "cancer villages" were conspicuously choking in smog while polluted rivers flowed by. In 2007, my colleagues and informants would rarely talk of pollution, speaking resignedly instead of the "heavy fog" outside, even on days where the *indoor* corridors outside our offices in Beijing were hazy. If pollution was the price to pay for rising living standards, there was no sense in lamenting. As Li Liu, a social psychologist I met while in Beijing, wrote at the time, "For some, the current environmental crisis is an inevitable consequence of China's transition from a traditional agrarian society into a modern industrial society . . .: for the sake of immense gratification in intensive consumption, we have to tolerate pollution; for the sake of speedy economic growth, China has to pay the price of environmental degradation" (Liu, 2006, p. 231). The resignation I had met early on in my fieldwork turned into a sense of anxious helplessness by the end of it. Back from Changde, during one of many weekend meals at a Changsha restaurant, we got to talking about what a gamble it was these days to eat out. A couple of doctors recounted a morbid joke that was making the rounds at their hospital: "Eating food will give us stomach cancer, drinking water will give us liver cancer, and breathing air will give us lung cancer." Their deadpan juxtaposition of vital activity with deadly outcome hung over the rest of the meal and beyond: urban living was toxic living in China.

In this chapter I will show how the sperm bank (*jingzi ku*) in China has emerged quite literally as a sanctuary of vitality amid concerns around food safety, pollution, declining population quality, rising infertility, and indeed a national "sperm crisis" (*jingzi weiji*). As a twist on Margaret Lock's concept of "local biologies," I suggest that "exposed biologies" have become a matter of concern in China (not to mention globally) in ways that have created a need for sperm banks within China's restrictive reproductive complex over the last three decades. As we will see, the problem of infertility

ENV.
FACTORS
IN PARTICULAR,
POLLUTION

Figure 6. Smog descends on a street.

has in recent years become inextricably bound up with rising concerns about the health effects of pollution on Chinese bodies. Lock originally proposed the notion of local biologies in her comparative study of the different ways in which aging was experienced in Japan and North America, arguing that further to the cultural constructions that surround aging processes, "it seems most likely that the traditional Japanese diet—low in fat, high in protein and natural estrogens—plays an important role in both low symptom reporting at the end of menstruation and in longevity" (Lock & Kaufert, 2001, p. 500). The concept of local biologies, then, allows us to account for how "biological difference—sometimes obvious, at other times very subtle—moulds and contains the subjective experience of individuals and the creation of cultural interpretations" (Lock, 1993, p. 39).

In contrast, exposed biologies are a side effect of modernization processes, as industrially manufactured chemicals and urbanized forms of living are increasingly held culpable for a range of pathologies, from cancers to metabolic diseases, respiratory troubles, cardiovascular conditions, disorders of sexual development, and infertility. Whereas "traditional" diets and lifestyles such as those found in Japan or Mediterranean countries are often lauded for their health benefits, "modern" diets and lifestyles—sedentary; high in fat, sugar, and salt—are blamed for their negative health impacts. This is "food as exposure" in Hannah Landecker's (2011) phrase; yet, we should be careful not to confuse exposed biologies with an individual's particular diet or lifestyle. As my doctor colleague's dinner joke highlights, it is impossible to avoid exposure when it is a part of vital activity —breathing, drinking, eating, working, and so on. Exposed biologies are tied to the moment when endocrine-disrupting, carcinogenic, or dysgenetic chemicals were "released into the environment in large quantities [especially] since World War II" (Colborn, vom Saal, & Soto, 1993, p. 378), exposing all, irrespective of diet or lifestyle; albeit modern diets and urbanized living are perhaps more likely to expose individuals to harmful chemicals in greater intensities. Indeed, scientists have argued that "it is now virtually impossible to identify an unexposed population around the globe" (UNEP & WHO, 2013, p. xv). Unlike the after-effects of disaster-intensified exposure that Adriana Petryna (2002) has ethnographically documented in post-Chernobyl Ukraine and Kim Fortun (2009) in post-Bhopal India, this is everyday exposure that affects most people in the world. Consequently, we can say that what Michelle Murphy has called "chemical infrastructures"—"the spatial and temporal distributions of industrial chemicals and their diverse effects on life" (M. Murphy, 2013, p. 106)—and the "chemical regimes of living" (M. Murphy, 2008) that form within them are now ubiquitous in all parts of the world.

In China, public health experts have recently pinpointed a perfect storm for exposed biologies: "rapid urbanization and changes in dietary and lifestyle choices" (Hu, Liu, & Willett, 2011, p. 552) linked to the spread of industrially processed foods (at times of dubious quality and safety); industrially contaminated water, which has been blamed by some researchers for the post-reform emergence of "cancer villages" (*aizheng cun*) (Liu, 2010; Lora-Wainwright, 2010); and the air pollution that regularly blankets many of China's cities, causing "between 350,000 and 500,000 people" to die prematurely each year from cancers and respiratory diseases (Chen et al., 2013, p. 1959). This is what Janelle Lamoreaux has called "a toxic China" where developmental and toxicological researchers have come to

understand the environment as "a lineage of personal and chemical exposures" (2016, p. 191). Over the course of my research I came to think of this
perfect storm as China's Anthropocene—a historical moment when anthropogenic effect was being detected, not so much in atmospheric carbon
dioxide levels, glacial ice cores, or sea levels, but rather in levels of carcinogens, mutagens, obesogens, teratogens, and endocrine disruptors found in
the human body. As we will see in the following pages, in China (as elsewhere), infertility has been directly linked to the exposed biologies that
have followed in the wake of post-reform industrial growth.

I begin by summarizing epidemiological debates on possible causes of
apparently rising infertility rates in China. I then go on to survey the science
of exposure when it comes to developmental sex disorders and infertility,
focusing in particular on testicular dysgenesis and endocrine disruption
hypotheses. I show how exposure to industrial chemicals, together with the
modern lifestyles that are seen as intensifying such exposure, have emerged
as culprits for apparently rising rates of infertility. While dysgenesis and
endocrine disruption hypotheses remain contested,[1] I subsequently demon-
strate how they nevertheless have taken on a social life of their own, circulating through alarmist news reports and expert meetings which in turn
have contributed to a socially diagnosed national "sperm crisis." Finally, I
argue that the quality-controlled sperm bank in China has emerged as a
sanctuary of vitality, a state-sanctioned site where "good-quality" sperm can
be collected and stored as reproductive insurance for individuals, for use by
infertile couples, and ultimately for the sake of the nation. As such, this
chapter examines how infertility has come to be problematized in China
today. For a medical technology like sperm banking to become routinized,
there must be a problem for which it is seen as a possible solution to (cf.
Koch & Svendsen, 2005).

ENGINEERING (IN)FERTILITY

As you approach the fifteen-story Reproductive and Genetic Hospital on
Xiangya Road in the northern part of Changsha you cannot help but be
struck by the crowds of patients milling around its front entrance. Some
have slept outside on the pavement in order to be among the first to enter

once doors open for the day. As described in the opening pages of this book, the building itself is incessantly abuzz as patients, nurses, doctors, janitors, and technicians navigate their way through the masses of people that can be found everywhere, in waiting rooms, elevators, hallways, and consultation rooms. The elevators were always packed, and much like my sperm donor informants, I would most often make my way to the sperm bank on the fourth floor using the back stairs, which were so narrow that one often had to turn sideways to make way for those on their way down.

Whenever I met with infertility doctors and nurses in the different clinics and conferences I attended, I always enquired about the extent of infertility in China, especially because national statistics can be hard to come by. And there are two rather standard answers that I would receive. Firstly, by now around 10 percent of couples of childbearing age have trouble conceiving without technological assistance and secondly, infertility is on the rise. The figures I heard most often were summarized by one of the doctors I met in Beijing in 2007 when he suggested that "there were five to eight out of 100 couples with fertility problems some twenty or thirty years ago, and this figure has increased to more than ten couples in recent years." Because of variations in methodology as well as quality concerns about past epidemiological studies of infertility, it is almost impossible to epidemiologically verify whether there has been an increase of infertility in China and if so to what extent. Moreover, it is probably no coincidence that 10 percent (the figure I heard most often) is also the most commonly cited percentage for global estimates of infertility. Nonetheless, a recent cohort study of newly married couples published in *Reproductive Biomedicine Online* is in line with what I was told when it concluded:

> The 12-month infertility rate was 13.6% among all of the eligible couples [2,151 newly married couples]. . . . The 24-month infertility rate was 8.5% among all of the eligible couples. . . . If we treated all couples who become pregnant within 24 months of trying as fecund regardless of the infertility diagnosis, however, the estimated infertility rate was 8.4% for all eligible women. . . . The infertility rates obtained by our study were much higher than those obtained by the two previous prospective follow-up studies in China (12-month and 24-month infertility rates were 5.2% and 1.7% in 1985 [Gao et al., 1989]; 9% and 5% in 1987 [Che and Cleland, 2002]). (Meng et al., 2015, pp. 94, 98)

Whether or not infertility rates are in fact rising in China—and they probably are—I have attended to the ways in which these kinds of figures as well as related narratives have circulated in China through media reports, conference presentations, as well as in my conversations with doctors, reproductive scientists, sperm donors, and infertile couples. It is clear that these numbers are actively mobilized to generate a sense of urgency around the problem of infertility, not least by the clinics that profit from infertility treatment.[2] What I am, however, sure about is that the rising demand for biomedical fertility treatment, which is manifest in the crowds found at any reproductive clinic in China, tells us nothing about whether or not rates of infertility are in fact rising. Even if "only" 5 percent of China's couples of childbearing age were infertile, there are still not enough clinics (an estimated 400 by now) to cater for their needs were they all to seek biomedical treatment.

When I have inquired as to why infertility rates might be increasing, there were broadly speaking two kinds of answers that I received. The first set of answers was directly linked to China's one-child policy, while the second set of answers concerned processes of modernization and their side effects. Married couples, I was told, are waiting longer to have a child because of their careers and ongoing societal transitions in general, a well-known demographic trend in industrializing countries (see also Wang & Yang, 1996). And even if this is the case in many other industrialized and industrializing countries, the one-child policy coupled with urbanization and economic growth is said to have intensified this trend to an extent that the average age of marriage had jumped by 1.5 years to around twenty-five during the 2000s, even surpassing thirty in cities like Shanghai by the end of the decade (Wang, 2013). With intense competition among the first one-child cohorts (currently in their thirties and twenties), for the best universities, best jobs, and indeed best marriage partners, the suggestion is that couples are intent on getting their careers established before they start families, much to the dismay of their parents (Bregnbæk, 2016; Sung, Brown, & Fong, 2017). Age, especially of women but also men, is of course the most reliable predictor of fertility; the older you are the more difficult it is to conceive "naturally," and with more people waiting longer to have their first child it would make sense to see an increase in the number of couples who have trouble conceiving without technological assistance. Hence reproductive deferral is most likely to be the key factor behind any rise in China's infertility rates.

Also considered an unintended consequence of the one-child policy, many of the infertility doctors that I met pointed to the iatrogenic shaping of infertile local biologies through multiple premarital abortions. As explained by Fu Ping, a doctor of women's medicine (*fu ke*) from Hangzhou TCM Hospital, at a conference on reproductive medicine held in Guangzhou in 2011:

> I have a female patient who was born in 1988 and she has not been able to get pregnant after two years of marriage. The reason is because she has had abortions many times since she was eighteen years old. This has resulted in tubal blockages, which lead to infertility problems. Some young women use abortion as a routine remedy. In fact, often abortion is an irresponsible behavior for their health, because artificial termination of pregnancy can make endocrine levels drop dramatically without a slow process of adaptation, which is a potential hidden blow to health. Repeated abortions make the body suffer a double blow and will gradually affect all aspects of functions such as premature aging, reproductive tract infections, sexually transmitted diseases, and even infertility. (quoted in *People's Daily*, 2011)

As we saw in the previous chapter, Zhang Lizhu had argued that infertility caused by tuberculosis was a Chinese particularity in the 1960s and 1970s. Yet these poverty-shaped local biologies had been reshaped in China's many urban centers by the end of the century. Damage caused by multiple abortions is one of the particularities of infertility in a post–one-child policy China. Given the difficulties involved in registering a child born out of wedlock or without a so-called "pregnancy certificate," which confirms a couple's eligibility to have a child in accordance with family planning laws, the suggestion is that more abortions are being carried out (up to thirteen million annually) than might be under different population policies, and that modern life is also leading to "increasing promiscuity" as more liberal attitudes toward sex are adopted.

This is not to say that other etiologies of female infertility have disappeared. Ovulation disorders, endometriosis, and polycystic ovarian syndrome (PCOS) are also implicated as they are in other countries, some of which have been directly linked to endocrine-disrupting chemical exposure

(Goodarzi et al., 2011). As Michelle Murphy has argued, "chemical injury, produced by industrial production or later by commodities, not only causes cancers or poisoning, but alter the material substrates of reproduction, mimicking or disrupting hormonal signals, mutating genomes, and thinning membranes" (2011, p. 35). Nonetheless, the suggestion is that family planning practices in China, which have explicitly set out to limit fertility, have in fact exacerbated the infertility of a considerable proportion of women who have undergone multiple abortions in order to avoid the complications of accounting for and registering an unauthorized child. This is iatrogenic effect—rather than toxic exposure—for those reproductive bodies that have undergone disproportionate numbers of abortions for bureaucratic (at times forced) or social reasons.

Now, while the burden of infertility is more often than not borne by women in China (see chapter 6), male factor infertility is of course also a factor in China's infertility rates, and it is to this side of the reproductive equation to which I will now turn in the remainder of this chapter. As already noted, sperm banks in China have been established in particular to tackle male infertility.

DECLINING SPERM QUALITY AND REPRODUCTIVE INSURANCE

One morning in 2012 while carrying out fieldwork at the sperm bank in Changsha, I came across a flyer in the waiting room for sperm donors, which was titled "Reproductive Insurance." I asked Li, one of the doctors who worked at the sperm bank, why this flyer was made available to sperm donors, as I presumed that healthy donors were not the target group for a technology that I had thought was most relevant for men with serious diseases such as cancer. And indeed most of the flyer was dedicated to explaining how reproductive insurance—freezing one's sperm for later reproductive use—was "good news for male patients with cancer who have not yet had children." Li responded by suggesting that some of their donors would perhaps in the future suffer from cancer, so they might consider preserving some of their sperm not only for recipient couples but also as an insurance for themselves. Moreover, he pointed out, some of

The main groups that reproductive insurance and *yousheng* insurance are aimed at:

1. Patients who need to undergo sterilization or males with serious diseases. For example, sperm can be cryopreserved before an orchiectomy, an operation on the epididymis, and chemotherapy or radiation therapy for patients with a cancer that will affect sexual function.

2. Men who want to prevent infertility caused by accidents. For example, soldiers going to war, astronauts, people who work in scientific research and exploration

3. People working in long-term jobs that affect reproductive ability, who are exposed to a large amount of volume radiation or poisonous substances. Before beginning work in these environments, they can cryopreserve their sperm, so if in the future there is a severe low sperm count or no sperm, they can use the frozen sperm for artificial insemination.

4. Men who are married and want to have children at a late age for work or career reasons

5. Patients with a low sperm count (oligospermia), low sperm motility, abnormal sperm, or obstructive azoospermia. The sperm from their testicles and epididymis can be cryopreserved for future, intracytoplasmic sperm injection treatment.

their donors might end up working in dangerous environments that could affect their fertility. On the back page of the flyer, the sperm bank listed five groups as potential customers of reproductive insurance for men (see boxed text). Reproductive insurance was thus offered to those men who were not planning to establish a family at the moment but who would like to minimize the risk of future infertility by freezing their "good"—or at least "better"—reproductive vitality today.

In recent years, freezing of eggs has emerged as a controversial issue in many countries as cryobanks now encourage young women to freeze their oocytes to counter an inevitable fertility decline while they finish their education and establish their careers (Mertes & Pennings, 2011).[3] Since extraction of eggs from women is only allowed in connection with IVF in China, only married women are eligible to undergo cycles of ovarian stimulation. As a result, freezing of eggs is currently not a legal option for young single women, which has led some well-off individuals to travel abroad to access this service (C. Zhang, 2015). Yet as we can see here, freezing of sperm is an option for men, married or not, who are advised by the sperm bank in its brochure to "anticipate infertility" (Martin, 2010) in the face of risks that dangerous or toxic occupations might impose on them or because they are deferring reproduction. This is possible because the regulation on Basic Requirements and Technical Specification of Human Sperm Banks issued by the Ministry of Health states: "The aim of sperm banks is to provide treatment for infertility, prevention of genetic disease, and reproductive insurance" (MoH, 2003c), without mention of marital status.

In China, concerns about declining sperm quality have contributed to a media-diagnosed "sperm crisis" in recent years. Yet, in the same way that claims of rising infertility rates can be hard to verify epidemiologically, so too are andro-epidemiological claims of declining national sperm quality. The science around aggregated sperm quality is contested both when it comes to whether or not there has been a decline in China's—or any other country's—overall sperm quality and whether or not anthropogenic processes set in motion by industrialization and urbanization in recent years are to blame. Nonetheless, ever since E. Carlsen and colleagues concluded in a 1992 global study that "there has been a genuine decline in semen quality over the past 50 years" (Carlsen et al., 1992, p. 609), it has become something of truism. In China, one of the first andro-epidemiological studies was carried out by researchers at the Science and Technology Institute of the National Population and Family Planning Commission in Beijing, who analyzed sperm samples from a total 11,726 men from thirty-nine cities and counties from 1981 to 1996, finding that sperm quality (measured as sperm motility) had declined at an annual rate of 1 percent, and normal sperm morphology rates decreased by 10.4 percent and 8.4 percent from 1981 to 1996, amounting to a total decline of 40 percent or more (Zhang, Wang, & Wang, 1999). Since then, a string of cohort studies have emerged, especially in the last five years or so, which have similarly concluded:

> In these five years [2007–2012], sperm concentration and the percentage of sperm normal morphology were decreased . . . [and] sperm concentration and the percentage of sperm normal morphology were also decreased (Jiang et al., 2014, p. 842);

We also found a decrease in sperm concentration during the four years of observation (Rao et al., 2015, p. 111);

We found evidence suggesting there may have been decreases in semen volume, sperm concentration, sperm forward motility, and total sperm count between 2008 and 2014 (Wang et al., 2016, p. 4);

And finally, most recently, staff at the sperm bank in Changsha examined their sperm quality records from 30,636 young adult men who applied to be sperm donors between 2001 and 2015 and found that "the semen quality among young Chinese men has declined over a period of fifteen years, especially in terms of sperm concentration, total sperm count, sperm progressive motility, and normal morphology" (Huang et al., 2017, p. 83).

Even though almost every andrologist whose research I have read or whom I have met in China has had reservations about such conclusions,[4] they have nonetheless expressed their reservations in ambiguous terms, which seemed to convey that they shared some kind of suspicion that sperm quality is indeed falling. Professor Guo Yinglu of the Institute of Urology, Peking University, put it like this: "Although the scientific speculation of gradual declining state of male sperm has been basically recognized by the medical field in the world, so far there is insufficient evidence to prove this" (quoted in *Sina News*, 2011b), while Li Hongjun of the Urology Department at the Peking Union Medical College Hospital told reporters at a news conference that "although these data may come from different research methods and standards and the results sound shocking, the global decline in sperm quality is undoubtedly a fact" (quoted in *Sina News*, 2008).

Published scientific findings were often corroborated by the gut feelings of reproductive scientists. During my fieldwork, one head of a sperm bank noted that "without accurate statistics, we cannot make the arbitrary judgment that mankind is facing a health crisis" while at the same time suggesting that, thinking back, "there were more people who could generate 60 million sperm per milliliter twenty years ago." Another doctor told a reporter from *Qingdao News* that whereas a test tube would have been full of ejaculate in the past, today it is only one-third full on average. "Human sperm density has decreased by half in sixty years," he explained, "and if it continues to develop like this, we cannot imagine the consequences in a further sixty years" (quoted in *Qingdao News*, 2005). And another sperm bank director suggested to me that "sperm quality has declined, but not to that terrible an extent." And so, we can say that while not necessarily an established scientific fact in China today, decreasing national sperm quality has in some ways become a scientific given, cemented by the symbolic traction that falling national sperm quality has gained as a form of social commentary, as we will see.

JINGZI WEIJI—SPERM CRISIS IN THE MEDIA

In 2008, I came across a news feature aired on the Shanghai News Channel. Against a montage of images showing crowded cities, high-tech laboratories, and urban workers, the commentator explained how:

> Five years ago, a sperm bank was founded in Shanghai, with the goal of providing sperm to infertile couples for artificial insemination. Five years on, according to many news reports, the sperm bank has found itself in great difficulties and the sperm crisis (jingzi weiji) era has begun. What has caused this sperm crisis? . . . With increasing industrialization, sperm quality worldwide is declining. Life pressure, smoking, drinking, pollution, lack of exercise, dressing the wrong way, and radiation from mobile phones and computers have all become hidden killers affecting sperm density and motility. . . . Since the day the sperm bank was founded, [Director] Li Zheng has faced two problems. One is the poor quality of sperm; the other is the shortage of sperm donors, which has directly caused this sperm crisis. (Shanghai News Channel, 2008)

Shanghai television was not alone in propagating this storyline. Indeed, 2008 turned out to be the year that a "sperm crisis" and a related "national emergency" were declared in the media. A health news report from December 2008 in Henan proclaimed a "national emergency in sperm banks in China" when only 37 out of 328 potential donors qualified for donation (Dàhé Jiànkāng Bào, 2008). In that same year Professor Cao Xingwu, chief physician at the Ministry of Health China-Japan Friendship Hospital, who had carried out research on sperm quality for some fifteen years, told a reporter from the Life Times that "If this trend continues, men will die without sons within fifty years!" Liu Dalin, a professor of sociology from Shanghai University, warned: "Do not let Man become an endangered animal" (quoted in *Sina News*, 2008). In June 2010, journalists put numbers to the crisis under the headline "Guangzhou Sees Alarming Increase in the Prevalence of Male Infertility" as they reported that "experts on male fertility from many hospitals in Guangzhou said that both sperm quantity and quality in Guangzhou are significantly decreasing. This view was shared by a large number of male fertility experts. Experts said, 'Now the sperm quality of a man in Guangzhou has declined by 50 percent compared with fifty years ago . . . the quality and quantity of sperm have declined, which is a problem we need to attach great importance to'" (*Xtata*, 2010).

To be sure, Chinese male fertility scientists and media are not alone in invoking the language of crisis and emergency; instead, they tap into growing global concern with anthropogenic effect. Much of hitherto social science engagements with the Anthropocene have concerned the ways in which humans and nonhumans (or "more than humans") are imbricated in environmental and ecological networks and entanglements (Latour, 2014; Tsing et al., 2017). This makes sense since the notion itself has emerged out of debates between geologists, climate scientists, and marine biologists about whether or not the scale of human modification of the Earth in the past century or so has been comparable to the kinds of meteorite strikes, tectonic collisions, and volcanic eruptions that are deemed to have punctuated previous geological eras. That is to say, the Anthropocene is the result of "human activity," "human influence," "human impact," "human modification," "human disturbance," or "human intervention" and as such scientists have been busy determining whether a "human imprint" can be perceived in sedimentation, carbon dioxide levels, glacial ice cores, rates of biotic change, sea levels, and so on. Indeed, an Anthropocene Working Group was formed in 2009 "to critically compare the current degree and rate of environmental change, caused by anthropogenic processes, with the environmental perturbations of the geological past" with a call to include botanists, zoologists, atmospheric scientists, ocean scientists, as well as geologists in this task (Zalasiewicz et al., 2010, p. 2230). As a result, social scientists have begun engaging with plant biologists, marine biologists, and geologists in novel ways to research multispecies life.

However important these social scientific investigations of new forms of living on a "damaged," "disturbed," or "modified" Earth have been, in theorizing the Anthropocene we must also shift focus from the Earth to the human body. For, around the same time that plans were being drawn up to form the Anthropocene Working Group, another group of scholars gathered in Copenhagen (in May 2007) for a workshop to discuss the possible effects of chemical toxicants found in consumer products on human populations. At stake, according to the workshop's organizers, was nothing short of the future of human reproduction: "We stand before a reproductive crisis which we should take just as seriously as global warming. . . . Our species is in danger. Climate scientists have long insisted that we have evidence of climate change, and now everybody knows we need to stop CO_2 emissions. We are saying the same thing about the reproductive crisis: we need to do something before it is too late" (quoted in *Politiken*, 2007).

Indeed, ever since Rachel Carson famously warned that in modern society "toxic materials become lodged in all the fatty tissues of the body" (1962, p. 170), epidemiologists, endocrinologists, oncologists, embryologists, andrologists, and other medical scientists have sought to measure not atmospheric carbon dioxide levels or sea levels, but rather levels of carcinogens, endocrine-disruptors, and other toxicants found in biological samples (blood, semen, tissue, etc.) taken from large groups of volunteer human subjects. Such research seeks to identify a toxic imprint within our cellular/molecular biologies and to determine whether this imprint is causative of pathology, that is, whether it is associated with diagnosed incidences of certain diseases, from cancer to heart disease and infertility. In this sense, exposed biologies have become yet another "natural" element (alongside the atmosphere, sediments, oceans, flora, fauna, etc.) within which a "human imprint" can be found. And, as we will see in the following section, amid media-led diagnoses of a "sperm crisis" male reproductive bodies have emerged as yet another site of contestation over anthropogenic effect.[5]

DYSGENESIS

The search for a "human imprint" within human bodies has been facilitated by a series of scientific hypotheses that have been formulated in the decades that followed the release of industrial chemicals into the environment in large quantities somewhere around the middle of the twentieth century (Colborn, vom Saal, & Soto, 1993). These include the chemical carcinogenesis hypothesis, the obesogen hypothesis, and the endocrine-disruption hypothesis. When it comes to human reproduction, two hypothesized syndromes stand out: the testicular dysgenesis hypothesis and the ovarian dysgenesis hypothesis, both of which suggest a link between exposure to endocrine disruptors and increasing rates of male and female infertility. For the purposes of this chapter I will focus on dysgenesis as a particular feature of male-exposed biologies (all the while acknowledging the importance of attending to female-exposed biologies in equal measure [see M. Murphy, 2008]).

The media-diagnosed sperm crisis or *jingzi weiji* in China can in some ways be traced to Danish andrologist Niels Skakkebæk's proposed "new concept that poor semen quality, testis cancer, undescended testis, and hypospadias are symptoms of one underlying entity, the testicular dysgenesis syndrome (TDS), which may be increasingly common due to adverse environmental influences" (Skakkebæk, Rajpert-De Meyts, & Main, 2001, p. 972). Skakkebæk's research group was the one that had organized the above-mentioned international workshop bringing together scholars from around the world with a common interest in the effects of endocrine disruption on reproduction. In a recent review article titled "Human Infertility: Are Endocrine Disruptors to Blame?" André Marques-Pinto and Davide Carvalho suggest that TDS symptoms "probably arise from intrauterine disruption of proper testicular development and function under ED [endocrine disruptor] exposure" (2013, p. R15). It is this disruption of proper testicular development that is thought to be causative of falling sperm quality as well as rising incidences of testicular cancers and sex disorders.

As Janelle Lamoreaux (2016) has shown, toxicological research into the effects of pollution on fertility and population quality in China has taken off in the last decade or so. Indeed, a report in the *South China Morning Post* from December 2013 suggested that the number of fertility studies funded by the National Natural Science Foundation of China has tripled in the last five years. In the news report, Liu Liangpo from the Institute of Urban Environment at the Chinese Academy of Sciences makes a disturbing argument: "Polluted water, unsafe food, bad air . . . so many things are threatening the reproductive capacity of Chinese people. If the situation gets worse, China's birth-control policy would become redundant" (quoted in *South China Morning Post*, 2013). Reproductive toxicologists throughout China have benefited from increased funding, and just as we have seen a flurry of epidemiological studies on apparently declining sperm quality in China, we are also seeing an increasing number of studies focused on the negative effects of pollution on male infertility. For example, Li Wu and colleagues concluded in a recent toxicological study that "that ambient PM [particulate matter from air pollution] exposure during sperm development adversely affects semen quality, in particular sperm concentration and count" (Wu et al., 2017, p. 219) just as Yinsheng Guo and colleagues have concluded that "occupational CS_2 [carbon disulphide] exposure can exert deleterious effects on male sexual hormones and sperm quality" (Guo et al., 2016, p. e294).

Now, just as the andro-epidemiological jury is still out as to whether there in fact has been a global or Chinese decline in sperm quality, so too is the toxicological jury on the dysgenesis hypothesis (underscored by the use of the qualifiers "may be increasingly common," "probably arise from," and "can exert"). Yet, the symbolic traction that dysgenesis has gained in China leads me to argue that it has become a media-aided scientific given. Take this selection of national and international newspaper reports that I collected while carrying out fieldwork:

- "Increase in male infertility is closely related to increasing pressure in day-to-day life and environmental deterioration" (*China Daily*, 2011a).
- "Various kinds of pollutions make sperm quality decline" (*Sohu News*, 2011).
- "Smog can affect reproductive ability" (*China Business Review*, 2011).
- "Smog crisis in China leads to increased research into effect of pollution on fertility" (*South China Morning Post*, 2013).
- "Male infertility rate on the rise—Radiation from cell phones, computers, and other electronic devices, air, water, and food pollution, combined with the sedentary lifestyle followed in cities are to blame for a possible 'quality decline' of sperm" (*China Daily*, 2009).
- "A controversial chemical found in plastic bottles, soda cans, and many other common products appears to adversely affect sperm in men. . . . [A] study of more than 200 Chinese factory workers found that those

who were exposed to bisphenol A, or BPA, were more likely to have lower sperm counts and poorer sperm quality" (*Washington Post*, 2010).

- "Pollution, stress blamed for poor China sperm count" (Reuters, 2007).

Through such media reporting, exposed biologies become salient. Biological difference is not the result of local lifestyles and diets; rather, it is related to the intensity, timing, and duration of exposure to industrial chemicals through the thoroughly mundane, vital daily activities of eating, drinking, breathing, working, and moving around. Many of the potential and qualified donors I interviewed brought up the negative effects of pollution when I asked them whether they considered infertility to be a significant problem in China:

> I have seen some news that two couples in ten have a problem. I think it is a very serious problem. . . . I think I want to do something. So yes it is a very serious problem. . . . Er, it is because the environment is not very good, so sometimes they want a baby but they can't have it and this is very disappointing. (twenty-two-year-old university student, Shanghai)
>
> I don't think there are a lot of [infertile] people; some people, but there are a lot of hospitals. The reason why many people can't have children . . . their own baby, is our environment. It means our sperm quality goes down. (twenty-one-year-old university student, Changsha)
>
> I have an aunt, they live next to a factory so they went for IVF; you know, pollution is causing infertility in China. As far as I know, my aunt, they went to get IVF and the reason is his [husband's] house is next to a factory and the environment changed so they went to the Changsha hospital. (twenty-year-old university student, Changsha)
>
> I know some information about this thing; there are about tens of millions of infertile people. I think the reasons are medical and more and more social pressure. Many people were fertile in the past, but they put off the time to bear children because of work and also because of social activities, environmental impact or other effects—all these slowly lead to infertility. Besides, a lot of people enjoy the nightlife and eat too much with an abnormal lifestyle; I think the fast pace of life is also not good for those people who want to have children. In fact, many factors are involved, not on their own, but because of the work environment or fast-paced life. (thirty-two-year-old office worker, Guangzhou)

As in the case of local biologies, biological difference stemming from exposed biologies can be sometimes obvious, at others subtle, imbricating subjective experience and cultural interpretation. In its most intensified forms, exposed biologies can lead to cancer and death, yet there are many other forms where symptoms may not be immediately life-threatening yet still impact people's lived lives in substantial ways. For example, sufferers of the contested condition known as toxicant-induced loss of tolerance (TILT) report headaches, respiratory trouble, mood changes, digestive problems, sleep disorders, and more, just as multiple chemical sensitivity (MCS) is blamed for muscle pains, nausea, and dizziness (see N. Shapiro, 2015). In China, as anthropologist Mikkel Bunkenborg has shown, the emergence of the notion of sub-health (*yajiankang*) in the 1990s can be linked to "apprehensions about the somatic effects of rapid modernization" (Bunkenborg, 2014, p. 128). Some studies have suggested that up to 70 percent of Chinese suffer from sub-health, which, much like TILT and MCS, is characterized by a diffuse set of symptoms such as tiredness, hair loss, poor sleep quality, a declining immune system, and more. One news report on CCTV from 2011 described its etiology as follows: "Sub-health has now become a major problem among city dwellers, especially white-collar workers and those with high education level. . . . For various reasons, many industrialized and developing societies are among the most seriously hit. Long-term stress, overtaxing physical and mental work, and environmental pollution all contribute to pushing a person into this condition" (CCTV, 2011).

When it comes to infertility, symptoms are not often noticeable until a couple is actively trying to achieve a pregnancy. And even if male infertility may not generate somatic discomfort, once diagnosed, the psychological consequences can be considerable for many men. They harbor feelings of shame, guilt, and inadequacy (see Inhorn, 2013; Tjørnhøj-Thomsen, 2009). Yet, Lamoreaux argues that the toxicologists she studied in Nanjing discourage guilt and embarrassment associated with disease by "pointing to the many possible causes of the conditions [they study], ones that go beyond individualized behaviors, such as air and water pollution, food safety and availability, and changing lifestyle habits" (2016, p. 189), and circulating narratives of anthropogenic dysgenesis do the same.

Even if epidemiologists, andrologists, and toxicologists usually temper their findings by suggesting that infertility rates "may be" rising, that sperm quality "is possibly" falling, and that this decrease is "probably" being caused by exposure to industrial chemicals, what I have argued is that these findings have nevertheless become scientific assumptions in China (and elsewhere) because of their symbolic efficacy as a form of social commentary. In their recruitment materials, some sperm banks highlight the detrimental effects of environmental exposure on male fertility:

> Do you wanna earn more money easily, without conflicts with your study? Do you wanna spend your spare time more meaningfully, doing something interesting and exciting? Yeah, now you can consider being a volunteer in the sperm bank . . .! Along with environmental deterioration, more and more males have become infertile, and some of them even need donor sperm insemination. Now, we are in need of sperm donors because many infertile couples are waiting. Generally they need to wait at least one year, and the long wait may cause anxiety, disappointment, and even divorce. So now we call on college students to engage in this honorable project! (recruitment flyer)

We can see then how infertility has come to be seen as a significant consequence of anthropogenic effect, a human-made problem: a side effect of China's efforts to engineer fertility through family planning and its economic policies, which in turn are seen to have led to reproductive deferral, intensified exposures, and modifications of lifestyle. So what, then, do China's sperm banks have to do with exposed biologies?

JINGZI KU—MINIMIZING EXPOSURE

"You see, we like to work here in the lab. It's quiet and cool, and we can enjoy chatting together." Li, one of the doctors working part time at the sperm bank, said this to me one afternoon as an assembly line of laboratory workers received sperm samples through a hatch that separated the outside clinical world from the good manufacturing practice (GMP) facilities of the sperm bank, where samples were analyzed and approved sperm prepared for cryopreservation (see chapter 5). The organization and layout of the sperm bank separates an unsterilized and chaotic front stage from a quiet, air-quality-controlled backstage. Staff at the sperm bank in Changsha worked on rotation, fulfilling the various required tasks of recruitment, reception, and semen quality analysis, and all of them told me how they enjoyed getting laboratory duty. Even if laboratory tasks were to some extent mechanical and laborious, it was quiet and cool in the lab, in direct contrast to the cacophonic, chaotic, and stressful clinic/sperm bank life that was going on outside. Moreover, the air quality of the laboratory was controlled to minimize risks of contaminating donor sperm, making for a cool and comfortable working environment, which was particularly attractive during Changsha's many hot summer months.

Sperm banks in China explicitly recruit among so-called "high-quality" (*suzhi gao*) university students, carrying out comprehensive medical screening of potential donors, and following strictly monitored GMP in their laboratories (more on this in ensuing chapters). There are many reasons why sperm banks recruit primarily from among university students, one of which is a suggestion that university students are in an age group that tends to have viable, if not lively sperm that has been less exposed to pollution, as one sperm bank administrator in Changhsa explained: "Compared to people who have already begun working, the students' lifestyle is healthier. Because after work begins, you have to . . . sometimes for work, you smoke or drink and this is not good for sperm quality . . . and in China, most of the students when they begin university, they haven't had a sex life before, so this is also good for sperm quality. And also because they are young, they are not impacted by the environment." His rather surprising views[6] were echoed by a twenty-year-old qualified donor I met in Shanghai: "I think it's better to choose donors among university students, as our environment and lifestyle is better than people in the society." And indeed, the Ministry of Health's Regulation on the Administration of Sperm Banks explicitly states that "Semen shall not be collected if the candidate . . . has had long-term exposure to radiation and hazardous substances" (MoH, 2003c, §16).

If my argument holds, the sperm bank with its tanks of quality-controlled sperm can be thought of as a state-sanctioned sanctuary of reproductive vitality—quite literally so—at a time where this vitality is increasingly seen as under threat. Aggregated sperm quality deterioration acts as a kind of metaphor for the degradation that China's rapid transformation into an industrialized nation is held responsible, a way to morally value the new forms of life and ways of living in China. The thing about "quality" (*zhì*) is not only that it is normative—the quality of something can be good or bad—but also that it can improve or deteriorate along normative continuums or scales. Such

Figure 7. Cryotanks at the sperm bank in Changsha.

continuums allow for an aggregated national sperm quality to be considered under threat, and hence in need of protection from all the pollutants, toxicants, and stressors that might damage it. It is little wonder that sperm bank staff enjoyed their rostered shifts in the air-quality-controlled lab, just as I did while carrying out my fieldwork. These hours were a welcome break from the traffic, smog, and constant crowds of people that the sperm bank laboratory's hatch held at bay, the only interruptions coming when the on-duty receptionist tapped on the window to indicate that the next batch of relatively unexposed sperm samples from university students had been delivered, waiting to be quality-controlled.

CONCLUSION

Jan Zalasiewicz and colleagues have suggested that more than an actual geological time, the Anthropocene is perhaps better understood as a "vivid yet informal metaphor of global environmental change" (2008, p. 7), which was "coined at a time of dawning realization that human activity was indeed changing the Earth" (2010, p. 2228). Similarly, I would suggest that fertility decline and aggregated sperm quality deterioration act as metaphors (among many others) for the degradation that China's rapid transformation into an industrialized nation caused. In a marathon interview with Lu Guangxiu held in May 2011, I was struck by one of her final reflections: "I think that of all the regulations from the Chinese Ministry of Public Health, those for human sperm banks and assisted reproductive technologies are the most successful, because all of these work, it really is going in a healthy way. I think that if we can do the same for quality security of our food it will work." This comparison of regulating sperm banks to the task of food safety assurance resonates in China today because of a sense that vital quality is under threat, deteriorating in all kinds of ways. In such a milieu, the sperm bank emerges as a guarantor not only of sperm sample quality but also of the very nation's vitality. It is through the sperm bank that the bottom end of such aggregated sperm quality continuums (those 1 to 2 million azoospermic men in China who are unable to produce their own sperm) are associated with the top end (those less-exposed, "high-quality" students who become qualified donors). The tanks of the sperm bank in Changsha contain much more than possible treatments for male-factor infertile couples; rather, these steel tanks are a form of national reproductive insurance, protecting the frozen life within from exposure to the smog, industrial chemicals, and mobile phone radiation that surround it.

4 Mobilizing Sperm Donors

<Xiangya sperm bank is in a state of emergency, please come and support it, if you are a man. Hunan University students, do you dare to come?>

This short message was posted on to the electronic bulletin board systems (BBS) of a number of Changsha universities in March 2011. The author was a recruiter from the Hunan Human Sperm Bank who wanted to catch the attention of as many young men enrolled at university as possible, simultaneously appealing to their consciences while challenging their masculinity. Indeed, his post caused quite a stir among students. It was shared and commented on, eventually prompting a local reporter from the Xinhua News Agency to pay a visit to the sperm bank:

> Recently this post on a Hunan University online forum drew a lot of attention from netizens. Was the information in this post real? This reporter approached CITIC-Xiangya Reproductive and Genetic Hospital, where the sperm bank is located. The vice president, Professor Fan Liqing, said that their sperm bank was one of the first sperm banks in China and that they were indeed currently in a state of emergency. Every year about 2,000 people come to donate sperm, and only 700 to 800 qualify. People wishing to receive sperm donations have to wait until 2012. (Xinhua News Agency, 2011)

Directors and managers of the twenty-three provincial sperm banks in China are in the news regularly, at times to refute viral rumors about goings-on in "mysterious" sperm banks, although most often because they see it as an effective means of getting their message out and to counter some of the disapproval that continues to surround sperm donation in China today. As a sperm bank manager from the province of Guangzhou put it to a journalist in March of 2011: "Now, most information on sperm donation is exchanged and spread among peers and through publicity; people also need a process to accept it slowly. So I hope that the press can guide this problem in a positive way. The majority of the sperm donors are college students, and we need to support and encourage them" (quoted in *Sina News*, 2011a).

This chapter charts practices of recruitment and donation in a country where sperm banks are in chronic states of "emergency" and fertility clinics face constant shortages of donor sperm as a consequence. The emergency is in some ways structural. In a country of 1.2 billion people with an estimated one to two million azoospermic men, the question is whether twenty-three sperm banks are enough. More significantly, Chinese regulations limit the number of women's pregnancies per donor to five (which for many years effectively meant five offspring, as a result of the one-child policy), an internationally restrictive limit when compared to Europe or the United States where some donors are known to have sired as many as 150 children (albeit sperm banks themselves suggest that the "normal" figure is between ten and twenty). As a consequence, a high throughput donation system has emerged in China, which sees the largest sperm banks bringing in as many as 3,000 potential donors for screening every year.[1] Reaching that figure, however, is a constantly uphill battle for managers and recruiters who face all manner of logistical, cultural, legislative, economic, biological, and medical hurdles. As we will see, in such a setting, strategies and campaigns of recruitment in China are best understood in terms of mobilization as sperm bank managers, staff members, and recruiters take on this task collectively.

At the same time, high throughput banking profoundly shapes donation processes and sperm bank socialities, especially if we compare these to donation processes in countries like Denmark or the United States. As I found out, those university students who make their way to a sperm bank for the first time are often surprised at the number of (would-be) donors, with waiting rooms packed during the busiest of periods. In cities outside of provincial capitals where weekly donation sessions are organized in borrowed facilities by a mobile sperm bank crew, masturbation conditions can be cramped and scheduling inflexible. And those students who do qualify as donors share the same kinds of questions and thoughts about their futures as donors in other countries might. Sperm donation remains strictly anonymous in China, an absolute requirement for the donors I spoke to, many of whom insisted that sperm donation would cease to exist in China if anonymity were not guaranteed.

In recent years, a number of scholars have analyzed blood donation practices in China as a "circulatory system" organized by an "economic logic that sanctions the extraction and circulation of human plasma" and enables "the production of biovalue in China's blood trade" (Adams, Erwin, & Le, 2009; Anagnost, 2006; Erwin, 2006; Shao, 2006). These studies have shown how predatory procurement practices in the 1990s put rural blood sellers increasingly at risk from reused needles and unsanitized equipment, eventually creating an AIDS epidemic in central China. As a result, such blood-selling practices were outlawed in 1998 and a series of high-profile public health campaigns were introduced to promote voluntary donation of blood (at times with compensation) as a glorious act that would contribute to the national good. Not only did these campaigns have to reassure potential donors that giving blood was now safe, they also had to counter "traditional" ideas that loss of blood as a vital bodily essence was detrimental to health. In their analysis of "how a nation which had a longstanding cultural obstacle to voluntary blood donations, as well as an emerging epidemic tied directly to blood donation practices, was able to produce a group of willing donors," Vincanne Adams and colleagues argued that these campaigns worked because they were able to distinguish compensation as a reward for glorious service to one's country from the unsafe, rural blood-selling practices of the past (Adams, Erwin, & Le, 2009, p. 416). For Kathleen Erwin, these developments raise the urgent question of "what does it mean for the Chinese social body to produce a population of blood donors whose vital essence is sought over and over again?" (Erwin, 2006, p. 152).

There are many parallels to be drawn here to the extraction and circulation of human sperm in China, and sperm bank managers consistently look to the recent successes of blood donation campaigns for inspiration in their efforts to recruit sperm donors. Sperm donation is similarly shaped by legal constraints that explicitly prohibit commercialization while allowing for compensation, just as recruitment campaigns also seek to dispel "old-fashioned thinking" about the potential harms of donating sperm. But this is where the similarities end. A restrictive limit on the number of couples a single donor's sperm can be used to impregnate means that, unlike blood donors, sperm donors can donate only once in their lifetime (albeit over a three- to five-month period consisting of approximately fifteen deposits). The task of sperm banks is therefore not to produce a group of willing donors whose vital essence can be sought over and over again; rather, it is to produce successive groups of willing sperm donors whose reproductive vitality is sought once. Moreover, with sperm donation, value is created through the screening of donors rather than from its processing into products outside of the body. In China's sperm economy, the so-called "low-quality" (*sùzhì dī*) rural villagers and "floating" migrant populations (*liúdòng rénkou*) who were instrumental in the formation of the blood trade in the 1990s were avoided in favor of so-called "high-quality" (*sùzhì gao*) university students. As such, I suggest that in China, reproductive bioavailability—as opposed to transplant bioavailability (Cohen, 2005, pp. 83–85)—depends on the cyclical mobilization (through recruitment), formation (through screening), and extraction (through masturbation) of successive populations of bioavailable sperm donors. It is the relatively unexposed and virile vitality of these bioavailable populations that is sought. This is a cyclic, rather than circulatory, tissue economy where sperm banks persistently exhaust the willingness of a given cohort of young men on university campuses only to resume once "fresh" cohorts have arrived. The Chinese term for sperm bank is *jingzi ku*, which translates as sperm "storehouse" or "warehouse," and, as we will see, their stocks can be thought of as a national semen reserve that is in a constant state of emergency.

GAOKAO—SCREENING BY PROXY

Every June, seven to nine million young Chinese students sit for their college entrance examinations, the so-called *gaokao*. The stakes are high as results are the most important university admission criteria, with only 0.2 percent of applicants making it into one of China's coveted top-five universities (Shanghai Jiao Tong University, Fudan University, Tsinghua University, Peking University, and Zhejiang University). Students are distributed into China's tiered higher education system according to *gaokao* scores and 40 percent of those who sit the exams will not get a place in any college. An entire industry of tutoring and extra training has emerged around *gaokao* and every June newspapers are filled with tragic stories of students who crack under the pressures of family expectations. This is how Zhaoju, a sperm donor and second-year BA student at one of Changsha's universities, recounted his *gaokao* experience:

> ZHAOJU: I was very nervous and looked forward to the university entrance test, as I can go to a good university if I have a good examination result. But I didn't know what I would do if I failed in it; maybe I would study another year for a retest or drop out. I tried my best to do it well and I had a lot of pressure from my family. So I was nervous about the test, but I looked forward to university life. Yes, the test lasts for two days and I was very nervous. As I studied for three years and all that I did was for these two days, I felt both excited and nervous. I felt sleepless; my parents tried to comfort me and let me sleep well. They made nice food for me, but I still stayed awake.

> RESEARCHERS: When did you get your results?

> ZHAOJU: I forgot the exact time, maybe July or August [2009]. It was a telephone inquiry, a kind of hotline for examination results. I was very excited because the test result came out and I was able to go to a satisfactory university. I felt a weight off my mind and both my parents and I were very happy about it. It's like I was sentenced in court and I was very excited about my results from the four subjects.

What Zhaoju did not realize at the time was that he was in some ways also de facto being screened by the Hunan Human Sperm Bank. Sperm banks in China consider university students to be their primary target group for recruitment, much like sperm banks elsewhere in the world. The choice to recruit primarily from among university students in China is both practical and a matter of quality control. "Our focus is on university students because they are a concentrated group and it's convenient for us to send them messages," explained one sperm bank administrator. And, as we saw in the previous chapter, university students are also considered less exposed, because of their relatively young age, both to environmental pollution and to the unhealthy lifestyles that working life is seen to bring with it. But there are further reasons, as made clear by sperm bank administrators and doctors in Changsha:

> Since we are not doing intelligence tests for every donor, by their having had the chance to go to university shows that they don't have any intelligence problems. . . . We have tried to attract donors from the army as well, to find some soldiers, but because of political reasons, there is no one who can take responsibility for allowing donation and so soldiers may not come out for donating. Also because in the army, they have very strict discipline and they can only have leave on weekends. That's also why they can't do this. And the second reason is that while we also want to recruit from other men in society, we don't know their genetic background and because some from this group of people . . . we are not sure what kind of people they are contacting. Some of them, maybe they have AIDS or they are addicted to drugs, that's why they need money, and they will certainly think of doing this kind of donation. This is also hard to find out. And for men who are already married, it's also very hard for them to finish the whole process of the donation, because they have to come here for a certain time. They can't guarantee they can come on time and also because of their age, their sperm quality is not as good as university students. These are all the reasons that we haven't recruited others than students. (sperm bank administrator)
>
> We can't do an IQ test, so we usually choose university students and government officials to provide samples. . . . Making students the main target can eliminate the possibility of mental disability, and their physical health is at its peak. At the same time they are relatively simple, psychologically affected much less than people who have started working. [But] we are not excluding other types and anyone who meets the requirements can become a sperm donor. (doctor)
>
> [We] have targeted colleges and universities for our publicity and propaganda because college students have relatively new ideas and they understand

the significance of establishing a sperm bank more readily. And the students themselves are of high quality (*suzhi gao*), they have fixed schedules in school, and infectious diseases can be controlled. (sperm bank director)

While one can certainly question whether university students in China are as shielded from psychological woes and infectious diseases as suggested in these quotes, what I am arguing is that *gaokǎo* nonetheless represents a kind of shortlisting of potential candidates, as it is from among these cohorts that around 95 percent of donors will be found. It is important to underscore that sperm bank staff consider this to be screening rather than selection per se, as explained by Lu Guangxiu when commenting on the fact that a sperm bank for academic and celebrity "notables" had been set up in China in the 1990s: "So far medical society hasn't decoded the genes related to intelligence, and there is no scientific proof that celebrities' descendants will be more intelligent. This is merely hype."[2]

Nevertheless, university entrance exams are considered to be a screening instrument that provides some kind of assurance about intelligence, mental abilities, and to some extent (mental) health. Consequently, in an important way, male students who qualify for university become (albeit unwittingly) bioavailable in the sense proposed by Lawrence Cohen, which is to say potentially "available for the selective disaggregation of one's cells or tissues and their reincorporation into another body" (Cohen, 2005, p. 83). With enrolment rates for higher education in China at around 19 percent, this particular bioavailable sub-population of male university students is considered in national education programs to be of particularly high quality (*sùzhì gao*) (see Bregnbæk, 2016; Kipnis, 2006; R. Murphy, 2004). Primed by such national discourses, a few of the potential donors I interviewed brought this up when I asked what they thought about sperm banks recruiting on campuses: "I have known about [sperm donation] for a long time. I have always been thinking that I can be a donor. Especially the college students, they are a crowd with high quality, and their sperm will help the offspring improve themselves." As Susanne Bregnbæk has shown in her study of what she calls the *Fragile Elite* (2016) at China's top universities, students both embrace and feel enormous pressures from being considered high quality. Doing well in the *gaokao* exams is considered an achievement—akin to a court sentence in Zhaoju's words—in the face of fierce competition to get into China's top-tier universities. Of course, targeting university students to donate their gametes is not unique to China in any way, as similar notions of "Ivy League sperm" and "Ivy League eggs" have circulated in American gamete markets as well (Almeling, 2007; Kr-løkke, 2009; Martin, 2017; chapter 2). The point being that when it comes to gametes, reproductive bioavailability is visibly circumscribed by assumptions about the kinds of qualities that nation-states as well as infertile couples appreciate and desire.

WORKER BEES

To be sure, while *gaokǎo* may well work as a kind of proxy screening instrument for sperm banks, which in effect generates a potentially bioavailable pool of millions of males on China's university campuses, university entrance exams in themselves do nothing to mobilize potential donors. Recruitment is a post-*gaokao* endeavor, and one that sees the pool of bioavailable males drastically dwindle from millions to a few thousand as recruiters hit what is sometimes described as a "bottleneck" (*píngjǐng*) by sperm bank staff, a bottleneck that makes the task of recruiting onerous. When asked at a conference on the ethical and social challenges of sperm banking, held in Changsha in May 2012, what their greatest challenge was, one of the attending sperm bank managers replied: "We know that throughout our country we are faced with the trouble of recruiting donors. . . . We still do not have a new manner in which to recruit new donors. What we do is propaganda time after time in each university and dormitory. So, the students know our sperm bank well but only around 3 percent of them would come here." While the statistic is an estimate, the point is clear: it is very difficult for recruiters to get students to the sperm bank. I met this reluctance on the part of male university students on numerous occasions, either when following recruiters on their recruitment trips to the busy, lush university campuses dotted along the foot of Changsha's Yuelu Mountain or when attempting to recruit male informants myself to ask them about their views on sperm donation. As one of the most successful recruiters at the Hunan Human Sperm Bank put it:

We go to the university dormitories and tell the students that this is a really great and noble action and tell them that they will be paid each time they come. But, in China there are three conditions we have to deal with when recruiting. First, there are students who do not understand these actions and they seriously object and they even don't open the door when we come to the dormitory: "bye, bye!" [mimicking a head peeking from behind a shutting door while waving dismissively]. The second condition is that some students, they understand these actions but they don't want to go to the sperm bank so they don't accept our flyers. And the third condition is that there are some students who understand and support this action and so they would come to the sperm bank. The most difficult part of recruitment is the administrators of the dormitories who don't understand our actions, so they don't want us to come to their dormitories, and we can't get in touch with the students.

The challenge for recruiters then is not only a practical matter of getting in touch with students but more importantly that the group of potentially willing sperm donors on a university campus is relatively small—3 percent of a cohort in the sperm bank manager's estimate. Indeed, at the Hunan Human Sperm Bank, they quickly came to realize that within a year of intensive recruitment, they would pretty much exhaust a given cohort. As a result they have developed a rotating scheme that takes them to the various university cities of Hunan in search of fresh cohorts of bioavailable males. Out of a total of six cities outside of the capital Changsha (where they recruit constantly but on rotating campuses), the sperm bank is active in three at a time, and after one or two years they move on to the next, only returning for a further round of recruitment after about three years when new cohorts have commenced their studies. As one recruiter described it, "We have a two-year cycle. In the first semester maybe 2,000 students will come to the sperm bank, in the second semester maybe 150 students will come, and in the third semester maybe just 100. There are fewer and fewer with time, and so then we move on to the next city."

I joined in on three of these weekly visits to cities outside of Changsha with a mobile sperm bank crew consisting of a receptionist (who received donors, handed out donation kits, and paid out compensation fees), a couple of laboratory workers (who assessed the quality of sperm samples and prepared qualified samples for cryopreservation), and a doctor (who medically screened first-time donors). We would meet by the sperm bank's

Figure 8. Men's dormitories on university campuses, a favored recruitment site for sperm banks.

minivan early in the morning as crew members loaded a cryotank together with a mobile sperm bank kit. This large yellow box contained a microscope, vials for preserving sperm, petri dishes for the bacterial smears that each stored sample is subjected to, a few white coats, latex gloves, hairnets, surgical masks, and a stethoscope. Access to facilities in the cities we visited had been negotiated with local women's hospitals that provided infertility treatment. Donors in these cities had to comply with the scheduled visits of the sperm bank crew. One of the sperm bank staff members rather poetically explained this cyclical, mobile sperm donation system one afternoon during our three-hour-long drive back to Changsha from the city of Yiyang with a replenished cryotank between us in the back seats of our minivan: "We are like the worker bees. We start in one field and when the flowers are finished we move on to the next one."

With a cyclic, high throughput style of sperm banking like that found in China, recruiters are perhaps the most important "worker bees" at a

Figure 9. Mobile sperm bank crew collecting donor sperm in Changde, Hunan Province.

sperm bank, as it is their task to bring in as many potential donors as possible for screening. Often former donors themselves, recruiters use flyers, face-to-face canvassing in male dormitories, and increasingly social media to encourage, lure, and entice students to the sperm bank. At a training session for recruiters I observed, a group of former donors were given ideas and suggestions from more senior recruiters as to how to catch the attention of fellow university students. They were in particular keen on exchanging ideas about how to gain access to dormitories on university campuses and also on how to reduce relatively high drop-out rates among qualified donors through moral support, encouragement, and follow-up phone calls. The elder recruiters were animated as they told funny stories of trying to sneak into various dormitories. Incentivized through bonuses to bring in potential donors for screening, recruiters are often creative in how they spread the word, as we saw in the beginning of this chapter.

Having observed recruitment and donation practices in both Changsha and some of the smaller cities like Changde and Yiyang, I noticed quite a difference in the kinds of atmospheres that characterized the inevitable waiting time for donors. The waiting room for donors in Changsha was often crowded with as many as 100 young men at a particular donation time slot, especially on weekends. One of my donor informants, a twenty-year-old studying at university, described the first time he arrived at the sperm bank on the fourth floor in Changsha: "This is not the donor room that I thought; I thought it would be, what should I say, . . . have several long seats and the doctor and the nurse would be more professorial, but they seem just like my grandmother! But one thing is exactly what I thought it would be: the donor keeps silent as death, just silent as in the grave, they are just looking at papers (the hospital provides us with several newspapers and magazines); that's quite good." Compare this to the scene that awaited us at the Women's Hospital in Yiyang one May afternoon in 2012. Having lunched just across the road, the sperm bank crew and I made our way to a ground floor wing at the north end of the hospital where they had reserved two rooms for three hours. The local recruiter, Cheng, met us as we approached the makeshift sperm bank. He was excited as he pointed to all the donors who were already gathered in the waiting area; many of them first-time donors, he exclaimed. As the sperm bank crew began setting up Cheng was constantly on his mobile phone calling students who had yet to arrive to encourage them to hurry. The mood in the waiting room was rather merry, even boisterous as many of the donors evidently knew each other quite well. Upon seeing the crew arrive, one of the young men who was already a qualified donor clapped his hands together and declared, "OK, let's get started!" much to the amusement of the other donors as well as the rest of us. Zhang, a recruiter from Changsha, later explained this difference:

> It's strange and interesting; in small cities recruitment of donors is easier. In Changsha it's hard because in Changsha we have built the sperm bank twenty to thirty years ago, and so when the student is approached he maybe knows our sperm bank already, and he will know in his heart that he won't like it. In the smaller cities many of them hear about this for the first time and we will change the thinking. . . . In Changsha, because Changsha has so many universities the students don't know the others so they are really shy.

In the smaller cities there aren't so many universities so the donors, maybe they know each other, so they would chat together.

At the conclusion of the donation session in Yiyang, one of the crew members patted the sealed cryotank while jokingly proclaiming, "1 million RMB right here!" All in a day's work. At the end of their extraction outings to Hunan's smaller cities, the sperm bank's worker bees would make their way back to the "hive" in Changsha; the recruiters to collect their remuneration and the rest of the crew to deposit their replenished cryotank at the sperm bank.

"DONATE YOUR SEMEN WITH COMPENSATION. WIN ENDLESS GLORY"

While Liu, a twenty-year old sperm donor who was studying at one of Changsha's universities, was waiting his turn to donate on a particularly busy day at the sperm bank in Changsha, he explained how he had initially heard about the possibility of becoming a sperm donor. His story was typical of most interviewed donors in Changsha, Guangzhou, and Shanghai: "One day, I'm playing computer games in my dormitory and some guy, another student, doing his rounds, gives me an advertisement—just like this paper—this advertisement provided some information about how to be a donor and the obligations and the rights on how to be a donor. I considered it for about a week and then I decided to be a donor."

Although many recruiters mobilize their own personal networks of friends and classmates, the flyer remains their most important means of communicating with potential donors whether through hard-copy canvassing or electronic dissemination via electronic bulletin boards and social media. Mass distribution of flyers in male dormitories and through social media is considered to be the most effective way of getting in touch with as many male students as possible. Sperm banks themselves prepare such official recruitment material in the form of printed flyers and announcements on their websites. The tone in these materials is often formal and factual, because according to the "Ethical Principles for Human Assisted Reproductive Technology and Sperm Banks," which were issued by the Ministry of Health in July 2003: "Donation of semen and ovum should be an altruistic act. Commercialization is strictly prohibited, but compensation for wages, transportation, and medical treatment can be made to donors. . . . It is prohibited to use commercial advertisements to recruit sperm donors. Sperm banks should seek socially acceptable and civilized means and measures to enroll as large a population of sperm donors as possible" (MoH, 2003b, pp. I.F, II.A.2).

Interpretation of these guidelines can lead to gray zones. Some recruiters take it upon themselves to make modifications to the official information they are provided with and look for novel ways of gaining the attention of fellow male university students. Quite often recruiters emphasize the compensation that sperm donors can expect, raising questions about whether some form of commercialization is taking place. During visits to Changsha, Shanghai, Guangzhou, and Beijing I amassed quite a collection of recruitment flyers, which I added to from the websites of sperm banks in Jiangsu and Shandong. In all I collected some twenty different flyers. (I do not specify from which sperm bank they originate in the following discussion.) While sperm banks also spread their message through websites as well as by giving interviews in local newspapers highlighting the chronic shortages of donors and "states of emergency" that they face, as already noted, flyer-bearing recruiters remain their most important means of reaching their target groups.

The sperm bank managers I spoke with would often compare sperm donation to blood donation, while at the same time lamenting that they were hampered in the ways in which they were allowed to advertise since the Ministry of Health's ethical guidelines emphasized "socially acceptable and civilized means and measures" of recruitment. Blood donation, they explained, is done openly with large campaigns using mobile donation units that are driven to visible locations around the city. Moreover, donors would proudly let others know about their deeds. This is not the case when it comes to sperm donation; therefore sperm banks must carry out their recruitment campaigns in a socially unobtrusive manner. During a researcher exchange visit to Copenhagen, two staff members from the sperm bank in Changsha had the chance to spend time at Danish sperm banks where they learned about recruitment strategies that were often humorous in more or less sexually explicit ways and included a bicycle shaped like a large spermatozoa, used to deliver frozen sperm to local clinics in Copenhagen while at the same time advertising for the sperm bank (see also Adrian, 2010; Almeling, 2011; Kroløkke, 2009). Pictures were taken and instantaneously shared through social media with colleagues back home in Changsha. When I asked whether they had been inspired to do something similar in Changsha they quickly retorted "Never! We have to be very low key because of conservative attitudes. It would be a scandal." Lu Guangxiu concurred, arguing that "I don't think Chinese people are open enough to accept advertising for sperm banks in magazines or on television because it is still a very sensitive topic. To respect donors, we'd like to keep everything private, including our advertising. Word of mouth is still the best and most effective way of attracting donors." This same theme came up in interviews with donors as well: "As we all know, China is quite a conservative country so we Chinese exist in this cultural atmosphere; we are also very conservative. Actually I don't think my parents would allow me to be a donor; I think for most of us our parents would not allow us to be a donor" (twenty-year-old student, Changsha).

In this cultural context, I found four distinct interpellation forms within the recruitment flyers that I collected, often constructed around slogans such as "Win endless glory" or "Donate sperm for the benefit of society." There were also explicit calls to move beyond old-fashioned conservative views: "Leaving behind traditional, old thinking and donating sperm, to help many miserable families find happiness and joy, is not only noble and humanitarian, but also contributes to society's progress and harmony." Each of the four forms of interpellation work to make sperm donation both familiar and acceptable in different ways. We saw earlier how reproductive science became a part of the nation's modernization program in the 1980s and how the improvement of population quality became a key family planning objective alongside the controlling of population growth. It is no surprise, then, that, as shown in chapter 2, some sperm banks on the one hand explicitly appeal to university students' personal pride by describing them as being of particularly "high quality" (*suzhi gao*), while on the other highlighting how their donation would contribute to the development of reproductive science and human genetics in China as well as "improve the Chinese people's quality (*zhonghuá mínzú sùzhì*)." Another flyer asked and answered the question "Why

> Excerpts from billboard with letters from recipient couples to donors
>
> "Many thanks to the sperm donors. We wouldn't be such a happy family without your sperm donation. Having a child is so important to a family. Having one has brought a lot of fun and happiness to the entire family. Our fate and life have been changed."
>
> "Thanks to your sperm donation, my husband and I got to experience being parents; our parents got grandchildren and became happier; our society became more stable and harmonious. You brought happiness to our lives!"

donate semen? Participate in 'superior birth' (*yōushēng*), healthy and beneficial projects for people and promote the balanced development of the population in the long term." This is the first form of interpellation found in recruitment materials.

Secondly, sperm banks are eager to appeal to the compassion and altruism of potential donors by vividly describing the suffering of infertile couples and the happiness that a sperm donor can bring to these families-in-waiting. One of the immediate impacts that the research for this book had in Changsha followed a presentation given in 2013 to staff at the fertility clinic and sperm bank on the donation process, in which I highlighted how some donors were interested to know more about how their sperm was used. The next time I visited Changsha in 2014, a large billboard containing blown-up scans of letters from happy mothers and fathers expressing their heartfelt gratitude to donors had been put on display in the donors' waiting room. This theme of providing infertile couples with happiness was by far the most common in sperm bank's recruitment materials as they interpellated compassionate and kind university students.

The third form of interpellation I found concerned the health of potential donors in two different ways. One of the "myths" that sperm banks were keen on countering concerned the harmfulness of masturbation. As already noted, I often heard the old Chinese proverb "one drop of sperm is the same as ten drops of blood" (*yi di jing shi di xue*) during my fieldwork, both from staff members and donors, a saying that had its origins in ancient

Chinese medical texts. Semen was considered to contain a man's vital essence and hence "losing" this essence through masturbation or nocturnal emissions was seen to be harmful to one's health (see H. Shapiro, 1998; Zhang, 2015). In one of the recruitment flyers I collected, this "misunderstanding" was tackled head on. The sperm bank suggested that research had shown that "an appropriate amount of masturbation, rather than causing harm, has many health benefits."

Although such information might allay some students' worries, my sense from speaking to many donors was that they were more than comfortable with masturbation and they often mocked the "old-fashioned" views of their parents' generation. And so, when it came to their health, what was more important was the medical screening that was part of the qualification process. Since health care has become increasingly privatized in China, the possibility of having a free health check was attractive to many students. Indeed, it was so attractive that drop-out rates were a huge issue in Changsha. In 2012, the sperm bank in Changsha experienced a 20 percent drop-out rate among qualified donors (161 out of 825 donors never returned to complete their donations once qualified). A major reason for this high drop-out rate was that some students would use the sperm bank's medical screening as a free check-up (indeed it was often explicitly advertised as such) and then leave it at that.

Finally, financial compensation featured prominently in much of the recruitment material. Official material produced by sperm banks would state compensation amounts in a matter-of-fact manner; however, as already noted, recruiters would often take it upon themselves to modify or add to the official flyers and materials they received from the sperm bank. Compensation for sperm donation is paid in cash per donation with a comparable amount "banked" for pay-out once the donor returns at the end of a six-month quarantine period (beginning from the day of the final donation) for a final HIV test (because HIV takes time to show up in blood tests). All in all, a qualified donor who donates the twelve to fifteen times asked by sperm banks (based on calculations concerning the five women's pregnancies per donor limit) can earn between 4,000 and 6,000 RMB, or, as I ended up calling it, iPhone money. Indeed, during a focus group interview with four university students carried out on the grassy campus of Changsha's Normal University, students were asked if they had ever considered becoming a sperm donor. The first to answer was Jin: "Maybe if I need an iPad one day!" Likewise, a couple of the online recruitment posts that I collected proclaimed: "Emergency! [Our] Sperm Bank is facing a shortage! We are seeking donors. Each qualified donor can receive an allowance for buying iPhone 6s!" and "No need to sell a kidney . . . [our] sperm bank can make your iPhone 6S dream come true."

When it came to highlighting financial compensation for donors, one of the more humorous recruitment pitches I encountered had clearly been modified by a recruiter who appealed to those students weary of nagging their parents for money:

> We often hear that someone isn't cool if he doesn't have a computer or a mobile phone; that the roommate on the top bunk just bought the newest PSP; that the hometown buddy in the same grade got a pair of really shiny Adidas sneakers. . . . We often find out that we need to pay this month's rent and Internet fee; that it's birthday time again and we need to treat friends to a big meal and fun activities; that a present is really suitable for the girlfriend; that this is a really useful but expensive textbook. What can we do? Ask our parents every single time? One year's tuition already costs up to 10,000 RMB or even more, and the monthly living cost is also a few hundred or more, how much more can the parents take? Even if they are willing, it's not worth suffering all their complaints. Lie to them? That is too cruel. We cannot find enjoyment by lying to parents. How can you solve these problems? Become a volunteer donor.

Perhaps inspired by this very flyer, Zhaoju, the second-year student whose *gaokao* story we heard earlier, explained why he decided to become a donor: "Just to make some money for living expenses. I will do something that I want to do with this money, such as travel or go some interesting places with my girlfriend. As my parents only give me a certain amount of pocket money every month, I don't want to bring them more burden. My parents usually give me 1,000 RMB every month, around 1,000 RMB to 1,500 RMB, but it's not enough for me sometimes." Now, while there is no question that compensation is a primary reason for becoming a sperm donor in China—as one donor put it "there will be zero donors in China without compensation"—there is more to it than commercialized transactions. Six thousand RMB is a considerable amount of money for most university students in China, yet sperm banks still struggle to recruit, as we saw earlier. Sperm banks would happily receive many more than the 3 percent of a given cohort they estimate will make their way to the sperm bank for screening, yet they seem to hit a bottleneck at around this mark every time. So, while compensation may be necessary for recruitment it is not sufficient in itself. In chapter 6, I will return to other considerations that play into a student's decision not to become a donor; considerations around genetic ties to offspring, possibilities of unwitting consanguineous marriage between half-siblings, and risks of privacy breaches. For now, let me turn to the socialities that coalesce around China's high throughput sperm donation practices.

THE FIRST TIME

One of the curious side effects of sperm donor mobilization in the dormitories of male university students is that relatively often groups of friends decide to come to the sperm bank together. One donor spoke of how sperm bank banter was a regular affair in his dormitory, not least because of the recruitment flyers that were often lying about in different dorm rooms. Some would yell out in the corridors for fun in the evenings that they were "off to the sperm bank!" And once in a while, as one sperm bank manager recounted:

> We once had seven students from one dormitory, they came together for their screening and physical examinations, but only one of them passed the examinations to be qualified. But in the end, this one didn't come for donation, because he was laughed at by the others. So this is also a privacy issue. This is why when we do lectures [on university campuses], we also choose some places that are considerate and private for all the potential donors. We think privacy from other students is important.

One afternoon in 2012 while I was carrying out interviews with first-time donors, a young man in high spirits arrived with some friends at the sperm bank. He seemed very confident, making boastful jokes about his manhood. One of the questions I always asked potential donors was what they thought about the prospect of potentially having five offspring that they would never meet. A look of consternation flushed over his face as he stammered, "R . . . really, five offspring?" He had thought his sperm was needed for scientific research purposes (also stated in recruitment material). It transpired that he had joined his friends that afternoon to come to the sperm bank without having read all of the information about donation. As I noted earlier, collective visits to the sperm bank by friends was also common in the smaller cities outside of Changsha. The social life in the sperm banks I visited were clearly affected by this tendency as such groups of friends often stood out (they could be rather boisterous) against the majority who were usually at the sperm bank by themselves, having confided only a minimum of close friends.

When individual donors were asked about their "first time" (the analogy is perhaps not so far off the mark!), they described being "a little nervous, and a little afraid"; "worried that other people might know I had come here"; "uneasy . . . there are so many people in such a small space, so I feel uneasy"; "nervous because I didn't do it before but I felt excited too"; "scared because I thought maybe this is a little dubious"; "very ashamed the first time, but now I accept this, because I am making a contribution to human genetics"; or "at first I thought this is a little dubious." This last point came up a few times, as first-time donors were concerned whether sperm donation was taking place in a legitimate way. As any cursory Internet searches on sperm donation in China will show, there is a shadow market for sperm (directly related to the constant shortage of sperm donors). As a consequence, some donors harbored suspicions and wanted to make sure that the sperm bank was legitimate. Zhang, a twenty-one-year old qualified sperm donor, described arriving at the sperm bank for the first time in this way: "You know this hospital . . . next to this hospital is a hotel, a third-class hotel [i.e., dubious] just to the left. I thought this is quite inappropriate." Another donor, twenty-six-year-old Guo from Guangdong, also emphasized trustworthiness when describing his first visit:

> It's just not the same as I knew from the Internet, as you know that the message on the Internet is not very accurate. Maybe this is due to different places with different economic development; the facilities, talent reserves, and environment inside the sperm bank are a bit different in every place, such as Shanghai or Guangdong. From having browsed the websites, I feel the facilities here are different from cities like Wuhan and Shanghai, so I

was a bit disappointed. Here it is so small, I do not know why. I think it should have a larger size with more staff as an official institution, as it will also have a psychological effect on the donor. Since sperm donation should pay attention to privacy, donors will think it's more professional and feel more assured if they do a better job on this aspect. And if the facilities are so-so with general sanitary conditions inside, he may feel that this place cannot be trusted.

Another twenty-one-year-old donor from Hunan Agricultural University in Changsha explained: "The only thing I worried about was that once my classmate told me that my sperm will be sold overseas, and that foreigners will do research to find some ways to harm us. So I asked my master's degree mentor from university about this, and he said that maybe this is true, but he wasn't sure. For me now, I don't worry too much about this, [but] this was my concern in the beginning." Sperm bank managers in China are very conscious of these worries. As a result, sperm bank staff emphasized the importance of providing "the best service to sperm donors who came to our department, giving them a welcoming reception, providing explanations patiently, and helping them to dispel any worries they had." Efforts were also made to make waiting time more comfortable through the provision of web-browsing computers, films, and subscriptions to some of the students' favorite newspapers.

While the issue of legitimacy was important for many donors, such concerns were nevertheless quickly addressed by sperm bank staff members who emphasized the strict Ministry of Health licensing requirements that they had to adhere to. What was harder to dispel were feelings of embarrassment and shyness. Two of the donors interviewed in May of 2011 mentioned a funny web forum post they had uncovered while carrying out some background Internet research of their own. The post had circulated on social media and had helped convince them that they would indeed go to their local sperm bank to see if they would qualify as donors. Here is a rather lengthy translation of an extract from the post, which was aimed at other students who might be considering donating:

> Volunteer sperm donation 2011–04–10 16:05:08
>   Oh, a little piece of cake ~ but it's very interesting.
>   Yeah! I really donated my sperm!

First of all, I want to say, if you have pornographic thoughts reading this essay, then I am sorry because here I cannot give you that kind of plot similar to *Tokyo Hot*; I will only write something about the details of a real sperm donation process. I hope to let more ordinary people know about sperm donation. In fact, sperm donation was never my intention, and I didn't have any preparation for sperm donation, but we got to talking about this thing two weeks ago. A few friends and I met for a banquet and were talking about sperm donation. Of course, at that time it was just joking, but we made a gambling bet to go to the hospital to donate sperm. The result, unfortunately, was that I lost the gamble. Crazy wine, alcohol emboldened me to say on the spot, "I will go to hospital for sperm donation." Actually we discharge semen every month several times, but it goes to waste. It is better to donate, and we lose nothing and have the opportunity to get a whole physical examination from the hospital. So this would be the first sperm donation experience in my life.

Originally I wanted to go to the hospital during the weekend for sperm donation, because I have a good rest during the weekend. (Donating will make me tired and exhausted, you understand!) But then I guessed that on the weekend the hospital's sperm donation [center] may not be open. So I decided to go Wednesday afternoon, no classes on Wednesday afternoon. I also found a lot of online information on sperm donation. I already have some experience about blood donation, but nothing on sperm donation, and I think everyone would be nervous if he goes to donate sperm for the first time.

First of all, I learned the basic requirements of sperm donation: age of twenty-two to forty-five years old, good physical health, being well psychologically, no family genetic history, semen concentration should reach 60 million per milliliter, motility should be beyond 60 percent. I think if a man qualifies for sperm donation, that means he is in fairly good quality. You know, not every man can be selected for the national sperm bank. If you do not believe this you can have a try, or ask your boyfriend to try!

I eat two extra eggs in addition to my normal lunch on Wednesday noon because as our old saying goes "one drop of semen equals to ten drops of blood," so this nutritional supplement is very important! After lunch, I take a bus to [the hospital]. (I did not know there is a donation place near our college; even if I knew this, I wouldn't donate there, being afraid of encountering classmates to avoid embarrassment.)

When I arrive at the hospital, I found many patients in the outpatient clinics. I am too embarrassed to go inside! I even want to retreat several times, but on second thought, I have already come, so no need to hesitate anymore. Finally I make up my mind again, and go toward one window to line up, but suddenly I saw a desk, two beautiful nurses talking nearby, and nobody there. So I move toward them, and I asked "Hi, sister, where is the sperm donation department?" My voice is very vague and low, so maybe they can't hear clearly. The bespectacled nurse asked, "What did you say?" I repeated in a whisper. They still did not hear, and said to me, "I'm sorry, I could not hear what you say." . . . Oh, my God! So I repeated a few times! ! ! At last I have to tell them very clearly "sperm donation! sperm donation! I want to donate sperm!" I shocked the two damn nurses (shuddering), then the two of them smiled and said, "4th floor hospital, sperm bank."

Sperm bank staff members are intent on making a donor's first time as comfortable as possible by highlighting professionalism while also actively working to dispel any worries or concerns that a donor might have. While drop-out rates are considered to be directly linked to the free health check that qualified donors receive as part of their screening, there is also a suspicion that shyness and embarrassment prevent some qualified donors from completing their fifteen donations. In this way, the emotional labor (Hochschild, 2012) carried out by sperm bank staff in their initial interactions with first-time donors is a crucial component of the sperm economy in China.[3] On-duty receptionists who coordinate afternoon sessions are key persons who work to manage (potential) donor affects, keep donation flows moving as quickly as possible, and encourage and comfort those who might have failed to qualify following their first donation. Let us now look at the specificities of such emotional labor in a context where sexual arousal is necessary for the extraction of reproductive vitality.

MASS DONATION

Anyone who has visited an urban park on a Sunday, traveled on a metro line, or indeed tried to commute in one of China's many mega cities will relate very well to the Chinese idiom "people mountain, people sea" (*rénshān rénhǎi*), often used in exasperation or resignation when lamenting huge crowds of people. There are people everywhere, and this has bearing on the way social life is organized in urban China. Whether going to a restaurant, a bank, a shop, or a hospital, chances are it's packed. The sperm bank in Changsha is no different. Housed in a hospital that carries out close to forty thousand IVF cycles and screens some four thousand potential sperm donors every year, there are thousands of patients, nurses, donors, doctors, janitors, administrators, and assistants going about their business; never a quiet moment, every available space in use.

As we saw in the opening pages of this book, first-time donors are often taken aback when they arrive at the sperm bank in Changsha: "In the beginning, I never thought there would be so many people at a sperm bank, but when I came here, I was very surprised, and I think the donation of sperm will spread." On the busiest days at the sperm bank in Changsha, some one hundred male university students show up to produce a sperm sample for analysis by staff at the bank. Some of them are qualified sperm donors, while others are there for the first or second time in an attempt to qualify. Once qualified, donors are asked to make a total of twelve to fifteen donations with at least three to four days in between, though in reality the number of donations is higher as even qualified donors' deposits are sometimes rejected if their quality is not good enough. In May of 2012, I kept a record of the number of donors who attended three-hour afternoon donation sessions in Changsha over a two-week period (see table 4.1) with numbers fluctuating between twenty-eight and eighty-eight. I observed similar numbers during my visit to Shanghai's sperm bank and at the donation sessions I attended in Yiyang and Changde, where between thirty and forty university students were in attendance. According to my own calculations, in 2012 the Hunan Human Sperm Bank alone received and analyzed around eighteen thousand samples (from the four cities it operates in at any given time), which averages out to around sixty per day. This is mass donation, which is in stark contrast to European and American sperm banks where sperm donors come and go in much less hectic and crowded circumstances, not least because sperm banks tend not to be located within fertility clinics (see Adrian, 2010; Almeling, 2011; Mohr, 2014).

When (potential) donors arrive at the sperm bank in Changsha they are directed to a waiting room filled with rows of orange tables and benches, which are often filled with students either waiting to use a private donation room or for semen analysis results. In Changsha, those students who have arrived by themselves rarely talk to each other, opting instead to mask their apparent embarrassment and shyness by staring into their

Table 4.1 Record of daily first-time, second-time, and qualified donor donations and number of accepted semen samples in Changsha, May 2012

	13 May		17 May		20 May		21 May		24 May		26 May		27 May		28 May	
	TOTAL	ACCEPTED	TOTAL	ACCEPTED	TOTAL	ACCEPTED	TOTAL	ACCEPTED	TOTAL	ACCEPTED	TOTAL	ACCEPTED	TOTAL	ACCEPTED	TOTAL	ACCEPTED
first-time donors	13	5	18	6	16	5	43	5	4	0	10	3	12	1	19	5
Second-time donors	3	0	3	0	4	1	6	0	5	1	2	0	8	0	11	3
Qualified donors	40	24	30	24	38	23	39	17	28	16	16	9	34	18	35	21
TOTAL	56	29	51	30	58	29	88	22	37	17	28	12	54	19	65	29

SOURCE: Author observations.

Figure 10. The waiting room for sperm donors.

phones, reading some of the newspapers and magazines that are lying around, or preparing for classes. One of the qualified donors I interviewed described how he would empathize with newcomers: "Sometimes some new donors will feel anxious. When I look at them I will feel it is just like me two weeks ago, yeah, then I will tell them, "Dude, don't be worried, I once failed too but then I passed it and now I am here as a successful donor.""

Every once in a while the relative silence of the waiting room is broken when a battered, plastic speaker crackles into life—"Number 54, please"—asking for the next donor to proceed into the donation area, which consists of five donation rooms. This is an area of the sperm bank that is sometimes described as "mysterious" in media reports, not least because of viral rumors that circulate through social media. As we have seen, most university students carry out their own Internet research prior to showing up at the sperm bank for the first time. While I was carrying out fieldwork in

2011, a rather pornographic Internet meme was making the viral rounds. The meme consists of a female dressed up as a nurse with latex gloves on masturbating a blurred-out erect penis. The caption reads, "Come and donate your sperm!" After fielding many curious phone calls and messages in the spring of 2011, the director of the sperm bank in Hubei, Xiong Chengliang, publicly refuted the viral rumors that were spreading about sperm donation: "There have been reports that sperm room nurses can help and that we will provide porn films. This is completely a joke! The volunteers use the masturbation method during the donation; we only provide them with some pictures" (quoted in Xinhua News Agency, 2011). Sperm bank staff in Shanghai and Changsha had likewise had to dispel rumors that had been set off. Even the funny Internet post describing a student's first time at a sperm bank excerpted above makes reference to this same meme: "I solemnly declare here, online pictures from some websites showing nurses helping people to take the sperm are very vulgar . . . but it is absolutely impossible that they provide you with an inflatable doll, let alone a living girl. Everything you do here should be DIY (Do It Yourself), or more professionally: masturbation."

Before entering the donation area in Changsha, a (potential) donor is asked to remove his shoes and wash his hands with soap. A receptionist explains the donation procedure thoroughly, including information on how to intimately prepare for the donation using disinfectant as a way to minimize the risk of infection. As noted above, the receptionist plays a crucial choreographing role at the sperm bank, welcoming students, keeping the flow of donors in the donation rooms as smooth as possible to minimize waiting times, and providing words of encouragement to make students feel as relaxed as possible. As emotional laborers, the receptionist and other sperm bank staff manage anxieties, allay fears, and instill confidence. The students are directed into private donation rooms and given the required paraphernalia, as explained by twenty-one-year-old Xin from Central South University in Changsha:

> XIN: Yes, a sample cup, some paper, and two cotton pieces; one is with a medical liquid and another one to dry. . . . He [the receptionist] would tell you that first you have to use cotton one to clean your parts, then you use

cotton two. . . . Then you can sit on your paper and
masturbate. Then do not open the sample cup at first
because some bacteria will come into the cup. When
you feel you are done you open it, finish it, and close it
and send it out to the doctors. Also the donor rooms . . .
have liquid to wash hands, a machine to dry hands
and some paper to clean.

RESEARCHERS: And how do you find the room, the facilities—do you
think it is comfortable?

XIN: Ehh, the donor rooms usually have a bed and a poster, a
poor poster, and some things to wash your hands. . . .
The facilities I think it is good you can switch the kind
of light; one is normal color and the other is pink, you
know, the pink color. I prefer this color actually; I think
the pink color is quite sexy, yeah, actually I think it's
good enough.

Since pornography laws in China prohibit sperm banks from providing
explicit material, there were usually a few pictures of partially nude women
on display in the sperm donor rooms I saw. But in the age of Internet and
smart phones, this was not seen as a problem by the donors, as almost all
interviewed donors confided that they brought their own stimulus with
them into the donor rooms:

The first time I saw the room I thought . . . but . . . you know to be honest I
have so many porn movies [laughing]! So I think to donate sperm, I think
it's OK. The first time I was nervous but I think it's OK. (twenty-two-year-
old student, Changsha)

Ummm, it's good. The pictures and light also are helpful. The environment is also quiet. . . . I felt a little awkward at first. As I only do masturbation by myself under the quilt, I am not adapted to do it in such a room, but
only for the first time. . . . I bring some videos too. (twenty-year-old student,
Changsha)

I don't need the pictures. I just imagine my girlfriend by myself. (twenty-
three-year-old student, Changsha)

The pictures are . . . how do you say . . . it is just girls with underwear so
you cannot . . . but before coming I knew about this because I had asked

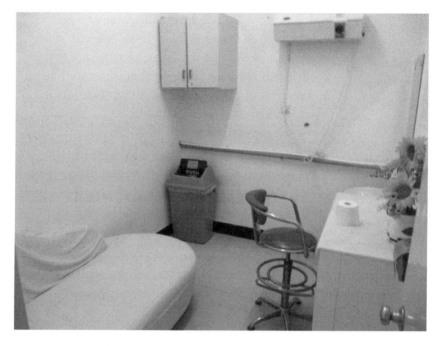

Figure 11. Private donor room for masturbation.

about this. The girls are not that attractive for me to . . . But OK I can download some on my mobile phone so that I can be 100 percent. (twenty-two-year-old student, Shanghai)

In some of the smaller cities where the sperm bank has rented space in local hospitals, donation facilities are not always optimal. In one of the smaller cities I visited, the thirty or so donors had to wait their turn in a small room with quite a thin door that was immediately adjacent to the waiting area. Indeed, hearing other donors was seen as a problem by a few of the donors I spoke to: "Of course it is nice but I think it is kind of . . . it is nicer than any of the hospitals in China but it also has some disadvantages. . . . They didn't offer a great environment for us to donate in because the soundproofing is bad; we can hear the others" (twenty-two-year-old student, Shanghai). Others suggested that on particularly busy days hygiene could be a problem with so many donors using the donation facilities. Nonetheless, all in all, my sense was that once initial awkwardness had been overcome, qualified donors did not find it too difficult to mastur-bate in the donation rooms. The biggest challenge was in the smaller cities where less-than-optimal facilities were borrowed from other hospitals. From my observations in the waiting rooms, twelve to fifteen minutes seemed to be the average time used per donation. This did lead to inevita-ble waiting time for the donors, as in Changsha there were five donation rooms for the, at times, 100 students who showed up compared with one or two rooms in the smaller cities. Having completed his donation, the (potential) donor places his sample into a stainless steel tray, which the receptionist then transports to a hatch that separates the donation area from the air-quality-controlled sperm bank lab.

Extraction in sperm economies requires arousal (see also Mohr, 2016), and as such sperm banks must facilitate masturbation by keeping it private and comfortable; yet with so many donors attending donation sessions in China this can be a challenge. China's high throughput sperm donation system has generated mass donation socialities—awkward silences in wait-ing rooms, hearing others as they masturbate, worries of being recognized by a classmate, teasing from fellow classmates when friends donate col-lectively, scheduled donation session times leading to peak times—which may well partly explain the difficulties not only of recruiting sperm donors but also of keeping them on board once qualified.

CONCLUSION

In this chapter, we have seen how each year potentially bioavailable sub-populations of sperm donors are formed through *gaokao*-screening. It is these cohorts of male university students who are mobilized through the labor-intensive recruitment practices involving face-to-face and online can-vassing by recruiters. China's restrictive limit of five couples per donor has generated a high throughput, cyclic sperm donation system wherein repro-ductive vitality is extracted through mass donation practices (massturba-tion?). Costs-per-donor are therefore considerably higher when compared to sperm banks in Europe or the United States. Despite explicit attempts to liken sperm donation to blood donation, the two remain distinctly sepa-rated. As we have seen, the national semen reserve has a constant shortage as sperm banks struggle to meet growing demand from fertility clinics. As a result sperm banks are in a perpetual "state of emergency."

Sperm bank socialities are shaped by this particular style of sperm banking, which has numerous (would-be) donors in close proximity to each other in waiting and donation rooms. It also has sperm bank staff members and recruiters working to the rhythms of their high throughput, cyclic donation system, which in turn is what shapes the various practice collectives that have coalesced in recent years at China's sperm banks. It is to the formation of such practice collectives that we now turn our attention.

5 Making Quality Auditable

The Julabo warm-water bath machine is gently rocking back and forth with the temperature set at 37.0 degrees Celsius. Inside it are ten lidded plastic cups in a shallow tub, each containing freshly delivered semen samples as they undergo liquefaction. Every once in a while the sperm bank receptionist who is busy coordinating the day's donations outside of the lab taps on the window of a hatch that is just to the left of the Julabo. The tap announces the arrival of the next batch of samples from the five donor rooms, which are in constant use. Sample cups labeled with donor name and number are delivered on a stainless steel tray, which is placed into the hatch. On this particular afternoon, five staff members are on lab duty dressed in light blue lab coats, surgical masks, latex gloves, and blue hairnets. Three of them stand along a four-meter-long lab bench while the remaining two are perched just opposite by a hooded clean bench that protects samples from contamination. Each is responsible for specific tasks. Huilan takes incoming samples from the tray and places them into the warm-water bath machine one by one. In front of her is a stack of donor ID books as well as a series of multicolored remuneration-slip pads. Samples are allowed to sit in the body-temperature water of the Julabo for about fifteen to twenty minutes. Once the first batch of samples from the afternoon's donation session has liquefied, Mei sets up in front of the sperm bank's phase contrast microscope.

On the busiest days, as we have seen, some 100 semen samples are analyzed. Mei plucks one of the labeled samples from the bath and opens the lid. Her first task is to look at the viscosity of the sample by stirring it around with a pipette and noting its volume. She then proceeds to pipette a few drops from the sample into a gridded micro chamber that slots neatly under the lens of the Nikon microscope, allowing her to count the number of sperm cells within 10 of approximately 100 visible squares when peering into the microscope. This number will then be multiplied by 50,000 to give an estimate of the number of sperm cells per milliliter of semen. She also assesses the aesthetics of the sperm cells, their shape, movement, and general liveliness in order to provide an estimated percentage of sperm cells that have good forward movement. To complete her assessment of a particular semen sample, Mei announces out loud her estimations of volume, sperm count per milliliter, and percentage of motile sperm. Ai, who is sitting just to her right, repeats these values out loud before writing them into an A3-sized ledger book, which contains the sperm quality assessments of every sample that is delivered at the Hunan Human Sperm Bank. It is these numbers that ultimately determine whether a semen sample will qualify or not. Disqualified samples are immediately binned into a yellow biohazard wastebasket just below Mei under the lab bench, whereas qualified samples are passed on to Lin who is waiting at the clean bench. Having finished assessing one sample, Mei proceeds to wipe the micro chamber dry with disinfectant and tissues, replace the disposable tip of the pipette, pluck the next sample from the warm-water bath, and repeat the standardized assessment procedure until all samples have been analyzed.

On any given day, samples have been provided by a mixture of first-time donors, second-time donors, and qualified donors, the last of which are usually the majority. Huilan's job is to keep track of just which category a specific sample falls under, as this has bearing on the amount of remuneration a donor will receive. The color of the remuneration slip reveals whether the day's sample has qualified or not. By far, most first- and second-time donor samples are binned, just as a considerable portion of the samples produced by qualified donors are. Since qualified donors are limited to

Figure 12. The assembly line in the sperm bank laboratory.

about twelve or fifteen qualified sample donations, there is some incentive to show up once in a while to produce a sub-par sample, as they will receive remuneration for these as well, albeit at a much lower rate. On the days that I observed workflows in the laboratory, between 40 percent and 60 percent of the samples from qualified donors were rejected.

Having heard Mei's sample assessment, Huilan fills out an appropriate remuneration slip and passes it back out through the hatch to the receptionist who will bring it to the waiting donor. Since the sperm bank is interested in keeping waiting times at a minimum, remuneration slips are usually returned to donors as quickly as possible so that they can take it to the cashier and be on their way. If a qualified donor's sample is accepted, Huilan also adds a note in the donor's ID book in a way that reminds me of getting a stamp in a coffee chain loyalty card. Once a donor book is filled up with around fifteen qualified donations, a completion payment awaits the donor, albeit six months later, once he has returned for a final HIV test.

The mood in the laboratory is often laid back. Staff members chat together, at times cracking jokes. The arrival of a visibly high volume sample might, for example, be accompanied by a quip like "Ahh, this must be a basketball player!" Gradually, as the afternoon's donation session wears on, more and more accepted samples are passed on to Lin and the air of the lab becomes unmistakably thick with the musky smell of so much semen, a smell that the surgical masks we are wearing do little to filter out. Lin is tasked with preparing each sample for cryopreservation, which involves mixing the sample with an appropriate amount of cryo-protectant made of glycerol and egg yolk. The cryo-protected sperm sample is then injected into three to five vials (depending on the original volume of the sample), which are clearly labeled with the donor's number and date of donation. It is these vials that will eventually be shipped out to fertility clinics for use in artificial insemination by donor (AID) or IVF treatment. Rong, who is sitting next to Lin, is tasked with preparing bacterial tests by smearing a series of petri dishes with leftover semen from the syringes used to fill the vials. Possible bacteria in individual semen samples will be allowed to grow on these petri dishes, and should a particular sample turn out to be contaminated with a bacterial infection, each vial will be retrieved from cryopreservation and destroyed.

Once all sperm samples have been analyzed, a cryofreezing ritual marks the close of the day. By then around 120 vials have been prepared for cryo-preservation from qualified samples. Vials are placed into a ThermoFisher controlled-rate freezer that brings the temperature of samples down at a speed that prevents as much damage as possible during the freezing process. Ai types her handwritten ledger book results into an Excel spreadsheet on a computer, which is located on the left side of the hatch, in the process removing any personally identifiable information from the logged sample numbers in the database. Once the freezer has rather loudly clicked and buzzed its way to well-below freezing temperatures, vials are taken out and transferred into a cylindrical cryotank's trays, which have been pulled out of the tank's liquid nitrogen using a steel rod and gloves. The storage room quickly fills up with the steam of liquid nitrogen as the sperm bank crew fits the day's harvest of vials into the square trays as one would Lego blocks and looks forward to finishing their day's work. In an interview with Huilan a few weeks later about her rostered shifts in the sperm bank lab, she says, "Sometimes I feel like I am working in a factory, a factory that produces sperm!"

Once *gaokao* results have secured admission to universities for the highest scorers, recruiters have done their job in getting as many male university students from the campuses to the sperm bank as possible, and the sperm bank's receiving staff have done everything they can to make donors feel comfortable during their first visit, yet another hurdle stands in the way of sperm banks' never-ending efforts to maintain, expand, and replenish their pool of donors. This hurdle was described by one director of a European sperm at a conference held in Changsha as "the eye of the needle" to highlight how hard it was for a potential donor to meet his bank's strict screening criteria. Since sperm banks in countries like Denmark or the United States require a much smaller pool of donors to cover the same number of families as in China, they tend to be much more selective in their screening, with qualification rates as low as 8 to 10 percent. One Danish sperm bank even made headlines in 2011 when disclosing that they had too many donors. An evening tabloid proclaimed, "We are drowning in sperm," on the basis of an interview with the sperm bank's CEO: "Our tanks are brim-full. We have more than 70 liters of sperm and almost 500 donors are currently in quarantine. We are rejecting huge numbers [of potential donors] and have had an enormous influx in recent years. At the moment we actually have 600 donors on our waiting list" (quoted in Ehrenskjöld, 2011).

Oversupply has never been an issue in China for the reasons outlined in the previous chapters. As a result, the "eye of the needle" is somewhat larger, although qualification rates are still low at around 15–30 percent of those who are screened. This does not mean, however, that sperm banks are in any way lax about their screening procedures. The Ministry of Health's management regulations for sperm banks are modeled on international standards from the World Health Organization. Higher qualification rates in China are a consequence of sperm banks' living up to these regulations as opposed to going above and beyond international screening standards, as some sperm banks in Europe and America do. Nevertheless, as we saw in chapter 2, low qualification rates are considered by some as yet another sign of a "sperm crisis" in China. Indeed, the sperm bank in

Changsha recently carried out a retrospective cross-sectional study in which they found that "the rate of qualified donors fell from 55.78 percent in 2001 to 17.80 percent in 2015, and the rate for 2015 was approximately threefold lower than the corresponding rates in 2001" (Huang et al., 2017, p. 83). Since willing male sperm donors are considered a scarce resource in China and each donor is limited to impregnating five women, sperm banks would of course prefer to have as many of them qualify as possible, just as they wouldn't mind nudging the state-set limit of five couples to perhaps eight or ten.

In this chapter, I will ethnographically chronicle routinized screening and quality control practices in the sperm banks I visited and show how these have contributed to the emergence of what can be thought of as a practice collective. This is the daily grind of sperm banking, as protocolled procedures are followed, adjusted, and developed day in and day out. The high throughput style of sperm banking in China creates a very particular atmosphere that emerges out of its regularized performance (cf. Fleck, 1979). In chronicling these everyday practices at the sperm bank, I will argue that quality control procedures can helpfully be thought of as technologies of assurance (*que bao*) understood as a configuration of strategies and techniques within which certain persons, activities, and/or objects come to be vouched for over others (Wahlberg, 2015). As one sperm bank director in China put it, "We collect sperm from our donors for the sake of providing treatment for patients. One of the goals is to offer a satisfactory pregnancy rate; the other one is to assure their offspring's healthiness." As we will see, assurance requires documentation—measurements of sperm quality, medical screening records, signed informed consent forms—and as such sperm banks in China are an example of what Matthew Kohrman in his ethnographic study of the making of disability organizations in China has called biobureaucracies—"institutions . . . undergirded by . . . a set of patterned ways for conceiving of and responding to normalcy and abnormality, health and pathology" (Kohrman, 2005, p. 3).

A number of ethnographic studies have shown us how, just like blood, sperm is considered a potentially dangerous bodily substance that needs to be meticulously controlled, screened, managed, selected, and contained in the reproductive bioeconomy. It was the HIV/AIDS epidemic that would usher in strict screening requirements for sperm banks globally (again similar to the case of blood donation), as fears of possible transmission through insemination spread (see Almeling, 2011). As a consequence, the "fresh" semen once preferred in insemination practices has been replaced by "technosemen," which Lisa Jean Moore and Matthew Schmidt have defined as "semen that has been technically manipulated in laboratory environments, has been collected from men who have been selectively screened for genetic and social characteristics, and has been rhetorically constructed by semen banks' industrial marketing strategies" (Moore & Schmidt, 1999, p. 340); although in China, I would replace those industrial marketing strategies with the state's family planning policies.

In her study of donor insemination practices in Taiwan, Wu Chia-Ling has argued that "in delineating the boundary between the safe and the dangerous ... doctors' configuration strategies ... devalued men of Taiwan's lower socio-economic class, not for their supposedly low IQs but for their supposedly higher probability of carrying diseases in the first place" (Wu, 2011, p. 105). Similarly, Stine Adrian, who carried out field-work in Denmark and Sweden, has argued that one of the sperm banks she studied "gives value to the sperm by emphasizing the high level of security measures taken into account in the process of cryo-preserving and storing the sperm" and as such "the sperm bank brands the sperm by narrating it as better and more secure than 'natural sperm'" (Adrian, 2010, p. 406). Sebastian Mohr, who likewise carried out fieldwork in Denmark, describes these security measures as legitimizing containment practices, which "help to secure donor semen's conversion into an exchangeable means of donor-assisted reproduction" (Mohr, 2016, p. 321).

Technosemen requirements have been enshrined in Chinese national law ever since the Ministry of Health promulgated the Regulation on Assisted Reproductive Technology, the Basic Standard Requirements of Human Sperm Banks, and the Rules of Administration of Human Sperm Banks in the 2001 to 2003 period. As a result, security measures and con-tainment practices can certainly be found in the production of technose-men in China today where (as we saw in chapter 3) sperm banks likewise devalue men from certain socioeconomic backgrounds because of suspi-cions that they may be drug users or carriers of infectious diseases. Nevertheless, in what follows, I shift analytical attention somewhat, away from the technosemen itself and toward what I have called technologies of assurance. In doing so, I will show how it is not just containment practices and security measures that make up daily routines in a sperm bank. Equally important are cultivation practices aimed at procuring a lively stock of sperm for distribution to fertility centers throughout China. As such, we will see how liveliness is cultivated as dangers are contained. The concentration of sperm cells in a given semen sample is one of the most important techno-indicators of liveliness and I will argue that it is analogously the premier task of sperm banks to concentrate producers of lively sperm into a high-quality pool of donors. On the one hand, sperm samples are to be collected, cryo-banked, and thawed in a manner that maximizes the possibility for a lawful recipient to become pregnant. On the other hand, transmission of disease (both infectious and genetic) should be prevented just as transmission of "positive" traits such as health, intelligence, and normal weight or height are to be promoted.

While much of the legitimacy work carried out by sperm banks in some European countries and America is aimed at the public, often conceived of as customers or markets, in China the assurance work that takes place in sperm banks cannot be detached from the state-centric reproductive complex that has shaped assisted reproduction into the technology of birth control that it is. Technologies of assurance have shaped the daily routinization of sperm banking in China by helping to legitimate it as a technology that contributes to and complies with the family planning objectives of the state—controlling population growth, improving population quality.

This chapter, then, is about the "daily grind" of sperm banking in China. My analysis covers three key areas of assurance, as sperm back staff members work to assure the *viability*, *vigor*, and *purity* of banked sperm. In doing this, they are no different from staff at sperm banks in other parts of the world, a point that is underlined every time sperm bank managers stress that they follow the highest international standards for screening sperm donors. Still, the high throughput form that sperm banking has taken in China as well as sperm banks' role as state-sanctioned guarantors of high-quality sperm shapes daily routines in particular ways that characterize the style of sperm banking we find in China today. At the same time, my point is that guarantors cannot guarantee; all they can do is *assure* by strictly complying with sperm bank administration requirements and rigorously following medical screening standards. As such, assurance is demonstrated through auditable practices—such as the ledger book of semen analysis results, standard operating procedures, informed consent forms, and the like—that must document how a sperm bank has lived up to these requirements and standards as a way to vouch for the quality of sperm stored in the bank's cryotanks. Sperm banks vouch for, rather than guarantee, the quality of the sperm that they provide for AID treatment in ways that legitimate sperm banking as a tool of family planning.

CULTIVATING LIVELY SPERM

Guang is listening attentively, brow furrowed. Hong, who is on duty as the sperm bank receptionist that afternoon, is reassuring Guang in the crowded waiting room: "Don't worry, it's very normal not to qualify the first time, that's why you have three chances. You see, your sample is not so bad. It should be 60 million but it's about 25. Here is some information for you to read so you can prepare yourself for next time." The card Hong passes to Guang lists a number of factors that can negatively affect the liveliness of a potential donor's sperm, although it must be said reads as a relatively accurate description of many young university students' daily lives:

- Medication (including vitamins, Chinese medicine, and Chinese patent medicine), smoking, drinking, chewing betelnut, thick tea, coffee, and drinks like Coke and Sprite
- Being in bad physical condition, overtired, having a flu
- Irregular life—lack of sleep, long periods using a computer, or staying up all night
- Being too stressed or low-spirited

Hong also stresses the need to abstain from sex at least three or four days before returning for a second try at qualifying. Later, Guang, a muscular young man, explains that he is a police cadet and when he read some information online about the sperm bank he decided to come and donate. "I was sure I would qualify, but I don't know . . ." his voice trails off. A week later, I bump into Guang again by chance on the back stairwell as I make my way up and Guang heads back down. As always the stairwell is packed so we can't stop, but Guang nods at me with a big smile. When I get to the sperm bank on the fourth floor, Hong confirms what I have already guessed: Guang had passed on his second attempt and had now been invited to return for a medical screening.

It is not uncommon for the 2,000–3,000 potential donors who come to the sperm bank in Changsha each year to fail their first donation. As a result, all potential donors are given three chances to qualify. The receptionist who receives first-time donors will often spend considerable time with those donors whose samples did not quite live up to the bank's quality standards, encouraging them to return and providing them with tips on how to improve their chances of qualifying, as Hong did with Guang. Moreover, mornings are often spent making follow-up phone calls in a bid to get students who failed the first time to return, while reminding them of how best to prepare. Unlike in organ or blood donation, bioavailability does not hinge on sperm donor–recipient matching (albeit a recipient couple may well be for social reasons interested in choosing a donor with the same blood type as the infertile man's). Instead, bioavailability in sperm donation is directly linked to the exceptional liveliness of a donor's sperm. Exceptional because the Ministry of Health's concentration standard of 60 million sperm cells per milliliter is four times higher than the World Health Organization's criteria for normal male fertility. This is deemed necessary because even natural conception can be hit-or-miss, but also since some sperm cells will inevitably not survive the freezing and thawing process. As explained by one of the sperm bank administrators: "If we would like to reach a 20 percent clinical pregnancy rate . . . then the quality of the donors' sperm should be better than normal people's."

This is what the workflow on the lab bench described at the beginning of this chapter has been designed to assure with the help of a phase-contrast microscope: a kind of viability assurance. As we saw earlier, the lab worker perched at the microscope has learned to count the number of sperm inside ten visible squares and estimate the percentage of sperm that are motile with "good forward movement." Since sperm quality assessment relies on the judgment of sperm bank staff, its routinization generates uncertainty, which in turn must be tamed. The *WHO Laboratory*

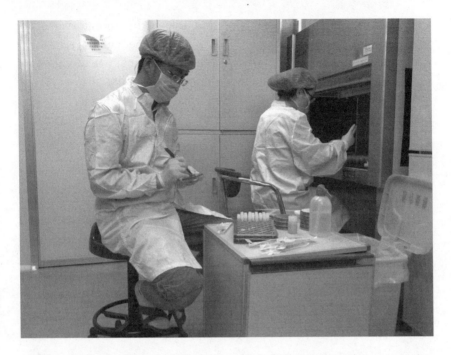

Figure 13. Preparing vials of qualified donor sperm for cryopreservation.

Manual for the Examination and Processing of Human Semen, which is used in China, makes a case for strict quality assurance:

> Since semen analysis is highly complex and procedurally difficult to standardize, quality control (QC) is essential to detect and correct systematic errors and high variability of results. The large discrepancies between assessments of sperm concentration and morphology in different laboratories ... underline the need for improved QC and standardization. Whatever its size, each laboratory should implement a quality assurance (QA) programme, based on standardized methods and procedures, to ensure that results are both accurate and precise. ... The fundamental parameters of sperm concentration, morphology, and motility should always be monitored by internal quality control and, where possible, by external quality control. (WHO, 2010, p. 179).

On a monthly basis, staff at the Hunan Human Sperm Bank hold "standardization sessions" where they share concerns and propose ways of ensuring uniformity of counting practices and handling procedures, not least since they rotate responsibilities and tasks in the laboratory in order to provide variation for staff members. Moreover, meticulous records are kept of the number of donors who visit the sperm bank; whether they are first-time, second-time, or qualified donors; the quality of their semen sample, as well as medical screening information. Central to technologies of assurance are processes of quantification as number of sperm per milliliter, motility grades, percentages of normal morphology, and milligrams of fructose per milliliter are observed, measured, counted, and recorded. Such numbers make sperm quality auditable and it is in this sense that we should read the Ministry of Health's sperm quality qualification criteria:

- semen liquefaction time less than sixty minutes
- volume more than 2 ml
- density greater than 60×10^6/ml
- forward motility greater than 60 percent
- post-thaw survival rate greater than 60 percent
- normal sperm morphology rate more than 30 percent

When these criteria are deployed in the quality control laboratory, the pool of bioavailable sperm donors shrinks once again quite drastically. By far most potential sperm donors will end up not qualifying because their semen samples do not live up to national criteria. This explains why considerable efforts are put into reassuring and encouraging first-time donors who do not make the grade in their first attempt, especially those who have "normal" quality sperm. With a little bit of coaching and information about preparation, the liveliness of the sperm of a number of those who fail in their first attempt can be improved. Such is the hope in any case.

In his study of Danish sperm donors, Mohr has argued that the practice of sperm donation generates embodied masculinities. For some, "being a sperm donor means to acquire a masculine self-image appropriated by biomedicine: measurements of sperm counts and sperm cell motility become part of how sperm donors think masculinity and male bodies" (2014, p. 170). Hence, embodied masculinities are in some ways an important part of cultivating lively sperm. When speaking to qualified donors in Changsha and Shanghai I would often be told how "happy" or "proud" they were upon learning that they had qualified, especially since it is not uncommon for a potential donor to fail to qualify on his first and second visits. Twenty-one-year old Gao from Changsha explains:

GAO: My motility is not so bad so they gave me a small white card and told me I have three times to pass the test. If I fail the three tests I am out. Then I was frustrated for a month after . . . a month after they sent me a text so that I came here again to do the second test; then I passed. After that they gave me this [takes out his qualified donor card] donor record and told me to follow the rules on this record card. This is the thirteenth time I come here.

AW: And how did you feel when you qualified, when you finally got the card?

GAO: I felt quite proud. You know this test is not only about the qualification, about my sperm. I am a man. Maybe this is also about my ability, you know *that* ability. . . . Yes, they told me they need very strong sperm so if we pass the test that would symbolize our health . . . that our sperm's health is quite good. But they also told me if we don't pass, that does not mean we are losers in sperm, just that we are not that qualified.

Hence, for some donors that I met making the grade as a qualified sperm donor was in some ways akin to getting a top *gaokao* result, putting you at the top of the rankings. As we saw in the previous chapter, just showing up at the sperm bank for the first time can be a nerve-wracking affair, not to mention waiting one's turn to masturbate on command. When twenty-two-year old Zhang was asked how he reacted when he was told he had qualified, he said:

Eh . . . from unqualified to qualified? It proves that I have reproductive ability. I felt happy about that. Also . . . I feel [laughter] . . . I didn't make it for the first two times and passed for the third time. I feel a bit . . . a bit happy. Are you asking about my feeling? I was a little bit nervous [laughter]. I was not living a disciplined life. I feel like I had some bad habits. Probably . . . I was a little bit scared about not being qualified the first one or two times. So . . . if one is "out of order," someone like me probably wouldn't come here the third time. Yes, once I learned about being qualified, I was pretty happy.

During my observations in the backstage laboratory where sperm bank staff were carrying out assembly-line quality control, it was not that uncommon for a first-time potential donor's semen sample to be of worryingly bad quality. One afternoon, I experienced what Cynthia Daniels has called the "paradox of reproductive masculinity" (see Wu's [2011] discussion of this paradox in a Taiwanese setting) in donor insemination practices, a paradox that was brought into sharp relief by the sperm bank's location within a fertility clinic in Changsha. Li called me to the phase-contrast microscope he was manning for the afternoon's quality assessments: "See, have a look, here we have someone who we will invite for treatment!" Although said in a humorous manner that was characteristic of the relaxed atmosphere in the air-conditioned laboratory of the sperm bank, Li was nevertheless both solemn and serious. I peered into the microscope and could immediately see that there was hardly any activity within the green grids that the microscope made visible. A few single sperm cells were moving about unhurriedly in an almost exhausted manner. This was the opposite of the liveliness that sperm banks actively seek out through their screening practices. In such severe cases, Li explained to me, a doctor on duty would have a private conversation with the potential donor:

> We ask him out to a private room, and have a warm talk, generally tell him the truth, but we are very careful about our words, we don't want to give him too much mental burden, but we must tell him the truth, and give him some advice on future fertility problems or other issues that may concern him, especially for those sperm donors we must discard. Our quality standard for the sperm donor is very high. Maybe the unqualified sperm donors won't have fertility problems in their own lives.

Once qualified, sperm donors are not off the hook when it comes to following the daily lifestyle guidelines that sperm bank staff members lay out for donors. Qualified donors have been chosen for their reproductive liveliness and through an incentivized system of paying more for each of the twelve to fifteen qualified samples that a donor delivers than for any sub-par samples that are produced along the way. Twenty-two-year-old Zhang from Changsha explains: "The doctor told me some information about how to be a qualified donor when I first came here.

Then I began to pay attention to meals and lifestyle as well as the taboos they mentioned. I tried to do everything according to what they said, such as meals, sleep on time, avoiding high temperature, soft drinks, and smoking." Having met many donors through the years of research, my sense was that qualified donors very quickly got into a rhythm that suited their studies and the logistics of getting to the sperm bank. The more seasoned donors who have been at it for a while learn relatively quickly how to optimize the quality of their sperm by following the liveliness tips they receive. Moreover, they have gotten at least more used to the masturbation facilities in the sperm bank than first-timers. Qualified donors knew that theirs was an approximately six-month commitment (with a single follow-up visit six months later) to maintaining certain regimes of abstinence, of looking after oneself as well as of making regular visits to the sperm bank. Some donors wanted to get donation over and done with as quickly as possible in order to receive the final payment, while others preferred stretching out their donation period to fit their schedules. Those donors who had girlfriends did find that abstinence could be a challenge, especially if they hadn't confided in their partners. Zhaoju told me how "if I have a special situation or I make love with my girlfriend, I will make some changes. I will change to Saturday or another time."

Hence, my suggestion is that to assure the quality of sperm that is banked, sperm bank staff engage in choreographed efforts to secure, cultivate, and maintain the collective reproductive liveliness of their highly selected bioavailable pool of qualified donors. This is done, first and foremost, through quality control at the bench because it is only with the help of a microscope that the viability of a particular sperm sample can be vouched for. At the same time, however, the microscope does not have the last say. Those potential sperm donors who do not meet national criteria are nevertheless encouraged, coached, and primed to work on their reproductive liveliness, not least because donors are in constant shortage. Knowing how hard it is to get male students to show up at the sperm bank in the first place, staff want to maximize the qualification rates of those who have decided that they would like to donate sperm. The sperm bank manager in Changsha receives weekly reports on donor numbers as well as their sperm quality, which allow him to monitor the liveliness of the sperm of both potential and qualified donors, and by aggregating the latter, the liveliness of the sperm bank's stock. As Hong told me, "We collect weekly statistics on concentration and post-thaw recovery rates and we also average them for the different cities we work in. Each week we must send these reports to the manager."

One of the effects of having a sperm bank located within a very successful fertility clinic is that it is constantly surrounded by rather astronomical growth rates. For example, as we saw in chapter 1, IVF cycles at the CITIC-Xiangya Reproductive and Genetic Hospital increased from 700 per year in 2002 to over 40,000 per year in 2016. In stark contrast, the sperm bank in Changsha was oscillating between 2,000 and 4,000 potential donors screened annually during the years of my research. This creates all kinds of pressures on sperm bank staff members in a bio-bureaucracy that constantly measures and monitors results as a part of its assurance practices. Management immediately reacts to falls in weekly numbers of first-time donors, as new potential city sites throughout Hunan are identified and negotiated, just as recruiters are encouraged to work harder in their efforts to get potential donors to the sperm bank.

During one of the afternoon sessions I spent observing semen analysis in the laboratory, I noticed that a high proportion of samples from both qualified and first-time donors was being binned rather than sent onward along the assembly line for cryo-preservation. I commented on this and Huilin said, "Yes, it can be seasonal, related to the weather." I was rather intrigued. I had never thought of seasonal fluctuations as a factor in sperm banking, but this was confirmed to me by the sperm bank manager who monitored the aggregated liveliness of all sperm samples coming in on a weekly basis. If a period of stagnating sperm quality sets in, receptionists at the sperm bank are instructed to remind donors of the active steps they can take to ensure the liveliness of their sperm. An interesting twist on this seasonal fluctuation was recently highlighted in a study by Wu Li and colleagues (2017) who assessed the exposure-response association between particulate matter exposure from air pollution and semen quality. The semen quality of 1,759 men from Wuhan who were partners of women undergoing assisted reproductive technology procedures was assessed and correlated with the air pollution readings from the days leading up to

Table 5.1 Number of screened candidates and qualified donors annually, Hunan Human Sperm Bank

	2002	2007	2010	2011	2012	2013	2014	2015	2016
Total screened potential donors	366	2,244	2,558	2,627	2,183	3,005	4,523	4,831	6,228
Total qualified	164	691	962	849	825	1,025	1,110	858	1,272
% qualified	45%	31%	38%	32%	38%	34%	25%	18%	20%
Total postqualification drop-outs	28	127	194	189	161	235	259	176	273
% drop-outs	17%	18%	20%	22%	20%	23%	23%	21%	21%

SOURCE: Hunan Human Sperm Bank annual reports.

the depositing of a semen sample in connection with fertility treatment. And sure enough, the study authors found an inverse correlation between exposure to particulate matter through air pollution and both sperm concentration and sperm count.

High throughput sperm banking requires a constantly replenished pool of good donors rather than the exclusive pool of "super donors" that some European and American sperm banks manage. The Ministry of Health's biomedical sperm quality criteria and audited quality control practices in the lab synch with the liveliness guidelines that the sperm bank has developed to improve (potential) donors' sperm quality through care-of-the-self practices. Together, these practices and strategies make up technologies of viability assurance.

PREVENTING TRANSMISSION

Not only is sperm as a biological substance more or less lively, as I have already noted, it is also potentially dangerous as bearer of genetic, sexually transmitted, or other infectious diseases. Moreover, donors themselves, masturbation rooms, and also the laboratories that handle the semen samples are potential vectors of bacterial infection. As a result, the production of technosemen has come to involve a series of procedures aimed at assuring not just the viability but also the purity and fitness of sperm. Assuring the health of donor offspring requires actively managing the collective health of qualified donor pools. We will recall that in one of the recruitment flyers distributed on university campuses, students are informed that "in order to assure the quality of sperm, and thereby ensure superior birth (*yōushēng*), every donor should have a systematized body examination, free of charge." The point being that, even if high-quality university students are considered less exposed, of better stock, more "pure," and more healthy than uneducated or working males by sperm bank managers, college entrance exams and microscope-aided assessments of semen samples are not sufficient for assuring sperm quality. Before the Ministry of Health introduced regulations stipulating that all sperm banks must be licensed and live up to sperm bank administration guidelines in 2001, there was not much quality control involved in sperm banking in China. In other words, as Lu Guangxiu described it, there were no procedures in place for assuring the quality of sperm—"they were not doing any selection of donors; everyone can be a donor; and they are also not doing any examinations of the donors." Today, there are strict requirements for medically screening, testing, and selecting donors as a way to minimize the risk of transmitting disease through sperm donation. These requirements have not least been informed by the transmission of HIV to millions of blood transfusion recipients in China in the 1990s. When it comes to sperm donation, however, transmission is understood both in terms of genetic and infectious disease. Assuring quality requires establishing procedures that minimize the risk of transmitting infectious disease and of inadvertently "breeding" genetic disease. Being able to cultivate and produce lively sperm is necessary, but not sufficient to become a donor.

Those donors who are able to provide a sample that meets national criteria after a maximum of three tries are invited to have a medical check-up with one of the doctors at the sperm bank as the next step in their qualification process. Following *gakao* and semen analysis, medical screening is the third bottleneck that can contribute to a further narrowing of the pool of bioavailable sperm donors in China. As put by a doctor responsible for screening potential donors: "Now, every college student in China must have a comprehensive physical before and after their entrance to college, so they are generally in good physical and mental health. Changsha has many universities, and students from good universities are more likely to come here. The college students are highly selected, and they are a high-quality population. And when they come here, they are selected yet again." Medical selection takes place through the sperm bank's medical check-up, which consists of a personal and family medical history consultation, a physical examination, and a blood test. The aim of such check-ups is to "catch" otherwise unnoticed diseases or abnormalities as well as to assess whether a person belongs to a high-risk category (e.g., drug user, multiple sexual partners, homosexual). If the biological sperm quality criteria serve as a key reference for laboratory workers peering through the microscope at the bench, then doctors at the sperm bank "see" through Article 16 of the Ministry of Health's rules on the Administration of Human Sperm Banks, which states that:

Sperm banks should carry out physical examinations and strict screening on donors. Semen shall not be collected if the candidate:

I.   has a family history of genetic disease or suffers from genetic diseases;
II. has a mental disease;
III. has an infectious disease or is a carrier;
IV. has had long-term exposure to radiation and hazardous substances;
V.   has failed semen examination;
VI. has other serious organic diseases.

The doctor will ask each candidate to fill out a medical history questionnaire as well as interview them about their past medical history, personal life history (e.g., whether they have had any long-term exposure to toxic substances), family disease history (to identify any potential risk of transmitting genetic disease) as well as sexually transmitted disease history. Here, the doctor relies on the honesty of each candidate as they have no capabilities for verifying their information. Indeed, one doctor told me how, in all his years at the sperm bank, he had only come across two potential candidates who stated that they were homosexual (considered to be "high risk" and therefore excluded from being able to donate [see Hoeyer (2010) for a discussion of the problems with the "high risk" category in donation practices]), both of whom became very angry at themselves for having been honest.

Secondly, a physical examination is carried out to ensure that the candidate has no physical abnormalities that might be visible, or genetic, sexually transmitted, or other infectious diseases. During one of the afternoons that I joined a crew from the sperm bank on a donation trip to Yueyang, one of the candidates whose semen sample had qualified and otherwise looked healthy turned out to have the skin disease ichthyosis. At the end of the day's donation and medical screening session, the doctor called me into a back room where he showed me a picture he had taken of the donor's arm on his phone: "We call this disease 'fish skin' and he told me that his grandmother also had the same condition, so we cannot accept him as a donor." The candidate was visibly disappointed that he couldn't become a donor, especially since he had initially learned that his semen sample had qualified. After he had left, the doctor continued, "You know we have maybe many cases of potential sperm donors who are discarded because they have family history of, for example, congenital heart disease. . . . We have had maybe about sixty sperm donors discarded for various reasons, mainly due to family histories although some due to personal medical history. . . . Fortunately the donors tell the truth but I think maybe only a few donors don't tell the truth and so there is a risk." On another occasion in the city of Changde, the sperm bank crew decided to reject a donor whose semen sample had qualified but who was considered to be too obese. Factors such as height and weight are taken into consideration for possible genetic reasons while sperm bank staff also implicitly uphold societal norms by talking about ensuring that their donors are "normal." When I asked Li, a doctor at the sperm bank in Changsha, whether they carry out any psychological screening, he answered:

> It's a good question. And I think this job is done by our recruitment staff when they are having the first talk with the sperm donors, so they can judge if the sperm donors have a normal psychological status. When the sperm donors come here, we have already carefully observed their interaction and communication. In the physical examination, I have a small talk with him, maybe very short, asking a few questions, such as "What's your major in university?," "What's the donation purpose?," "Do you have some worries about donation?," or "Do you know the purpose of your donation?." If they have some worries, we must do some examination. In the following days through their donation, all staff in our sperm bank should observe, to see if they are behaving abnormally or weirdly. So everyone [at the sperm bank] should be involved in the selection of sperm donors.

Such psychological screening is not necessarily written down in the form of guidelines but my informants told me of examples where one qualified donor was consequently observed conspicuously talking to himself while in the waiting room or where a potential donor spoke "too much" about wanting to "spread his genes." In both cases, these donors who had otherwise qualified were rejected.

Genetic screening was a topic that many of my informants suggested remained a problem because it relied on the honesty of donors regarding their family history, as mentioned above. Because of anonymity requirements, the sperm bank would of course never contact parents or other relatives should they harbor suspicions about possible medical history in a family. Some sperm banks in Europe and America have introduced targeted genetic tests as part of their medical screening procedures, for example, for the relatively common cystic fibrosis gene. Given the sheer volume of potential donors screened in China's high throughput sperm banking system, to do this is deemed too costly. On the other hand, given the restrictive limit of a maximum of five impregnated women per donor, doctors pointed out that there was statistically less chance that a disease that is inherited through an autosomal recessive or dominant pattern would be passed on to offspring. While I was in China in May of 2011, a story broke back home in Denmark about a Danish sperm donor who inadvertently had passed on the potentially serious genetic disease NF1 to numerous offspring (see Mohr, 2016). I was asked to relay information about how the health authorities were handling the case, not least because of worries about liability. To date there have been no known cases of inadvertent transmission of genetic disease through sperm donation in China.

Finally, a blood sample is taken from each donor who reaches the medical screening stage, which is subject to a battery of standard tests to check for chromosome disorders as well as various communicable diseases such as hepatitis, HIV, and HPV. Blood chemistry analysis takes the form of numbers where certain measured values—biomarkers—which lie outside a norm may indicate disease. For hepatitis and HIV, specific diagnostic tests are run to confirm presence or absence of the virus in a blood sample. While positive test results for hepatitis and HPV are relatively common, the sperm bank in Changsha had only had one case of HIV, which was promptly forwarded to the Center for Disease Control in Hunan Province in accordance with legal requirements.

As part of their priming of sperm donors, sperm bank staff impress the importance of hygiene and health maintenance upon all qualified donors in the instructions they give them. In an information leaflet intended for newly qualified donors, the sperm bank asks donors to "maintain good health habits, preferably taking a shower the night before [donating]. (We have high requirements for health and a bacterial culture is made from every sperm sample.)" Clinical settings themselves are of course notorious breeding grounds for all kinds of bacteria, not least because of the high numbers of people who pass through a Chinese hospital on a daily basis. Sperm samples can therefore become contaminated as they make their way from penis to cryotank. For this reason, sperm banks uphold their good laboratory practices aimed at minimizing the risk of contamination both for the sake of the health of its workers and to safeguard the purity of its prime material: sperm samples. Donors must leave their footwear in lockers before they enter the donor room area. They are instructed to wash their hands thoroughly before and after masturbation just as disinfectant wipes are provided for cleaning their genitals before and after along with hygienic paper towels for sitting on in the donor rooms. Donors are instructed carefully as to how they should collect their sperm by ejaculating into the plastic cup and immediately closing the lid. Once they have finished masturbating into the plastic cup and washed their hands again, donors must place their samples into a stainless steel tray outside of the door, which is then transported to the hatch that separates the donor area from the laboratory.

Within the laboratory, workers wear lab coats, hairnets, and face masks while working. And the staff member in charge of cryo-preserving qualified samples must also prepare smears of each sample on a petri dish, which is cultured for twenty-four hours to make sure the sample doesn't contain any bacteria. All of this to avoid inadvertent contamination of a semen sample with bacteria. I was only told of a single case where a family had accused the sperm bank in Changsha of transmitting an infectious disease to a newborn; however, medical records on file (which include blood test results and semen sample smear test results) showed that the infection did not have its origins in the donor sperm.

The results from the medical history interview, physical examination, blood tests, and smear tests are meticulously recorded in a qualified donor's file, which is stored away and kept for a minimum of seventy years in case a sperm bank is ever held liable for transmission of a disease to an offspring born with the help of donor sperm and also to allow couples and donors to consult the sperm bank when their children are going to marry. As stated in the informed consent form for donors and recipient couples: "In order to avoid the very remote possibility of inbreeding, the sperm bank has created a permanent computer database of sperm donation and supply, and provides free consultation for sperm donors and receivers." Bound by family planning laws, sperm banks are responsible for helping to improve the quality of the newborn population by screening their donors in ways that will prevent the birth of children with serious diseases. Hence, alongside viability assurance, health assurance plays an equally important part in the daily workings of a sperm bank as the staff members seek to prevent transmission of genetic and infectious diseases while at the same time promoting transmission of "good" traits such as normal height, eyesight, and weight. Just as the collective reproductive vitality of the sperm bank's pool of qualified donors is to be cultivated and assured, so too is the collective health, vigor, and strength of this same pool to be screened and assured.

CONCLUSION

Sperm quality is directly linked to its liveliness (which needs to be actively cultivated), its purity (which is under threat from infection and in need of protection from contamination), and its innate traits (which are "hidden" in its DNA). Assuring this quality, as we have seen, relies on a series of techniques and procedures, each of which cumulatively vouch for each particular sample. In a sense, we can see them as analogue algorithms, designed to sift through a mass of potential candidates in order to identify a qualified donor whose sperm will maximize chances of pregnancy while also assuring the health of offspring, thereby contributing to the improvement of the quality of the newborn population. *Gaokao* vouches for the intelligence and social status of a donor, the laboratory bench and biological sperm quality criteria vouch for the viability of a sample, medical checkups vouch for the health and genetics of the donor and his semen, and GLP procedures vouch for the safety of a sample. Starting with an entire cohort of male university students, a series of screenings and tests whittles down the pool of bioavailable candidates until only the best-qualified donors remain.

What I have argued in this chapter is that taken together, these techniques and practices constitute a technology of assurance that contributes to the formation of particular practice collectives. There are no guarantees in a system of assurance, as there are numerous ways in which quality can be compromised. To minimize the risk of compromising quality, safeguards are installed in the form of protocols, standard operating procedures, and guidelines. It is these guidelines and protocols that come to be "internalized" by staff to the extent that they constitute reference grids through which sperm samples or donor candidates can be viewed, assessed, and cat-

Figure 14. Cryopreserving the day's quality-controlled donations.

egorized while at the same time shaping the mood and workflows within the sperm bank. Sperm quality has to be made auditable as a matter of assurance. As I pointed out earlier, assurance requirements are not peculiar to sperm banks in China; sperm banks throughout the world are bound by similar requirements. Indeed, Michael Power has argued that in recent decades, throughout the world, a "market for assurance services has emerged which demands a tight coupling between quality performance, however that is to be defined, and processes to ensure that this performance is visible to a wider audience" (1999, p. 60). Nevertheless, I have shown how such assurance practices are shaped by China's reproductive complex, which in turn has generated a high throughput style of sperm banking that requires a constantly replenished pool of good donors rather than an exclusive pool of "super donors." As biobureaucracies in China, sperm banks are first and foremost committed to and required to make their assurance practices visible to the Ministry of Health, which is responsible for licensing them. Yet, in a time of increasing conflicts between hospital staff and patients (see chapter 6), I noted how sperm banks were increasingly also worried about their liability in case a genetic or infectious disease were to be transmitted through donated sperm.

We will recall from chapter 3 how food quality, air quality, and water quality are all considered to be under threat in urban China today. The same can be said of sperm quality. It is in this way that sperm banks in China act as state-sanctioned guarantors of good quality, much more so than their counterparts in some European countries or the United States, which explicitly assure their stocks of sperm for their customers in commercialized settings. And so, while technologies of assurance and the techniques they employ might well be global, the form they take in China is directly related to a style of sperm banking characterized by mass donation, assembly-line sperm quality analysis, cultivation of the liveliness of cyclically replenished donor pools, and medical screening to assure the quality of donor offspring.

6 Borrowing Sperm

In the early months of 2011, twenty-three-year-old Mu from Daduo town in the city of Xinghua gave her husband the joyous news that she was pregnant. The couple had been trying to conceive since they had married in January 2010 and finally the wait was over. Ahead of them lay the kind of expectant preparations that pregnancies bring with them. Mu asked her husband and mother-in-law to accompany her for the first visit to the local maternity ward where the obstetrician routinely calculated an expected birth date based on Mu's last menstruation.

But Mu was not pregnant. She had lied to her husband and in-laws. And far from a time filled with practices aimed at ensuring a healthy birth, Mu's fake pregnancy would be a race against time to get hold of a baby that she could present as her own by the end of the year. Mu confided her quandary to her mother and together they set about trying to find a child. Through Internet searches, Mu quickly learned that she would not be eligible to adopt a child through official procedures, at least not within the urgent time constraint she was under. Instead Mu and her mother made discreet inquiries through an acquaintance who worked at a maternity ward about whether they could pay their way to adoption, offering a total of 8,000 RMB to both the family of a newborn adoptee and the doctor who would take care of the paperwork. This plan also failed.

Meanwhile, Zhang Jinbing and Ju Yong-xiang from Xinghua city had found out that they would become first-time parents in exactly the same month that Mu's deception began. And indeed, Ju's genuine pregnancy came to term on October 30, 2011, when she was admitted to the Eastern Obstetrics Hospital in Xinghua as she went into labor. That night she gave birth to a healthy girl, whom they named Ke Ke. Yet Zhang and Ju's joy was short-lived as they woke up to their worst nightmare early on the 4th of November. "My daughter is gone!" Ju cried as Zhang leapt out of the adjoining bed. "Ke Ke was supposed to be lying in the cradle in front of her mother's bed, but we woke up around 5 A.M. and found her gone," Zhang would later explain. In the confusion that followed, Zhang took matters into his own hands and demanded to see surveillance video from the preceding night. And sure enough, scratchy footage from a minute past midnight showed a woman wearing black pants, a blue jacket, a scarf, and a hat hovering around the doorway to the maternity ward on the fifth floor. At 00:18, the surveillance footage showed the same woman on her way down the stairs with a baby in her hands.

Mu's mother was waiting for her outside the hospital. With time quickly running out on their deception, in the weeks before that night Mu and her mother had begun keeping an eye on expectant mothers at a local maternity hospital. As a measure of last resort, they had decided to abduct a newborn from one of the wards. Once they had the baby in their hands, Mu and her mother flagged down a taxi under cover of the night. Their plan was to take the baby to the local hospital in their hometown north of Xinghua in order to get a birth certificate for "their" new child. They told hospital staff that the child had been born on the way to the hospital and were admitted into a ward. In the morning, they called Mu's husband and in-laws to tell them the "wonderful news." Yet, by then, a manhunt was under way and local media had been mobilized by Zhang to help find his stolen daughter. The media attention paid off, as a taxi driver called police to inform them that he had picked up two women with a baby late at night on November 4 and dropped them off in Daduo town. Not long after, some sixty hours following her abduction, Ke Ke was reunited with her sobbing parents. Mu and her mother were taken into custody and charged

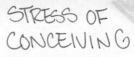

with the kidnapping of a child. Upon confessing to the crime Mu explained how she had become increasingly distraught by many unsuccessful attempts at conceiving. She had mooted the possibility of not having children to her husband on more than one occasion: "He said that if I can't get pregnant, he would abandon me." Faced with such a predicament, Mu and her mother had hatched their desperate and eventually criminal plot to bring home a newborn baby.[1]

As countless ethnographic studies from around the world have shown us over the years, more often than not, the onus of infertility falls almost entirely on women, even though male factor infertility is as likely to be the root cause of a couple's infertility. In Ecuador many women consider infertility as "god's punishment" (Roberts, 2012, p. 34); in India Aditya Bharadwaj has written of the "gendered experience of infertility" (2016, p. 74) where it is women rather than men who are considered barren; just as Karen Throsby has shown how when IVF fails in the United Kingdom the burden of responsibility falls mostly on the woman (2004, p. 137). As we saw in chapter 1, when Zhang Lizhu and her team analyzed the 6,300 letters they had received from infertile couples (mostly women) from around China by the early 1990s, they concluded that many of them had extremely low self-esteem, many had deteriorating marital relationships, some had divorced, some had family conflicts, and many did not work anymore. In a more up-to-date study, Joseph Lau and colleagues (2008) interviewed 192 infertile couples in Dengfeng County, Henan Province, using quality-of-life scales, concluding that stress resulting from infertility is associated with lowered quality of life.

Marcia Inhorn has argued that involuntary childlessness is often unrecognized or at the very most under-recognized as a public health problem in so-called "high fertility" countries "where children are highly desired, parenthood is culturally mandatory, [and] infertility is a socially unacceptable condition, leading most infertile couples on a relentless 'quest for conception' that may eventually involve resort to new reproductive technologies" (Inhorn, 2003, p. 1838; see also Evens, 2004). In such sociocultural contexts, "infertile people's suffering is often exacerbated" (Inhorn & van Balen, 2002, p. 6). Indeed, this is what Lisa Handwerker (1995a; 1998; 2002) found when carrying out her ethnographic studies at infertility clinics in Beijing. Through interviews with infertile women and men,

Handwerker concluded that China's "birth policy aimed at reducing births has ironically led to the further stigmatization of infertile women" as the pressures to have "one child" had intensified (Handwerker, 2002, p. 310). One of her informants insisted that: "I am sure the pressure to have children in China is greater than in any other country. . . . I feel so much pressure because of the mandatory birth certificate which provides me with permission to have a child. I have had to turn in my certificate the last three years because I couldn't have a child. I felt terrible. Here they give you permission and then you can't even give birth" (Handwerker, 2002, p. 302). Similarly, bioethicist Qiu Renzong, who had played a key role in the drafting of China's ART regulations at the turn of the millennium, has argued that: "Living in a Confucian pro-natalist society, couples known as infertile are always under grave psychological and social pressure. They will always ask themselves 'what is wrong with me?' They may be stigmatized in the community. Especially for women, everything depends on if she can deliver a boy. As a result, they will make every effort to treat their infertility" (Qiu, 2003). And finally, this is how a clinician who counsels and treats thousands of couples each year at the department that carries out up to 3,500 cycles of artificial insemination by donor (AID) each year in Changsha put it:

> For women, especially in China, I think most of the women—because I see both patients for AID and IVF—I think that women in China are more tolerant of the male's infertility but the men in China are less tolerant actually. So many of the men if they know it's the woman's problem they just come in and are very frustrated and say that they will divorce them or something like that. They will argue in front of you and I think most of them will not have a good result. But I think the women are more tolerant, they really are.

Herein lies the problem of living with infertility for couples in China (and indeed elsewhere)—it gives rise to burdened (*fùdān*) lives filled with sadness, family pressures, and stigmatization. It is in this sense that psychologist Xiao Shuiyuan of the Central South University in Changsha has argued that "surely a majority of infertility has a biological origin; however, suffering with infertility is not only a biological problem, but also a psychosocial process. . . . Improving the quality of life [*shēnghuó zhìliàng*] of the couple and the family should be considered the primary purpose of treatment" (Xiao, 2008). The family nightmare involving Ke Ke's abduction was playing out on national media during my fieldwork, covered by newspapers and television channels, initially in efforts to mobilize people in the frantic search for Ke Ke and subsequently to cover the tearful reuniting of Ke Ke with her parents. It was a compelling media drama that gripped many, including myself. With an estimated 10 percent of the childbearing population in China having fertility troubles, this tragic story is but one among millions, which highlights the anguish and desperation faced by many who are unable to conceive as they plan and pursue various options to have a child.

In this chapter, I focus on a very particular form of fertility treatment, namely AID. With the routinization of sperm banking in China over the last decade or so, AID has emerged as a realistic and acceptable option for many couples living with male factor infertility who are intent on forming a family. Realistic and acceptable in the sense that it is available (albeit with long waiting lists in many parts of the country), more accessible than, for example, IVF (3,000 RMB per AID cycle compared to 30,000 RMB per IVF cycle[2]), and in demand (as attested to by the chronic shortage of sperm donors). The aim of the chapter is not to provide insights into the experience of how couples live with male factor infertility as such; rather, it is to trace the form that third-party fertility treatment[3] has taken in a country where childbearing is a matter of filial piety and patriliny *as well as* of maintaining relations with friends, neighbors, and acquaintances (cf. Stafford, 2000).[4] In this way, the chapter provides an account of, firstly, how couples with male factor infertility[5] in China are able to "borrow sperm" (*jièyòng jīngzi*) from sperm banks and secondly, how couples and donors reason about third-party conception. In doing so, the chapter shows how fertility clinic–brokered strategies of what might be thought of as "hearth" management and trouble (*máfan*) avoidance are pursued by recipient couples and donors alike.[6]

I begin on the ninth floor of the CITIC-Xiangya Reproductive and Genetic Hospital where every Monday, new married male patients arrive in the morning to provide a fresh semen sample for analysis by the hospital's laboratory staff. In an inversion of the donor screening process, diagnostic pathways at the Hospital narrow down potential recipients of donor sperm to those who are confirmed as unable to produce their own sperm. Those patients who are diagnosed with azoospermia at the fertility clinic in Changsha are more fortunate than others in some ways since the hospital is home to China's largest sperm bank. Waiting lists are much shorter in Changsha as a result (and indeed the clinic attracts couples with male infertility from around the country because of this), and the sperm bank even distributes sperm to over forty other fertility clinics throughout China. Nonetheless, given the overall chronic shortages of donor sperm in China, we will see how recipient couples have little choice when deciding which donor to use and consequently how a shadow economy of illegal sperm continues to operate.

In the second half of the chapter, I move on to show how those couples who are given the option of AID reason about the use of third-party gametes. These couple's reflections are counterpoised with those of clinicians and sperm donors about what it means to make third-party babies in China today where infertility is highly stigmatized and kinship continues to be configured around ideas about male lineage and notions of filial piety. The received wisdom in China among doctors, patients, and donors alike is that infertility treatment in general and use of third-party gametes in particular should be kept a secret from all but the very closest loved ones, which means that couples will even insist that it is best not to tell donor children how they were brought into the world. Anonymity and secrecy are highlighted as essential by both recipient couples and donors, not least because both groups are intent on avoiding future trouble.

MONDAY MORNINGS

The scene outside of the CITIC-Xiangya Reproductive and Genetic Hospital that I described in the opening pages of this book is the same every morning, six days a week. The entrance is always teeming with people. A whole micro-economy has emerged around these crowds as local restaurants, pharmacies, and shops take their custom while landlords hawk rooms to rent nearby for those who have traveled from afar by distributing small business cards to anyone who will take one. Obtaining an admission ticket sets patients on standardized diagnostic pathways, which ultimately branch off into relevant treatment pathways. Everything has been calibrated to facilitate as efficient a flow of large volumes of patients as possible.[7] First up are a series of high throughput diagnostic tests to help determine what the primary cause of infertility is, although up to a third of cases will not have any biologically discernible causes.

While I was carrying out my observations at the sperm bank and fertility clinic in Changsha, Monday mornings at the ninth-floor clinical laboratory were reserved for newly admitted male patients. On a few of these Monday mornings I would make my way up the crowded backstairs to the ninth floor to observe work at the laboratory. The scenes that played out on these mornings are among the most vivid from my fieldwork. The noise explosion was intense as soon as one walked into the corridors that led to the clinical laboratory. Some forty to fifty men were more or less forcibly edging their way toward a small hatch that separated the corridor from the lab. I would deploy similar tactics to make my way through to the laboratory's entrance, which was located beyond the hatch toward the end of the corridor. Unlike these men, however, I was not carrying a "fresh" semen sample in a labeled plastic cup (similar to those used in the sperm bank on the fourth floor) in my inside jacket pocket (each patient having been instructed to keep samples at body temperature). Having made my way through the masses I would enter the laboratory and take up my observational perch on a stool in a corner incredulously watching as a large cardboard box quickly filled up with three-cup-high stacks of semen samples.[8] On the busiest Mondays, up to 150 semen samples are delivered, with a total of three laboratory staff carrying out microscope-aided semen analysis.

Even if couples who were newcomers to the hospital in Changsha had previously visited other (often less-resourced) fertility clinics, both men and women were still asked to pay for and undergo a full set of diagnostic tests in order to build up individual patient files in the hospital. Since the hospital in Changsha is one of the most renowned fertility clinics in China, those couples who do show up already know that they have a problem with their fertility; they are unable to conceive through intercourse. But not all of them arrive with an accurate diagnosis, just as a considerable number are dealing with "medically unexplained" infertility. As a result, all new patients follow standardized diagnostic protocols prior to being counseled on which forms of treatment are relevant for them, often in the form of lectures to an audience of similarly diagnosed couples.

Since almost all new male patients are asked to give blood and semen samples, the volume of tests carried out by diagnostics laboratories is enormous. To minimize the inevitable sample mix-ups, the hospital introduced a fingerprinting system to verify the identity of patients. For this reason, patients are asked to physically hand in their own blood and semen samples to the relevant laboratories. They are then given a receipt with a date and time for when they can return to collect their test results. Once a male patient has collected his test results, he will be told to make his way to the unit for men's fertility on the first floor to sign up for a consultation with a doctor, who will regularly see fifty to sixty patients every day, which works out to some ten thousand patients a year. That is a serious caseload by any measure. Quite a few times during my stays in Changsha I joined visiting fertility doctors from both America and Europe on their site visits at the hospital (as the world's largest fertility clinic, the hospital is involved in various international collaborations). On one such occasion, astounded by the caseloads in Changsha, one of the visiting fertility doctors jokingly said that complaints from staff members back home would no longer be accepted! Patient consultations often lasted no longer than two to five minutes as doctors quickly reviewed diagnostic test results in the green patient files that lay stacked on their desks, asked medical history questions, and carried out physical examinations in small, curtained-off areas. Consultations were often interrupted by nurses providing extra information to doctors or impatient patients inquiring when it would be their turn. With three or four doctors working in adjacent cubicles at a time, noise levels were high and privacy was in scarce supply. After a morning spent observing consultations, I sat down with Li, an infertility doctor, to ask him what the most difficult part of his job was:

LI: The first is our explanation with these patients. Maybe some of them find it hard to understand and maybe they strongly believe they have some severe disease but actually don't have one. There is something very interesting in China; many males believe they have some kidney problems—they say their kidney is not strong (*shènquē*). From traditional Chinese medicine [laughter] they have a strong belief. Maybe their symptoms are not very severe, maybe only something like going to the toilet during the night. They think it's very severe. But when I tell them they don't have this kind of [kidney] disease they don't believe me. . . . Or maybe they think they have prostate problems but they actually don't. You know, for something that is called "chronic prostate infection" (*qiánlièxiàn yán*) you can see many advertisements on the Internet or on television or radio but this is from some bad hospitals.

AW: You mean, they just want to earn some money?

LI: Yes! So it is very difficult to say that "actually you don't have this disease," but it's very interesting that almost every patient they say themselves that they have such a disease. . . . Another difficulty in my clinic is that we have too many patients so we don't have enough time for every patient so maybe some patients are unhappy.

AW: When there are so many people to help in China that can be very frustrating?

LI: Yes. But you know I want to say that another problem is that of bad hospitals. Even in Changsha there are maybe about ten hospitals, and some of them may mislead our patients. So we have some conflict between our explanations, but we can't say too much.

Indeed, in recent years, doctor-patient relations have deteriorated to frightening lows in China (Song, 2016). Violence toward hospital staff and even cases of murder brought about by miscommunication, unrealistic expectations on the part of patients' family members, and fraudulent practices on the part of some doctors are now relatively common. In the years that I carried out fieldwork the fertility clinic ended up installing security gates in different parts of the building. And toward the end of my fieldwork I encountered a number of angry outbursts from some patients who had failed yet another cycle of treatment. My clinician informants had expressed disillusionment to me in talks over meals at the weekend, and in one interview a visibly exhausted gynecologist in charge of treating infertile couples put it like this:

DOCTOR: You know . . . the relationship between the doctor and the patient, so the trust between them, is very poor so it is really hard to get a patient's trust. . . . We are not like the

cardiologist or surgeons where when you come you have this
indication, you have to do the surgery. What we have is, as
I talked about before, you have many options: you can have
unexplained infertility, you can have expectant management,
you can have IUI or you can have IVF or you can have ICSI.
So for them, so the cost, the time is totally different for these
treatment options. So when you suggest to the patient you
need to be very patient, with all these patients and you have
to explain to them over and over. Most of them they just do
not trust you especially after several failed AID cycles. If
they have four AID cycles and they do not get a successful
pregnancy and they come to see you again maybe they will be
very frustrated and they do not believe you anymore. Maybe
so they will say to you . . . maybe some of them even calculate
like this "so for every cycle we have 25 percent, and after four
cycles that's supposed to be 100 so how could this not be?"
So that so you have to explain to them. . . .

AW: Yeah, I have been here quite a few times now and you see. . . .
I mean there are sometimes angry patients in the hospital so
you do see that they react.

DOCTOR: Yes, they rush in, they say they will kill you, "I will burn the
hospital" [sighs loudly], throw a bomb in the hospital, geee!
Many doctors say this conflict is very disappointing. I think in
modern society the doctor is supposed to be respected because
if you respect your life you have to respect the doctor, but in
China I don't know what has happened, but this actually
happens all over.

As we saw, in consultations with male patients, doctors spend a lot of
time convincing many of them that they do not have a fertility problem. Yet,
there are of course those male patients who *do* have severe male infertility
problems (an estimated 2 percent of all men in China). For many years,
sperm donation was the only realistic option for these couples. However,
much like in the rest of the world, the technology of intra-cytoplasmic
sperm injection (ICSI) has transformed the way in which male infertility is

treated in China (see Inhorn, 2004). As long as a single sperm cell can be found and retrieved from a semen sample or surgically from the testes, a couple can choose to try injecting that sperm cell into an egg cell in the hopes that it will fertilize and later implant. The rise of ICSI (as well as techniques to surgically retrieve sperm cells from testicles rather than ejaculate) has also meant that fewer couples contemplate using donor sperm. As a form of IVF (requiring that women take hormones to stimulate egg production, which are then laparoscopically retrieved), ICSI is ten times more expensive than AID, which does restrict its accessibility. Still, given the option, most patients would prefer using their own sperm if at all possible. One doctor noted how during his first two or three years of working at the hospital in the early 2000s "my main patient population was more for AID but now I have more for ICSI."[9]

As I have noted earlier, however, there are an estimated one to two million men in China who are azoospermic (unable to produce their own sperm cells) and so the clinic in Changsha regularly receives patients where AID is the only option they can offer. Negotiating such diagnoses with male patients is not always easy, as described by a clinician who provides AID treatment for eligible couples:

> So most of the people who suffer from male infertility, it's kind of like maybe they care more about . . .they kind of feel not that self-confident. They just feel even shy to talk to the doctor so the wife will do the talking and say "Oh, it's his problem" and the guy will feel very guilty and not that comfortable. Yeah, so just to ask for help . . . or . . . many of the men, maybe they have consulted a doctor in another hospital and they come here alone to have more sperm tests. It is kind of like they don't believe that "how could that be?"! I still have many men who cannot believe this. These men can be very tall, and also very strong, and when he first comes in and he first talks to me and says, "So you see, this diagnosis of azoospermia, you see, is that even possible?" It's kind of like they say, "I'm so tall and so strong, it cannot be possible!" But actually it *is*. So maybe for this group of patients, maybe they suffer more psychologically. Many of the men even choose divorce from their wife; they do not tell the wife the problem and they divorce the wife. They divorce the wife, they do not tell the real reason and then they try to find a female with a child so they kind of like pretend [to be the father], so others will not find out. That is also a problem. Yeah, they really hurt, I think.

Li, whose morning consultation session I observed, agreed: "It is very hard [for men] to accept and many are astonished. But for the patients in our hospital maybe 90 percent before they come to our hospital they have already known that they have no sperm; only around 10 percent don't know. In this group some find it unbelievable, and sometimes they have some sense that something might be wrong. But for some it is unbelievable and they refuse to accept it."

And so we can see how in a diametrical inversion of the sperm donor screening process, high throughput diagnostic tests for infertile couples who arrive at the clinic in Changsha can clear a man of having fertility problems, indicate moderate to severe sperm quality problems, or confirm azoospermia. This last group has not made it through the "eye of the needle" as qualified donors do; rather, they have ended up at the very bottom of sperm quality assessment scales with literally no or very few sperm cells to assess. With the rise of ICSI (for those who can afford it), sperm donation has become a fertility treatment of last resort, once all other fertility treatment options have been explored and deliberated upon (including adoption, as we will see). It is to this group of misfortunate patients and their engagement with third-party conception in China that I will now turn my attention.

AVOIDING TROUBLE AND GOSSIP

Sitting in a meeting room on the fourth floor of the fertility clinic in Changsha that has been reserved for interviews on a warm day in May 2012 is forty-year-old Zhiguang, a day-laborer from Anhui Province. Zhiguang's face is weathered and bronzed as he looks wearily across the meeting room table:

> ZHIGUANG: I have been very upset. I have been seeking treatment for fifteen years. I started when I was twenty-five, and now I'm forty. I have spent a lot of money in many places, but still haven't been cured. My situation is there is no sperm. It can't be cured. I have been to Shanghai and Hefei. I've spent over 100,000 RMB. I have all the receipts at home. Hospitals I have been

to? I can't remember all the small ones. Bigger ones,
I went to Shanghai and spent a lot of money in vain. I
lost my hair and became bald because of the medicine
I took. Too much pressure. I'm forty already. There
won't be any chance for me if I don't get this done now.
Shanghai, Nanjing, Hefei. Big hospitals, two or three.
Small ones, I lost count. Small hospitals, private prac-
tices, and men's hospitals.

RESEARCHERS: What kind of treatments have you received?

ZHIGUANG: Treatments? I was diagnosed with prostatitis
(*qiánlièxiàn yán*), but it was not that. No sperm, azoospermia. It can't be cured and I'm aware of it. My
current treatment is the only way, right? I tried AID in
other places as well. They had their own sperm banks.

RESEARCHERS: When did you come to this hospital for the first time?

ZHIGUANG: Last year October in the lunar calendar. I have been
here three times. I found this hospital online and then I
called them to get more information. Myself and my
wife both got treated for it [infertility]. That's why we
spent so much money. For seven years, a lot of money
was spent. The doctor at Anhui Hefei Hospital said
that both me and my wife had problems. The doctor
didn't tell the truth. Later the doctor said what I had
was azoospermia. He said I've had it since childhood
and there is no cure for it. I've wasted a lot of money.
I don't have other options.

RESEARCHERS: What has been the most frustrating thing for you in the
last years of trying to have a baby?

ZHIGUANG: When I heard this diagnosis from the doctor, I cried a
lot. It was really painful. My wife didn't know about it
at the time. I left the water running from the tap and
cried in the bathroom. I wanted to die. I wanted to kill
myself. I really wanted to commit suicide. My wife gave
me a lot of pressure. I wanted to kill myself.

RESEARCHERS: Have you talked to your family and friends?

ZHIGUANG: Yes, I have. For my family, they have agreed, if we can
have a baby successfully, they will treat the baby as my
own. As parents we shouldn't have preferences for children. All the kids should be raised and grow up well.
We have signed up for it. People in my hometown village do look down on me. I went to work in the city and
all the money I earned was spent on the treatment. I
don't have any money; I took out high-interest loans.
Too much pressure. If I could succeed with this one try,
it would be the best. We have an adopted child and our
relationship with her is good; she doesn't know she
is adopted. My wife wants to have another one. . . .
My wife's parents and my wife give me the pressure. My
parents, if I explain to them, they will listen to me and
show understanding. Other people, they don't know
much about my situation and they won't show understanding. . . . I told my parents. I can't tell friends, I'm
absolutely keeping it a secret. My wife's parents don't
know either; there's no way to tell them. It's definitely
confidential.

While every couple's story is of course unique, there are nevertheless strik-
ing similarities not just within the accounts of those ten AID recipient
couples interviewed for this book, but also within accounts of living with
male infertility collected from around the world (see Bharadwaj, 2016;
Carmeli & Birenbaum-Carmeli, 1994; Inhorn et al., 2009). Distress, self-
doubt, hope, travels to reproductive clinics, pressure from family members, marital troubles, money spent, misdiagnoses, thoughts about
whether a third-party child is "ours" or "mine," comparisons to adoption,
secrecy: all are elements in quests for conception involving male infertility
globally, albeit shaped by availability of treatments, cultural notions of
masculinity, as well as the particular form that socio-cultural expectations
of bearing children can take. In patrilineal China—where kinship imaginations revolve in important (albeit not all-encompassing) ways around

filial piety, son preference, and the securing of a man's lineage—male infertility and third-party reproduction is most often managed by the infertile man's family. One sperm donor informant invoked an oft-cited Confucian teaching to explain family involvement in a couple's reproductive matters: "Their parents must be concerned about this issue. We have an old saying: 'There are three things about not being filial, the first of which is no offspring' (*buxiao yousan, wuhou weida*). . . . Sometimes to carry on the family name is quite a concern for parents. . . . Normally, a human being should be continued and the life of the family should be continued. Yes. It [a couple's infertility] is fundamental for their parents" (see also Zhang, 2015, p. 35).[10]

From interviews with both infertile couples and sperm donors, it became clear that one of the biggest concerns on both sides was not so much secrecy in itself; rather, it was the management of who should know what. By keeping their use of reproductive technologies a secret from all but a minimum of family members or close friends and their use of donor sperm from even fewer people, couples wanted to avoid the gossip of their in-laws, family, neighbors, friends, and other acquaintances. Likewise, confidentiality was considered an absolute necessity by all interviewed donors because they did not want "trouble" (*máfan*) later on in life should a donor child suddenly appear to disrupt their imagined future family life. One of the ads posted on a university web forum by a sperm bank recruiter in May 2011 was quickly tagged with this question from a student: "What will you do if a group of children come to find you twenty years later?" This is a version of what Sebastian Mohr (2015) has called "kinship trouble," which arises when connections to third-party children are negotiated in particular cultural and juridical settings. Interviewed couples and donors *had* confided in someone, whether family member or close friend, as part of their own deliberations. For recipient couples, it was often the man's family who was confided in regarding use of donated sperm and not the woman's, for fear that the woman's family would break up their marriage. Moreover, like Zhiguang (who had adopted), while the following four infertile men had all considered adoption, they preferred AID treatment. Here is how they reasoned about who should know what and their preference for pursuing AID:

In the countryside the pressures are bigger than in the city. There is a lot of pressure [to have a child] from outside, mostly from parents and partly from relatives and neighbors. I have talked to my close friend. You have to open your mind to the right person. My family members know but my wife's parents don't know this [about fertility treatment]. I was very worried that if this is known by her parents and relatives, they will try to break up our marriage. We had considered adopting my younger brother's baby before the treatment, but the doctor recommended us to take more treatment using the donor, and to have children by my wife. Having a half-genetic descendant will be better. (twenty-six-year-old, Guangdong Province)

There is nothing I can do anyway. This thing was destined to be. My life is doomed and this cannot be changed. It would be best to be able to cure it [my condition] but this medicine is not so developed. I did consider adoption, but my wife didn't approve. She has hopes for us to have our own baby. My wife's parents only know that we are having treatment by artificial insemination, but they don't know we are using other people's sperm. (thirty-nine-year-old, Hunan Province)

We would have to wait until after having a child before considering adoption. If I have no children, and go to adopt a child, then the neighbors will talk things about you; there will be problems with adoption. We have never considered not having children. Impossible. Firstly for family reasons, we would like our own children, and then what about when we get old? (twenty-eight-year old, Hunan Province)

I have had to bear a lot of pressure, and when we came to seek treatment, we had to hide our objective. This time when we came here for treatment, we lied to our friends that we needed to come and buy something. The less people know the better. I only let a small number of people know about this and I will try to raise the baby as my own son, have some emotion with the baby from a sperm donor. My wife is very supportive. She asked me to come every time, and to pretend that we are using my own sperm, because if I am not here, other people will be suspicious that we are using other's sperm. My parents know that we are here at the fertility clinic but my wife's parents don't know. If my wife's parents knew this, they would try to break up our marriage. My parents have supported me a lot. . . . . I think that adoption is very different from a baby born by my wife. If we adopt a child, it will lead to a lot of gossip and rumors around us so we chose IUI [intra-uterine insemination] treatment. It's a better option to use a donor, to have a baby born by my wife. But only me and my wife know about using donor sperm. Others don't know this. (twenty-nine-year-old, Guizhou Province)

At the fertility clinic in Changsha, insemination takes place on the fifth floor where between 2,000 and 3,500 cycles of AID are carried out each year with a 25 percent pregnancy rate (see table 1.1). Many couples will try four to six cycles before pursuing other options. Moreover, bearing in mind the price differential compared to IVF, AID is one of the most accessible ARTs, which helps explain the diversity of socioeconomic backgrounds among recipient couples that I met. The clinician responsible for insemination of women with donor sperm who had experienced increasing numbers of angry outbursts from patients confirmed the tendency for recipient couples' to inform close family members on the man's side of the family rather than the woman's:

> I think most of them don't talk to anyone [about using a sperm donor]. Only the couples know. But in China you know there is still some kind of thinking . . . it's very interesting (I don't know if you asked the patients about this) that some of the women's mothers-in-law, that is, the man's mother, will accompany the daughter-in-law to our department to have the AID treatment but not the woman's mother, only the man's mother. If there is anyone accompanying the women it is supposed to be the male's relatives, so, like, the male's sister or the male's mother. So some of them, they will talk to the man's relatives because it is the man's problem so they have the . . . they are kind of more likely to keep the secret because it is their own son or own brother. Because I think maybe even in an extreme situation the man's mom will not reveal it because I think most of the relatives from the man will say it is a shame on them. So it is not only the man but the man's family I think is also ashamed so maybe they are more able to keep the secret.

At the same time, she continued, it was not only family pressures and negotiations of which relatives to confide in that were at stake. The (in) fertility of couples of childbearing age is very often subject to the evaluations of others (i.e., gossip), making concealed AID a form of reputation management:

> What they want is the pregnancy. They have the pregnancy and they have the child, which is easier for them to explain. But for some of them, I think even most of them, who want to adopt a child, they will move to another place. So adopt a child, move to a new city, and start a new life where no one knows. They will get the child to be registered officially and then move to another city and start a new life. Because . . . so you know, I don't know what is the situation in the U.S. but in China there is a lot of gossip from the neighbors, and in China I think neighbors are closer than Westerners are because the Westerners do not care maybe. . . . You can even be neighbors

for ten years and do not know what your neighbor does, whether they have child. But in China it's like all these neighbors, maybe within one or two months everyone knows whether you have a child or how many children you have, where your husband or wife works blah blah blah so [laughter] it creates more pressure for those infertile couples. . . . Yes, so [with AID] you have the pregnancy and you have a child and I think many of the families will be stable so they will just bring up the child and it's good.

Similarly, a couple of qualified donors from Changsha suggested that:

I know people in foreign countries usually choose to adopt a child. But because of our traditional concepts in China, people will choose to use the sperm bank to give birth to a child. They hope the offspring can continue their genes and blood. If they choose to adopt a child, the kid won't look like them. For the child born from sperm donation, nobody will question the process of his birth. If I were the husband, after a period of consideration, maybe I could persuade myself to accept the sperm donation. I will feel grateful to the sperm donors, because they give me a good chance to be a father. Why shouldn't I do that? (twenty-year-old student, Changsha)

I think they will choose AID, coming to the hospital. As for adoption, it could be more popular abroad. Traditionally, I think it is easier for people to accept the child from one's own belly. At least it looks like one's own child. If someone is adopted, the kid himself/herself knows that he/she is not born by the parents. Once he grows up, or he started to have some thoughts, I think he/she will do something that is hard for us to imagine. (twenty-four-year-old student, Changsha)

And so we can see that what binds the forms of reasoning about third-party conception we find among recipient couples, donors, and doctors alike in Changsha is an emphasis on avoiding gossip, rumors, and talk as a way to manage reputations and avoid potential trouble. In *Drink Water, But Remember the Source*, the anthropologist Ellen Oxfeld makes a case for taking gossip seriously in her analysis of the moral discourses she identified while dissecting all the personal disputes and controversies that she had encountered in the rural village of Moonshadow Pond in Guangdong Province. While gossip can harm and hurt individuals in devastating ways, Oxfeld argues that its ubiquity in China (and indeed throughout the world) tells us something about how relations and actions are codependent; what one does is very often evaluated and assessed by those who are a part of one's life. Women risk being stigmatized as a "hen that can't lay an egg" (*bu chia dan de mu ji*), just as infertile men risk being seen as unmanly. Indeed, in his ethnography of the impotence epidemic in China, Everett Zhang (citing Thomas Gregor's work in Brazil) makes the point that when it comes to sexual and reproductive failure a man's "reputation . . . rides precariously on the shifting currents of community gossip" (Zhang, 2015, p. 35). While infertility is often a biological condition, social diagnoses of the inability to produce offspring are bound up in moral assessments of the qualities of individuals, couples, and families, as is evident in the depictions of male infertility given by a couple of qualified donors in Changsha (see also Bharadwaj, 2016):

> For the man, for the husband, it is quite pathetic, you know, if you have some matters with this area [of male infertility] others including your relatives, your neighbors, your parents, even your wife would then regard him as a loser and a failure. The husband would feel inferior and he would feel he is quite useless because he cannot produce a child. (twenty-one-year-old student, Changsha)
>
> You can't pass on your generation if you have no kids and you will have no motivation in your life or goals to strive for. I think parents are very great. They make efforts in their life all of which are for their children. If they don't have their own child and just live for the sake of their own life, they will feel passionless. A man will feel much pressure if he is infertile. Others will talk about it and his wife will also look down upon him. (twenty-year-old student, Changsha)

At the same time, as already noted, it is not only infertile men, their families, and their wives who are keen to avoid gossip and trouble. Take this sperm donor's ambivalent reasoning about why he thinks anonymity and confidentiality are crucial:

> I think normally over 90 percent of the donors would not tell their parents. Especially when I have graduated from university, even several years later, I think confidentiality will be very important. If I have my own family at that time, it should be confidential, anonymous. If the confidentiality work is not so good, once the child gets to know that . . . if something happens, he or she got to know about this information through some way. If they came to us, this will do harm to my own family. This will be hard to explain as well. . . . Yes, very important. If . . . if it is possible [that they find out], it will not only

do harm to my own family. It will cause very, very many troubles. I think I
don't want any . . . eh . . . questions in and around me and my wife, my child,
children, my family, my parents. . . .

    I don't think I will tell my family or friends. As for my parents, I probably
will mention it at some point. My wife . . . I probably will talk with my wife
as well. But I don't think they will be happy about that. I do not want them
to be troubled by this problem. Because [laughter] . . . because it is confidential. They probably cannot accept it or understand it. . . . What I want to
say is that the confidentiality work from the hospital must be really good
and careful. For example, I think the Internet should not be wiretapped by
hackers. . . . I'm saying, I am not 100 percent [laughter] 100 percent [laugh-
ter] trusting. . . This should be confidential, but probably will cause some
consequences, if they find us. . . . We will have our own family at that time,
once this kind of situation happens . . . once the kids grow up and come to
find me. . . . If the information is open, the kids could easily find me and . . .
once this happens, it will be very troublesome in all senses. (twenty-year-old
student, Changsha)

Another donor had only confided in a very close friend, being likewise
concerned about how other people might view his actions:

I talked with one of my friends; he is in Beijing now so far away. . . . We
talked by computer, MSN actually. He was against . . . he didn't agree. . . .
He is my best friend, a boy, we grew up together and he thought that if I
wasn't so eager to get the money then I wouldn't have to be here. . . . But
something happened and I ended up coming here. Normally, for someone in
my position, we would not want to be a donor. I only know me and another
guy from my department [at the university] who came here to be a donor.
First, you know, the Chinese culture is quite private and we Chinese do not
want to go to a hospital especially in this area [of infertility]; we would
think it is a sign that this guy has some issues. Second, I am unmarried and
I . . . actually in my mother's eyes I am always a good boy, but we both know
this is not true! For certain reasons this is regarded as strange behavior, you
know, this area [of sperm donation] is not so popular in China. . . . So confidentiality is quite important, as I said, Chinese are quite conservative and
privacy was the first thing I had concerns about, then the compensation and
other things like convenience. Regarding privacy, actually they would ask
for our parents' phone numbers but they told us they would not call our
parents, but I am still a little worried about that. . . . Maybe I would tell it to
my wife but never to my parents. My parents they are a typical Chinese old
couple and they may not accept it but my wife, maybe she would be as open
as me. (twenty-one-year-old student, Central South University)

Both recipient couples and donors engage in various negotiations of who to confide in. When male infertility is at stake recipient couples tend to confide in the man's family, fearing that the woman's family would break up the marriage and that neighbors and friends would gossip about them. More than some kind of absolute secrecy or confidentiality, however, the fact that both recipients and donors actively manage (or seek to manage) who knows what when it comes to sperm donation and AID reflects the ways in which certain troubles or problems that threaten to disrupt normalized family forms ("affairs of the hearth") are envisaged on the part of both donors and recipients.

The medicalization of third-party reproduction through sperm banking in China and the upholding of a strict double-blind system whereby recipient couples and treating doctors do not know the identity of the donor allow for visible pregnancies for recipient couples and never-to-be-known offspring for donors, which in both cases do not need to be socially explained as a result. We might say that AID in China is surrounded by efforts to manage potential trouble on the part of donors, recipient couples, and fertility clinics alike. Hence, the management of whom to confide in on the part of donors and infertile recipient couples as well as the active separation of donors from recipient couples by clinics are important features of the style of sperm banking that prevails in China today.

Of course, this management pertains treatment processes and does not preclude further kinship trouble down the line should the proverbial cat be let out of the bag. Moreover, however secretive they might be about using/being a sperm donor, couples and donors do have concerns regarding the new forms of relating to which third-party reproduction inevitably gives rise. I will return to these concerns at the end of this chapter.

SEPARATING DONORS AND RECIPIENTS

Before donor sperm became available in China, involuntarily childless couples living with male infertility had to adopt or, as Margaret Sleeboom-Faulkner (2010a) has discussed, an infertile man might instruct his wife to sleep with another man to solve their infertility problems; the opposite of those cases of informal surrogacy arrangements analyzed by

Jie Yang (2015) where the man sleeps with another woman in order to "overcome" the infertility of his wife. A modern-day version of such arrangements led one of the fertility clinics I visited to introduce strict monitoring of their sperm collection area for husbands as well as ID checks after having experienced some couples using "male impostors" when delivering semen samples for treatment (as a way to circumvent the need to ask/pay for donor sperm). In separating reproduction from sex, reproductive technologies like sperm banking have medicalized third-party reproduction and relocated ethical negotiations from the bedroom into a clinical domain.

The strict separation of donors from recipients was enshrined in the Ministry of Health's Ethical Principles for Human Sperm Banks from the outset of legalization in 2001: "In order to protect the interests of the donors and the recipient couples as well as the offspring, donors and recipient couples should be kept blind of the other; donors and medical staff who provide assisted reproductive technology should be kept blind of the other; and donors and future offspring should be kept blind of each other" (MoH, 2003b, p. 2.5.1). When I brought up the fact that many European countries have repealed sperm donor anonymity with doctors, donors, and recipients, most counter-argued that this was simply not conceivable in China today. In the words of a donor twenty-one-year-old donor from Changsha: "I think it should not be open for at least fifty or one hundred years. I think it is possible. . . . [laughter] I think in at least the next fifty years we cannot achieve such an open system. . . . But it is not possible, it is not possible for now." His views were corroborated by a telephone survey that was carried out by the sperm bank in Shaanxi province that asked 240 sperm donors and 68 male patients who were undergoing or had completed AID with their wives about anonymity. They presented their results at a conference on social and ethical challenges in sperm banking held in Changsha in May of 2012:

> Only 6.7 percent of the donors we surveyed would continue to donate sperm openly, 10.8 percent of them are uncertain, and 82.5 percent would not donate. 41.9 percent of male patients clearly expressed they would give up treatment if the donation was open while only 18.6 percent of them stated that they would be willing to continue treatment. . . . . Our survey indicates that most donors refuse to donate semen, and most male patients refuse to

accept donor semen without anonymity. . . . [Hence,] open sperm donation
is currently not suitable. Anonymous semen donation is a more realistic
option in China.

And so for now, the strict separation of donor and recipient through a
double-blind system is a defining feature of sperm banking in China. In
Changsha, the sperm bank and AID clinic were formerly located on the
same floor, only to be separated on to different floors some years ago.
Similarly, in one of the sperm banks I visited away from Changsha, which
was housed in the same building as a fertility clinic, the separation of
donors from infertile couples was also spatially reinforced. One of the
sperm bank staff there explained to me that they had recently introduced
a separate entrance for sperm donors in order to avoid their having to
walk past infertile couples to get to the sperm bank. As we will recall from
the opening pages of this book, some donors feel anxious when having to
push past the worried faces of infertile couples on their way to the sperm
bank, yet this concern was not the only one that attempts at spatially separating donors from recipients were addressing. When donors and recipients are too close, confidentiality can potentially be breached, as recalled
here by a sperm bank administrator in Changsha:

> I remember one donor . . . it's because several years ago, we still had the AID
> department and the sperm bank on the same floor, so the patients could see
> the donors. There was one donor who also lives in my district, so we know
> each other, and that man works for the police and he is very tall and hand-
> some. At that time, when he visited the sperm bank for sperm donation,
> many patients saw him and said: "I want that one, I want that one!" So I had
> a very deep impression of that donor, and several years later, the donor
> asked me: "How many offspring do I have?" And I didn't tell him. But after
> that, we divided the AID department and sperm bank on to different floors.

At the same time, a further pressing concern was that having donors
and infertile couples too close together might lead to clandestine deals,
potentially between a medically unscreened university student who did not
qualify and an infertile couple. The commercialized sale of human gametes
(whether sperm or eggs) is illegal in China, although a shadow black market does exist, not least because of the chronic shortage of sperm donors.
In 2008, a series of news reports set out to expose this black market. An

undercover reporter in Jilin Province recounted his investigation of a web forum posting where a man had advertised that he was willing to provide sperm to an infertile couple for 20,000 RMB. The reporter met with the twenty-two-year-old university student ("he looks exactly like a film star") who set out the following terms for selling his sperm: "The first is that you are willing to do this; the second is that child born has nothing to do with me and you are responsible for all the costs for the child; the third is that no personal information is disclosed on both sides in order not to cause any harm" (News163, 2008). Similarly, a news reporter in Heilongjiang Province responded to an advertisement he found taped on to a street-side wall in Harbin that read:

> Do you feel upset because you can't have a child? Do you feel helpless because there is no suitable sperm source? Our sperm selling company is willing to offer you good-quality sperm and can help you solve your problems and troubles. . . . The company has strong men of different ages available.

In this case, the reporter met with Mr. Wang, a middleman who had put together a catalog of eleven sperm donors chosen from among his friends and a relative who he could arrange to provide fresh donations at a location decided by the recipient couple. As a middleman, Mr. Wang ensured a certain distance between donor and couple. He operated according to a tiered pricing system, which, he told the undercover reporter, was worked out "according to the condition of body and education level: Married men with children can only prove their fertility, but their physical condition is not as good as young people, so they charge low fees. Students are young and strong; they can enter university and graduate studies, which shows that they have higher IQ, so they charge higher fees" (*Lifestyle News*, 2008).

Both reporters interviewed local government officials who confirmed that such selling of sperm was illegal in China and, more importantly, that buying sperm on the black market entailed serious risks for vulnerable couples: "And this so-called company, the sperm provided by them hasn't undergone a rigorous inspection and its quality and sanitation are very difficult to guarantee, so it is easy to be contaminated by some kind of infection" (quoted in *Lifestyle News*, 2008). Moreover, government officials pointed out that unlike sperm donors who donate through licensed sperm banks, anyone selling his sperm on the black market was legally liable as the father of any resulting offspring, a fact that DNA paternity testing could be used to confirm. Put in another way, the separation of black market donors and recipient couples is unenforceable.

NOT KNOWING YOUR *SHENSHI*

In this chapter, I have made the case that the style of sperm banking that has coalesced in China is organized around strict separations of donors from recipient couples and vice versa. This does not mean, however, that donors and recipients are indifferent toward each other. Those couples in need of a donor are provided with a limited amount of social and biological information about potential donors on an Excel spreadsheet with the following columns:

- donor number
- number of live births
- blood type
- race [90 percent of Chinese are Han, but there are also fifty-five minority ethnic groups]
- physique (high, middle, low)
- height and weight
- shape of face (round, square, triangular)
- skin color (yellow with some white or yellow with some black)
- eyelid form (single or double)
- educational level (bachelor, master's, doctorate)
- special hobbies

However, there are rarely many donors to choose among, as a doctor at the clinic in Changsha explained: "Generally we meet the blood type, height, and perhaps some special demands. Because maybe at any given time there are only thirty sperm donors available to choose from [for all couples in AID treatment at the hospital]." Although one of the interviewed women expressed interest in seeing pictures of the donors (which is not allowed in China), others maintained that they were not that interested in knowing more about the donors than what was provided on the Excel sheet. They were mostly concerned that the hospital should select healthy donors and a few were happy that donors were chosen from among university students.

This kind of distance-keeping is well known from existing studies about secrecy and donor insemination among heterosexual infertile couples (see Daniels & Taylor, 1993; Wahlberg & Gammeltoft, 2017) and it was likewise confirmed by a doctor at the AID Department in Changsha:

> I think most of them do not want to compare with the donor and tell the donor they are the recipients because they do not want the donor to have any rights. . . . The recipients are more afraid of being contacted by the donor. So what they want is that . . . they want to see [information about] the donor and try to understand more like where he comes from, what is his hobby, just to take a look but they do not want any contact. . . . They are very afraid. The most asked question is whether the donor will have any contact with them because maybe they are afraid that maybe after several years the donor will come to the family and take the baby away.

Each of the ten infertile couples who were interviewed maintained that they would not tell their future child that he or she had been conceived with the help of donor sperm. Their reasoning was similar in each case—they were concerned that sharing this information would potentially break up their family. In the words of a thirty-nine-year-old day laborer:

> If this information was to be known it would result in a lot of conflict in my family. If it was in the open, we will feel a lot of pressure from our parents and friends. They will say that the baby is not the real son of the father. There will be a lot of gossip from people around us. That's why we will keep the secret. If we tell the truth to the child, when the child grows up, it will affect the child's thinking, and will be bad for his life. The child will think that I am not his real father.

Empathizing with the wishes of infertile couples to keep their use of donor sperm a secret a donor suggested that:

> If I were the boy of AID I would be eager to find my biological father. So it is difficult to run this mode [of being open] in China. I think the father

would be OK, but the mother will feel sad. After all, the mother spends too much time and energy to raise the kid. If the kid leaves to find his real father, the mother maybe can't afford it. And the kid will also blame his biological father for neglecting him. (twenty-one-year old student, Changsha)

And another donor shared his unease about possibly being contacted by donor offspring if strict confidentiality was not maintained:

> I talked with a friend [also a donor] about this. We agreed that we can make some money while helping other people, and we also talked about how our donation should be kept confidential (*baomi*). If this information was to become open, the children will maybe find us twenty or thirty years later. You know, those children do not know their own genetic origin (*bu zhidao ziji shenshi*). Confidentiality should be thorough. In the future these children may find us, and this may affect our families at that time. (twenty-two-year-old student, Changsha)

In an interview with the *People's Daily* newspaper from 2005, Lu Guangxiu was asked whether withholding information from donor offspring about their biological origins was fair:

REPORTER: People also worry that when the child grows up and find out the truth of his or her origin, that it will be human nature for the child to want to look for their biological father, but by law they have no such right. Isn't this a dilemma?

LU GUANGXIU: It is indeed a dilemma. However, by regulation and due to our social situation, finding the biological father is not allowed. Even so, there are still those who believe that the children have the right to know the truth. Therefore it is a dilemma. The donors we choose are strictly suitable for certain scenarios. Artificial fertilization is considered only when males don't have sperm and can't produce sperm, or with some special hereditary diseases. So we choose donors strictly for certain situations and do as little artificial fertilization as possible. (Li, 2005)

And so, for now, separation of donors and recipient couples in order to prevent the disruption of their respective (future) "hearths" outweighs concerns about the right of donor offspring to know their biological origins in China. At the clinic in Changsha, I was told of a case from 2005 where a couple had been married for eight years without a pregnancy. The husband suffered from azoospermia and was also in poor health. They decided to try for a child through AID but did not tell the man's parents that they were using a sperm donor. After two cycles of AID the woman became pregnant; however, five months into the pregnancy her husband's health deteriorated. He then told his parents about having used AID and that he and his wife were expecting a child just before he passed away without leaving any will. His parents rejected the child's inheritance rights only to be sued by their daughter-in-law since their son had signed an informed consent form in which he acknowledged that he was "bound by the same rights and duties as with a child born from a natural pregnancy." We can see, then, how AID troubles kinship, introducing emotional and legal apprehensions and even threatening families to the point of being broken up. And it is this concern with family "harmony" that currently undergirds China's legally enshrined principles of anonymity and confidentiality in sperm donation.

From their perspective, some donors had very clear thoughts about their future donor offspring and the families they would be brought up in, while others less so. Here is how five donors reflected on who should be eligible to receive donor sperm:

> I do not care. I do not know them, and they do not know me either, so I do not care. I never think about it. There is no relationship with the situation of the family, and if couples want a child, all of them can get my donation. (twenty-two-year-old student, Changsha)
>
> I never think about it. Maybe the infertile couples . . . they should be educated and from a different province, not in Hunan. The couples should be healthy, without genetic disease. (twenty-two-year-old student, Changsha)
>
> Actually I hope they have a good family, at least; they are from my sperm. But you cannot predict anything and if the couple has enough money to come here to get their children they may have enough capability to raise their kid well. (twenty-one-year-old student, Changsha)
>
> I don't know this, I really don't know. . . . I hope the baby will be born in a family with good conditions; after all, it's my sperm. . . . But I will not

think about it anymore as I don't want to give myself much pressure; I think it's not good for me too. Sometimes, maybe, I will think of those women and maybe I will come across my child someday. I think it's better not to tell the children. They won't know this in their childhood anyway, but they may think about it during a rebellious teenage phase. (twenty-year-old student, Changsha)

I want the family to be harmonious. . . . They should have a nice relationship after the kid grows up. And the kids should grow up healthy and happy, happily. Make him a useful person for the society. This kind of family . . . In order to . . . It is quite natural. Because, because . . . it is not easy [for the infertile couple] to give birth to such a child. If, if the child was born, and he grows up, I think it is pretty sad if the couple's relationship . . . or they get divorced. Eh . . . That must be very important. The couple should be as lovely as possible. I don't want them to divorce. They shouldn't have come to the hospital and give birth to this kid if they get divorced someday. . . . Concern . . . I will not be concerned about the kid. Even if I am, it would be nearly nothing. I think we have a relation between supply and demand through the hospital. They want me to supply my . . . my . . . thing. Through the hospital, I got the compensation and do not harm myself. Offspring . . . [laughter] it . . . eh . . . I think, as I said before, we do not need to meet. . . . It will be fine as long as they are living a healthy and happy life and the family keeps complete. I will not think about him/her. I will not care. I will not . . . yes. (twenty-four-year-old student, Changsha)

It remains to be seen whether sperm donors in China will end up regretting that they will never get to meet their donor offspring. As we can see, some of them do have hopes for these offspring in terms of the kinds of families they will grow up in and how they might cope with learning they have been conceived using donor sperm. As it stands, however, confidentiality and anonymity are seen as preconditions for sperm banking in China today.

CONCLUSION

We have seen in this chapter how the use of donor sperm in the treatment of male factor infertility has become acceptable for an increasing number of involuntarily childless couples in China. Fertility clinic–brokered strategies of "hearth" management and trouble avoidance among recipient couples and donors have emerged out of routinized sperm banking and AID in China. Donor sperm is currently made available primarily to married couples who are living with male infertility (but also couples in which the male is considered to have a genetic disease that is "not suitable for reproduction"), while single women and lesbian couples are legally prohibited from accessing donor sperm. Much like all other forms of medical treatment in China, diagnostic and therapeutic pathways in fertility clinics are highly standardized and have been tailored to cope with enormous flows of patients. There is little time for counseling during consultations; rather, all patients are diagnosed according to standardized protocols (physical examinations as well as semen and blood sample analyses for males), which then indicate possible treatments. With the rise of ICSI (which remains out of reach for many because of cost), AID is now supposed to be a treatment of last resort, reserved for those couples where the man suffers from such severe male infertility conditions as azoospermia.

Bearing in mind patrilineal kinship imaginations (the "lineage paradigm" [Stafford, 2000]) and close relations between friends and neighbors in China, it is perhaps of little wonder that confidentiality and separation are maintained between family members and in-laws in infertile couples as well as between sperm donors and recipient couples, while secrecy about having donated (on the part of the donor) and having used donor sperm (on the part of the couple) is upheld. A man's family members (rather than the woman's) are most often a part of couples' therapy management groups when male infertility is at stake, to avoid censure from the woman's family. The double-blind system that characterizes the style of sperm banking that has emerged in China is a strategic form of "hearth" management that both recipient couples and donors mobilize in order to try to avoid gossip and troubles.

To be sure, much more research is needed with families who have chosen third-party conception, as this chapter has provided but a glimpse into the kinds of deliberations that donors and recipient couples go through. What remains to be seen is how good families are at maintaining the secrets they have pledged to keep in the years to come, and whether third-party children will in fact end up disrupting lineages in families affected by male infertility, as in the case of grandparents who wanted to disown their son's child upon learning that he had been conceived through donor sperm. With sperm banking having been routinized only relatively recently, the first major cohort of third-party children from around the mid-2000s has yet to reach adulthood. Will they begin to seek out their *shenshi* as well as donor siblings, as we have seen in many other countries? The question is, can AID families and donors keep a secret?

Conclusion

ROUTINIZATION

The style of sperm banking found in China today is very different from those found in other parts of the world. It is not so much the techniques of sperm banking that are different—all sperm banks, regardless of where they might be located, require cryotanks, liquid nitrogen, vials, phase-contrast microscopes, medical screening criteria, donor recruitment strategies, as well as private donation rooms and plastic containers for semen sample collection. What I have argued throughout this book is that what *is* unique is the *style* of sperm banking we find in a particular place, at a particular time. Ethnographically, and to some extent historically, accounting for the style of sperm banking that has developed in China has required what I have called an assemblage ethnography, which has taken as its object the conditions of possibility and modes of problematization that have allowed for sperm banking to settle into a routinized medical practice. Hence, through my ethnography of sperm banking in China I have tracked the routes of routinization whereby this medical technology came to be: 1) socio-historically (re-)produced and entrenched within China's restrictive reproductive complex (in chapters 1, 2, and 3); 2) an established and habituated part of health delivery, which is to say a standard of care for a given condition that is sustained in a fixed setting through routinized, daily practices (in chapters 4 and 5); and 3) a normalized part of daily life, in the sense that it is made available to, accepted, and used by its (un)intended users in a routine, commonplace manner (in chapter 6).

In doing so, I have argued that over the course of the last thirty years or so sperm banking-AID in China have settled alongside ligation operations, contraception, and sterilization as technologies of *birth control.* Assisted reproductive technologies like IVF, sperm banking, and AID could only be legalized in China in 2003 in the form of "one-child ART," whereby infertile couples' efforts to achieve wanted pregnancies using ARTs in order to have one child were to be controlled in strict accordance with family planning policies. The use of donor sperm in the treatment of male infertility had to take place within the framework of national family planning objectives to control population quantity (by limiting treatment to those couples living with azoospermia who are able to provide copies of their marriage and pregnancy certificates to a fertility clinic) and to improve population quality (as the medically screened, high-quality sperm collected by sperm banks can help secure "superior births" (*yousheng*) in the newborn population). I have also argued that the problem of infertility in China has come to be inextricably bound up in scientific and popular discourses about the toxic effects of industrialization, and as such sperm banks in China have emerged as state-sanctioned assurers of the nation's reproductive vitality. More than repositories of donor sperm to be used in the treatment of particular infertile couples, the high throughput and cyclic screening, collection, storage, and replenishing of relatively less exposed, more lively stocks of sperm from high-quality university students in China can be thought of as a kind of national reproductive insurance. Finally, through this assemblage ethnography of the routinization of sperm banking in China, I have shown how AID is accessed by many couples living with male infertility (often in consultation with members of the man's family) using strategies of hearth-management that revolve around confidentiality, anonymity, secrecy, and a visible pregnancy that does not need to be socially explained in the same way that an adoption would. At the same time, in a country where filial piety (*xiào*) and the securing of male lineages are almost synonymous in the shaping of family life, third-party sperm can generate thorny kinship troubles. Consequently, both donors and recipient couples take active steps to avoid the gossip of in-laws, parents, other family members, neighbors, and friends.

One of the core arguments in this book has been that it is through routinization that practice collectives emerge and particular styles of sperm banking take form, characterized by mass mobilizations, assembly-line laboratory shifts, the managing of large groups of (potential) donors, and the maintaining of strict anonymity and confidentiality. Practice collectives are post-translation, emerging as they do out of the roll out and, in China's case, the mass scaling up of particular medical technologies. This is why I have made the case that as particular medical technologies traverse the continuum from experimental to standard of care, we as social scientists must relentlessly and empirically attend to the routes of routinization they follow and the effects of these, whether unintended or not. And while globalization undoubtedly shapes these routes of routinization in important ways and we may well speak of global reproductive assemblages as doctors, techniques, equipment, couples, and gametes cross international borders (Inhorn, 2015), the reproductive complexes and governance that takes place within them remain anchored in certain places, at certain times.

By investigating the routinization of sperm banking it has also been my intention to provide unique insights into some of the ways in which life (*shengming*) and living (*shenghuo*) are being valued in China today. In recent years, a string of anthropological studies from China have addressed questions of what an adequate life, a moral life, or a good life in China might be. This is not surprising given the profound economic, demographic, social, and environmental transformations that China has been undergoing over the last three decades or so, some of which are documented in this book's chapters. Arthur Kleinman and colleagues have suggested that "China's extraordinarily fast and compressed modernization may have created a special cultural version of the divided self . . . [,] the new ideal of having a life of one's own replaced the previous call for a life devoted to the socialist cause" (2011, pp. 16, 23). In a similar vein, Everett Zhang has argued that "along with rapid economic development, there has been, in official discourse, an abandonment of the ethos of sacrificing life for the revolutionary cause, and an emerging appeal for valuing life" (2011, p. 1).

And, in her anthropological study of students at elite universities in Beijing, Susanne Bregnbæk contends that such a transformation will perhaps never be quite complete since "students struggle to reconcile the . . . contradictory social imperatives of self-sacrifice and self-realization" as they seek to achieve "a life worth living" (2016, p. 14).

In this book, I have adopted a different approach to studying vital valuations in contemporary China by shifting analytical focus away from "the new subjectivity of Chinese and the changing moral context" (Kleinman et al., 2011, p. 24), and toward a particular concept, namely *zhì*, which, as we have seen, translates as "quality," "substance," or "nature" and informs notions of population quality (*renkou suzhi*), the quality of a person (*suzhi*), sperm quality (*jingzi zhiliang*), and quality of life (*shenghuo zhiliang*). Each of these forms of vital quality is normative in the sense that each can deteriorate or be improved along good–bad or high–low continuums. When it comes to sperm banking in China, it is good quality that is to be assured at population, individual donor, and cellular levels in ways that will hopefully improve the quality of life of infertile couples who live with male infertility. Having children has long been a part of what makes life good in China. What I hope to have shown in *Good Quality* is how a reproductive technology like sperm banking has contributed to new forms of estimating, assessing, and measuring vital quality as a crucial component of daily efforts to improve life at the level of the population, the family, the individual, and indeed the cell in China.

Coda

In February of 2017, I returned to Changsha once again to present a draft of this book. It is always something of a nerve-wracking affair to get feedback from the people whose work you have researched and written about. Much to my relief, and notwithstanding important critiques of the book's chapters, which have been incorporated into the final draft, staff members at the sperm bank appreciated the account of their work found in *Good Quality*. Let me conclude this book by recounting two moments from this week-long visit.

During one of our lunches, an anecdote was shared about a provincial family planning agency that had started asking for a 5,000 RMB deposit to grant married couples a pregnancy certificate, a deposit that would be returned upon the birth of their second child. Regardless of whether this anecdote is true (apparently the National Health and Family Planning Commission has refuted it), I put it to my colleagues in Changsha that perhaps, after the difficult inception and routinization of ART described in this book, we are at a moment in history where the fertility clinic is poised to replace the abortion clinic as one of the most important family planning institutions in China. While it is too soon to have a clear indication of the effects of the loosening of family planning laws in China in early 2016,

Yi Zeng and Therese Hesketh recently put forward this tentative conclusion: "The effects of the new policy may be less than expected. There is now clear evidence that the role of fertility policy is diminishing fast, and that fertility in contemporary China, as elsewhere, is socioeconomically determined. . . . Surveys of fertility preference undertaken over the past two decades show that China has indeed become a low fertility culture" (2016, p. 1932). During our exchanges I mentioned some of the fertility awareness campaigns that my colleagues Søren Ziebe from University Hospital Copenhagen and Lone Schmidt from the University of Copenhagen had been involved in in low-fertility Denmark (which has one of the highest proportion of assisted births in the world). Lu Guangxiu asked if I could share some of the campaign materials with her as she prepared for an International Women's Day talk on reproduction that she was scheduled to deliver.

The second moment arose after sperm bank staff members had given me detailed feedback on the book manuscript on the following day. While they largely agreed with my account of the particular style of sperm bank-ing found in China and of their work as a practice collective, they also insisted that I should include in the book some of the changes they have made to their work practices over the last few years, not least, they said, as a result of our decade-long collaboration. Sperm bank staff described these changes as a shift from having been "protocol-centric" to now being "donor-centric." They summarized these changes under the following seven points: 1) they now hand out letters of thanks to both qualified donors and those who end up not qualifying, and display letters of thanks from recipient couples to donors in the sperm bank's waiting room; 2) they have prepared a FAQ leaflet on sperm donation and reproductive insurance, which all donors are provided a copy of; 3) instead of having specified donation time slots, the sperm bank is now open from 8 A.M. to 5 P.M. Mondays to Saturdays and from 8 A.M. to 12 P.M. on Sundays, allow-ing maximum flexibility for donors and fewer peak times; 4) waiting areas for sperm donors have been upgraded with new PC facilities and televi-sions; 5) a special nurse for first-time donors has been employed whose primary task is to provide reassurance and answer any questions; 6) a standardized satisfaction survey is given to all donors and the sperm bank receives about four hundred of these every month for analysis; and 7) they have brought down donor waiting times to around twenty minutes.

Partly as a result of these changes and partly as a result of expanding their recruitment strategies to reach not just university students but also university graduates who are employed, the Hunan Human Sperm Bank had for the first time ever screened over six thousand potential donors in 2016. At the same time, however, qualification rates had fallen from some 35 percent to around 20 percent. As a result, and since medical technologies are always evolving, we will always need further ethnographies of assisted reproductive technologies like sperm banking in China and beyond.

Notes

1. After the completion of fieldwork for this book, in 2016, the Hunan Sperm Bank doubled the number of screened potential donors from 3,000 in 2013 to 6,000. I will return to this remarkable rise in screenings at the end of this book.

2. Ever since Chairman Mao Zedong, in a newly Communist China, had in a 1944 speech suggested that "of course the new medicine is superior to the old medicine," relations between biomedicine and Chinese medicine have been strained as the Communist Party in China has supported modernizing and scientificizing Chinese medicine (see Taylor, 2005, pp. 16–17; see also Wahlberg, 2014b).

3. In late 2015, the Chinese Communist Party announced that it was relaxing its family planning policies to allow all couples the possibility of having a second child. There had been exceptions to the one-child limit for some families prior to that, e.g., in some rural areas couples whose first child was a girl could "try again," and throughout the country if a couple gave birth to a child with a "serious condition" they would also be given permission to have a second child. As of 2016, however, all married couples can apply for and be granted a qualification of pregnancy certificate for a second child (see Zeng & Hesketh, 2016).

4. This is because a single donor in Europe or the United States can "sire" anywhere between twelve and even over one hundred offspring, which reduces cost per donor considerably and likewise substantially reduces the number of donors required by sperm banks to serve the same number of families (see chapter 4).

5. According to George Marcus, multisited ethnography "moves out from the single sites and local situations of conventional ethnographic research designs to examine the circulation of cultural meanings, objects, and identities in diffuse time-space" (1995, p. 96). Likewise, Gregory Feldman has made a case for what he calls nonlocal ethnography when studying the "migration apparatus [which] activates and proliferates without central coordination, without tight networks among its technicians, and without a detailed master plan, all of which render it an evasive object of empiricist field research" (2011, p. 378). The kind of assemblage ethnography of a medical technology I am proposing is site-bound, as it is in such sites that we observe and gain an understanding of the form that, e.g., sperm banking takes in a country like China. That site then multiplies as the ethnographer follows connections—whether regional or global—that emerge out of a particular site in order to cartographically map out the conditions of, in my case, China's reproductive complex within which sperm banking is firmly entrenched. The single site thus remains crucial in assemblage ethnography.

6. As should be clear by now, with the term "assemblage ethnography" I am not invoking Gilles Deleuze and Félix Guittari's concept of the assemblage as lines; rather, I am using it in the Foucauldian sense, as a way of describing the systems of relations that make up an apparatus or *dispositif* (see Legg, 2011 for a helpful discussion of how the two relate). It may perhaps make more sense therefore to call them apparatus ethnographies or *dispositif* ethnographies, but as an ethnographic methodology the term "assemblage" is for me the accurate descriptor.

7. As such assemblage ethnography should be seen as distinct from what Jarret Zigon has called "assemblic ethnography," which he suggests "chases and traces a situation through its continual process of assembling across different global scales and its temporally differential localization in diverse places" (2015, p. 515). For Zigon, a situation is a nontotalizable assemblage, whereas when it comes to assemblage ethnography, it is the cartographic mapping of forms of problematization that take place within a totalizing *dispositif* that is at stake (cf. Ferguson, 1990; Foucault, 1991; Rose & Miller, 1992).

8. In my view, one of the first assemblage ethnographies, as I define them, was James Ferguson's classic *The Anti-Politics Machine* (1990), even if he did not call it that. In it, Ferguson makes the point that "unlike many anthropological works on 'development,' this one takes as its primary object not the people to be 'developed,' but the apparatus that is to do the 'developing.' This is not a book about the Basotho people, or even about Lesotho; it is principally a book about the operation of the international 'development' apparatus in a particular setting" (Ferguson, 1990, p. 17).

9. This, of course, remains an important comparative task in itself, and it is an approach that has characterized a good part of the anthropology of infertility and ethnographies focusing on assisted reproductive technologies around the world (see, for example, Bharadwaj, 2016; Inhorn, 2004; Roberts, 2012).

10. Such a practice collective is different from Lave and Wenger's notion of "communities of practice," which have been defined as "groups of people who share a concern or a passion for something they do and learn how to do it better as they interact regularly" (Lave & Wenger, 1991). Lave and Wenger developed their notion of communities of practice to help analyze processes of social learning that emerge out of regular interaction. In contrast, the notion of practice collectives allows us to examine how, for example, scales of operation contribute to a particular mood in the lab, in the reception room for new donors, or on minivan trips to cities outside of the capital to collect donor sperm.

11. I concur with historian Jiang Lijing (2015) who has argued that the "full [Chinese] story shows how IVF technological transfer from more developed countries to China was not one of unmodified, unidirectional imports." See also Gürtin (2012), who suggests that ethnographic studies of reproductive technologies from around the world "increasingly negate a unidirectional model of technology transfer. It is not (any longer?) a case of exporting ARTs 'from the West to the rest,' but rather a range of dynamic and pluridirectional exchanges between multiple contexts that dis-locate and re-locate these technologies and practices" (p. 83). And finally, in her analysis of the beginnings of IVF in India, Barnreuther (2016) highlights the importance of "the production of science and technology in the Global South" (p. 75).

12. Michael Whyte has proposed the methodological notion of episodic fieldwork "to emphasize the significance of absence and return for fieldwork relationships and the ethnographies that rest on these relationships" (2013, p. 112). His point is that long-term engagements in particular field sites often entail return visits, which engender particular forms of social bonds and relations as "catching up" and "updating" becomes an intrinsic part of an ethnographer's relations with informants and collaborators. Sometimes absences are short while at others they may be lengthier and may lap over with periods of major historical change, which has certainly been the case for me when it comes to family planning policies in China. In such cases, Whyte argues, returning to a field site involves being brought up to date in ways that generate novel insights into historical processes.

13. The first conference on Social and Ethical Challenges in Sperm Banking was held in Changsha in May 2012, bringing together participants from all of China's sperm banks as well as from Europe. The second conference was held in December 2012 in Copenhagen and was titled "Selective Reproductive Technologies—Routes of Routinization and Globalization" and gathered social scientists from around the world (see Wahlberg & Gammeltoft, 2017).

14. Throughout the book when excerpts from interviews are provided I use the initials "AW" when I have carried out the interview on my own and the term "Researchers" to indicate that an interview was carried out with assistance from a translator.

CHAPTER 1. THE BIRTH OF ASSISTED
REPRODUCTIVE TECHNOLOGY IN CHINA

1. This is my best estimate based on the knowledge I have gathered visiting various fertility clinics around China. There is no official tally of the total number of IVF babies in China. China's largest clinic in Changsha had helped bring 73,461 IVF babies to term by March 2015.

2. ARTs were developed in China at the exact same time that the "one-child" policy was rolled out across the country. The policy never was strictly speaking a one-child policy, as there were many exceptions in rural areas as well as in cases where a couple conceived a child with a serious disease. In 2016, the policy was adjusted into a two-child policy, allowing all couples a second child. Early indications are that the easing of the policy has not resulted in a significant increase in births.

3. For Zhang Lizhu's background story I rely on Jiang Lijing's extensive account (2015) as well as my own interviews with members of staff at the Beijing Third Hospital, attendance at workshops, and archival sources.

4. The Cultural Revolution lasted from 1967 to 1978 as a social movement initiated by Chairman Mao Zedong, who called for the cities' educated to go and work in rural areas: "It is necessary for the educated youth to go to the countryside, and be re-educated by the poor peasants" (quoted in Zhou & Hou, 1999, p. 12). The Red Guard, a mass of high school and university students who supported Mao Zedong, persecuted local party leaders, teachers, and other intellectuals whom they saw as enemies of Maoist thought. Scientists were among those groups who were targeted by the Red Guard, in often violent ways as described by Frank Dikötter: "In the onslaught of the Cultural Revolution, teachers, researchers, and scientists were repeatedly persecuted, harassed, and tortured, as Red Guard organizations inflicted sustained damage on research centers and educational institutions" (1998, p. 121).

5. This was also the case in the United Kingdom, where Robert Edwards and Richard Gardner, long before the world's first IVF baby Louise Brown was born in 1978, developed the technique of embryo biopsy (see Bhatia, 2017; Franklin & Roberts, 2006).

6. Today, ethical review boards have become a required authorizing institution for much biomedical research. In China, such reviews remain relatively new to the country (see Wahlberg et al., 2013) and there are certainly numerous questions that can be raised about the ethics of early ART research in China. Such questions are, of course, equally relevant in every country where experimental ART research has been carried out, whether in India, Denmark, or the U.K.

7. *Yousheng* is often translated as "eugenics" but it is more accurately translated as "excellent birth" or "superior birth" and is used to denote all efforts aimed at ensuring the birth of a healthy child, from genetic counseling to taking care of

oneself during pregnancy, prenatal care, and screening (see Sleeboom-Faulkner, 2010a; chapter 2). See Frank Dikötter's chapter on "'Inferior Births': Eugenics in the People's Republic of China" for a historical account of how eugenic theories circulated in China in the latter half of the twentieth century, culminating in the promulgating of the Law on Maternal and Infant Health Care in 1995 (Dikötter, 1998, pp. 119–83).

CHAPTER 2. IMPROVING POPULATION QUALITY

1. I will return to this in detail in chapters 4 and 5 where I ethnographically examine the recruitment and screening of sperm donors and the assessment of sperm quality at the sperm bank in Changsha.

2. Which of course does not mean that this concept cannot have subjectifying effects as it circulates and comes to inform patterns of self-constitution and interpellation (see Sturgeon, 2010).

3. A number of scholars have discussed this "spiritual" aspect of rénkǒu sùzhì in the English-language social science literature (Anagnost,1995; Bakken, 1999; Fong, 2007; Greenhalgh & Winckler, 2005; Kipnis, 2006).

4. See Matthew Kohrman's Bodies of Difference (2005) for an important ethnographic account of the difficult emergence of a notion of disability rights in China and all of the obstacles and stigmatization that disabled persons continue to face in China. Also, Zhu Jianfeng has described how a "quality assurance regime" has emerged around prenatal care in urban China, which encourages women to use all available means to avoid giving birth to what doctors call a "defective newborn baby" (Zhu, 2013, p. S39). Finally, in the introduction to Tine Gammeltoft's account of selective reproduction in Vietnam, Haunting Images (2014), she explains how "during fieldwork in Hanoi, I was often struck by the fact that official Vietnamese framings of selective reproduction were characterized by a nearly complete absence of reference to choice or individual preference" (2014, p. 17). It is therefore important to distinguish between the different ways in which selective reproductive technologies come to be routinized in different parts of the world (see Wahlberg & Gammeltoft, 2017).

5. For in depth discussions on what constitutes a "serious disease" in the United Kingdom see Scott (2005) and Wahlberg (2009).

6. As we will recall from chapter 1, Lu Huilin's early work on medical genetics and reproductive technologies was informed by a concern for the strength of China's population, which he felt had been weakened during the final years of the Qing dynasty around the turn of the twentieth century because of widespread opium-smoking (see also Fay, 1997).

7. Similarly, in spiritual terms rural and migrant populations are described by some as being of "low quality" (sùzhì dī) in comparison to "high-quality"

(*sùzhì gāo*) urban dwellers who are considered more "cultivated" and "civilized" (Anagnost, 2004; Sturgeon, 2010).

8. These requirements also disqualify single women and lesbian couples from ART treatment in China.

9. ICSI is a form of IVF where a single sperm cell is injected directly into an egg for fertilization. In normal IVF sperm and eggs are mixed together in a dish and allowed to fertilize "on their own." ICSI is typically used in cases where a man has very poor sperm quality, although in recent years numbers of ICSI cycles have grown vastly as ICSI can "guarantee" fertilized eggs in a way that normal IVF can't (see Inhorn, 2016b; chapter 6).

10. The use of sperm banking in the treatment of male infertility will be the subject of the remaining chapters.

CHAPTER 3. EXPOSED BIOLOGIES

1. My informants at the sperm bank in Changsha have rightly pointed out that even if environmental pollution is implicated in rising rates of male infertility and falling sperm quality, there are other factors that play a much more important role when accounting for rising rates of overall infertility, such as reproductive deferral, lifestyle changes, changing sex life patterns, and the spread of sexually transmitted diseases. My argument in this chapter is not that pollution is the prime culprit for apparently rising infertility; rather, I show how it has gained traction as a kind of social diagnostic of some of the many dramatic transformations China is currently undergoing.

2. In *Infertility Around the Globe* (2002), Marcia Inhorn and Frank van Balen show how infertility in so-called high=fertility countries is often not recognized as a public health problem even though the suffering and stigmatization that infertile couples around the world experience are often more intense because of cultural expectations and socioeconomic needs. There are not many governments in the world that cover infertility treatment as part of state-run healthcare programs.

3. Facebook and Apple made headlines in 2014 when they began offering to pay for female employees to have their oocytes frozen—which requires women to go through a cycle of ovarian stimulation that is not without risks to health— sparking a debate about whether this wasn't once again a case of blaming women for the structural discrimination they face on the labor market.

4. Reservations exist not least because inconsistent methodologies for sperm quality assessment made it difficult to compare with historical data and also because some were convinced that lifestyle changes and increased sexual activity among young men, rather than any kind of biological deterioration per se, were the most likely explanation for any measured drop in aggregate quality over time.

5. As I have already noted, it is important to keep in mind that even if it is a fact that aggregate sperm quality levels are falling around the world, reproductive deferral remains the most important factor in fertility transitions from high to low fertility.

6. I will leave it to others to empirically challenge this sperm bank director's take on the relatively less exposed biologies and healthier lifestyles of university students today in China. What I am analyzing here is how ideas about exposure shape recruitment practices.

CHAPTER 4. MOBILIZING SPERM DONORS

1. As noted in the introduction, the sperm bank in Hunan managed to double the number of potential donors they screened to 6,000 in the years after my fieldwork concluded. I will return to this in the conclusion.

2. We saw in chapter 2 how ideas around the possibility of selecting for traits such as IQ are part of what some see as a contribution to the improvement of population quality in China.

3. See Svendsen and Koch's analysis of what they describe as "emotion management" by researchers and research subjects involved in a pharmacogenomics research project. In a similar way to sperm bank staff, researchers are interested in enrolling and maintaining voluntary subjects in their project, which requires various forms of emotional labor (Svendsen & Koch, 2011).

CHAPTER 6. BORROWING SPERM

1. The abduction of Ke Ke made national headlines throughout China in November 2011. I have reconstructed the details of Ke Ke's kidnapping from the following sources: *Shanghai Daily* ("Nurses Vanish as Baby Is Stolen from Hospital," November 7, 2011); *Law and Society* ("'Stolen' Baby Girl Found by Police: Suspects Are a Mother and Daughter Pair," November 8, 2011); *China Daily* ("Woman Made Careful Plans for Late-Night Hospital Baby Snatch," November 8, 2011); *China Daily* ("Stolen Baby Returned to Parents," November 8, 2011).

2. IVF requires women to undergo hormone treatments for ovarian stimulation followed by an invasive procedure to retrieve eggs (in China women are offered full anesthesia), fertilization and incubation in the laboratory, and then transfer of embryos into the womb. Insemination with donor sperm does not require any of these steps, which accounts for the large price differential. ICSI and IVF with donor sperm are also used in the treatment of male factor infertility, both of which are ten times more expensive than AID.

3. Since egg donation is only allowed by women who are willing to donate any spare eggs from their own IVF treatment, it is a very rare form of third-party conception in China compared to sperm donation. In the same way that there is a black market for sperm, as we will learn in this chapter, so too is there a black market for egg donation. Some couples who have the resources for it may also travel overseas to access donor eggs. Nevertheless, when it comes to third-party conception in China, sperm donation is by far more prevalent.

4. Charles Stafford has argued that the "'lineage paradigm' of Chinese anthropology . . . has helped sustain the impression that Chinese kinship is, in essence, an extreme and non-fluid version of patriliny: a male dominated system of rigidly defined agnatic groups, of kinship given by birth, of immutable connections, of exclusion, and of women who have power only as disruptive outsiders" (2000, p. 38). While not dismissing patriliny as an important mode of relating in China, he suggests that two other incorporative systems of Chinese relatedness must not be overlooked: "'the cycle of *yang*' (which centres mostly on parent-child relationships) and 'the cycle of *laiwang*' (which centres mostly on relationships between friends, neighbours, and acquaintances)" (ibid.).

5. As we saw in chapter 2, donor sperm is also made available to couples when the male is found to have a genetic disease considered "medically inappropriate for reproduction." These cases are, however, few in comparison to the use of donor sperm in the treatment of male factor infertility.

6. In third-party conception involving donor sperm there are of course multiple families at stake, those of the infertile male and the female, that of the donor (both current and future), and of course that of the infertile couple should they succeed in having a child. Following Stafford, we will see in this chapter how a "constant involvement in affairs of the hearth, children, and marriage" (Freedman quoted in Stafford, 2000, p. 35) comes from a wide group of family, neighbors, and friends. It is in this sense that efforts to control who knows what (i.e., to keep use of donor sperm secret from the male's in-laws, neighbors, and acquaintances on the part of couples, and to keep sperm donation a secret from parents and other acquaintances on the part of donors) can be thought of as strategies of "hearth" management.

7. Over the years that I carried out fieldwork in Changsha I witnessed how the hospital transitioned into a modern e-hospital. Since 2016 patients have been able to book times and make payments using the popular WeChat app, which has considerably lessened the amount of queuing time couples face.

8. I never did get used to the sheer scale of operations in the hospital even after many, many stays in Changsha. Diagnostic tests, medical procedures, drug regimens, etc. were pretty much the same as those used in Europe, yet daily logistics were always multiplied by a factor of 100. But the incredulity was mine; for my informants who worked in the hospital and in general lived in urban China, there was absolutely nothing strange about the scale of operations. "This

is China," they would often remind me, "people mountain, people sea" (*rénshān rénhǎi*)!

9. In the period 2007 to 2016 annual cycles of AID have fallen from 3,440 to 1,597 while ICSI cycles have risen from 1,197 to 6,415 in Changsha.

10. See Susanne Bregnbæk's *Fragile Elite* (2016) for an account of how notions of filial piety are currently under pressure in China and of how university students negotiate moral quandaries in their often strained relationships to their parents who have sacrificed everything to give their children a good education and possibilities in life.

References

BOOKS AND ARTICLES

Adams, V., Erwin, K., & Le, P. V. (2009). Public health works: Blood donation in urban China. *Social Science and Medicine, 68*(3), 410–18.

Adrian, S. W. (2010). Sperm stories: Policies and practices of sperm banking in Denmark and Sweden. *European Journal of Women's Studies, 17*(4), 393–411.

Almeling, R. (2006). "Why do you want to be a donor?": Gender and the production of altruism in egg and sperm donation. *New Genetics and Society, 25*(2), 143–57.

———. (2007). Selling genes, selling gender: Egg agencies, sperm banks, and the medical market in genetic material. *American Sociological Review, 72*(3), 319–40.

———. (2009). Gender and the value of bodily goods: Commodification in egg and sperm donation. *Law and Contemporary Problems, 72*(3), 37–58.

———. (2011). *Sex cells: The medical market for eggs and sperm.* Berkeley: University of California Press.

Almeling, R., & Waggoner, M. R. (2013). More and less than equal: How men factor in the reproductive equation. *Gender & Society 27*(6). doi: 0891243213484510.

Anagnost, A. (1995). A surfeit of bodies: Population and the rationality of the state in post-Mao China. In F. D. Ginsburg and R. Rapp (Eds.), *Conceiving the new world order: The global politics of reproduction* (pp. 22–41). Berkeley: University of California Press.

———. (2004). The corporeal politics of quality (*suzhi*). *Public Culture, 16*(2), 189–208.

———. (2006). Strange circulations: The blood economy in rural China. *Economy and Society, 35*(4), 509–29.

Bakken, Børge. (1999). *The exemplary society: human improvement, social control, and the dangers of modernity in China.* Oxford: Oxford University Press.

Bärnreuther, S. (2016). Innovations "out of place": Controversies over IVF beginnings in India between 1978 and 2005. *Medical Anthropology, 35*(1), 73–89.

Barry, A., Osborne, T., & Rose, N. (1996). *Foucault and political reason: Liberalism, neo-liberalism, and rationalities of government.* Chicago: University of Chicago Press.

Becker, Gay. (2000). *The elusive embryo: How men and women approach new reproductive technologies.* (1st Ed.). Berkeley: University of California Press.

Bharadwaj, Aditya. 2002. Conception politics: Medical egos, media spotlights, and the contest over test-tube firsts in India. In M. Inhorn and F. van Balen (Eds.), *Infertility around the globe: New thinking on childlessness, gender, and reproductive technologies* (pp. 315–34). Berkley: University of California Press.

———. 2003. Why adoption is not an option in India: The visibility of infertility, the secrecy of donor insemination, and other cultural complexities. *Social Science & Medicine, 56*(9), 1867–80.

———. 2016. *Conceptions: Infertility and procreative technologies in India.* New York: Berghahn Books.

Bhatia, R. (2017). The development of sex selective reproductive technologies within fertility, inc. and the anticipation of lifestyle sex selection. In A. Wahlberg & T. Gammeltoft (Eds.), *Selective reproduction in the 21st century* (pp. 45–66). Basingstoke: Palgrave Macmillan.

BIONET. (2007a). 1st workshop report: Informed consent in reproductive genetics and stem cell technology and the role of ethical review boards. Ethical Governance of Biological and Biomedical Research: Chinese-European Co-operation. http://www.bionet-china.org/pdfs/BIONET _1st_Workshop_Report.pdf.

———. (2007b). Cases for discussion—Assisted reproductive technologies. Workshop on informed consent in reproductive genetics and stem cell technology and the role of ethical review boards, Beijing, 1–5 April.

Bregnbæk, S. (2016). *Fragile elite: The dilemmas of China's top university students.* Stanford, CA: Stanford University Press.

Bunge, R. G. & Sherman, J. K. (1953). Fertilizing capacity of frozen human spermatozoa. *Nature, 4382*, 767–68.

Bunkenborg, M. (2014). Subhealth: Questioning the quality of bodies in contemporary China. *Medical Anthropology, 33*(2), 128–43.

Burr, J. (2009). Fear, fascination, and the sperm donor as "abjection" in interviews with heterosexual recipients of donor insemination. *Sociology of Health and Illness, 31*(5), 705–18.

Carlsen, E., Giwercman, A., Keiding, N., & Skakkebæk, N. E. (1992). Evidence for decreasing quality of semen during past 50 years. *British Medical Journal, 305*(6854), 609–13.

Carmeli, Y. S., & Birenbaum-Carmeli, D. (1994). The predicament of masculinity: Towards understanding the male's experience of infertility treatments. *Sex Roles, 30*(9–10), 663–77.

Carson, R. (1962). *Silent spring.* New York: Fawcett Crest.

CCTV. (2011, 9 August). 70% of Chinese suffer from "sub-health" problems. Retrieved from http://english.cntv.cn/program/china24/20110809/103624 .shtml.

Chen, Q. (2005, 14 September) Keeping policy-making process transparent. *China Daily.*

Chen, Z., Wang, J. N., Ma, G. X., & Zhang, Y. S. (2013). China tackles the health effects of air pollution. *The Lancet, 382*(9909), 1959–60.

China Business Review. (2011). Smog can impact humans' reproductive ability and immune system. Retrieved from http://hsb.hsw.cn/2013-11/05/content _8516735.htm.

China Daily (2007a, 21 May). Birth defects rise as checkups slide. Retrieved from http://www.chinadaily.com.cn/china/2007-05/21/content_876472.htm

———. (2007b, 30 October). Baby born with birth defects every 30 seconds. Retrieved from http://www.chinadaily.com.cn/china/2007-10/30/content _6215074.htm.

———. (2009, 2 April). Male infertility rate on the rise. Retrieved from http:// www.chinadaily.com.cn/cndy/2009-04/02/content_7640758.htm.

———. (2011a, 7 November). More than a million men sterile in China. Retrieved from chinadailycom.91song.cc/china/2011-11/07/content _14051476.htm.

———. (2011b, 8 November). Woman made careful plans for late-night hospital baby snatch. Retrieved from http://www.chinadaily.com.cn/cndy/2011-11/08 /content_14053814.htm.

———. (2011c, 8 November). Stolen baby returned to parents. Retrieved from http://www.chinadaily.com.cn/china/2011-11/08/content_14053907.htm.

China News Center. (2011, 7 November). Nurses vanish as baby is stolen. Retrieved from http://www.chinamedia.com/news/2011/11/07/nurses-vanish-as-baby-is-stolen/.

Cohen, L. (2005). Operability, bioavailability, and exception. In A. Ong & S. Collier (Eds.), *Global assemblages: Technology, politics, and ethics as anthropological problems* (pp. 79–90). Malden, MA: Blackwell.

Colborn, T., vom Saal, F. S., & Soto, A. M. (1993). Developmental effects of endocrine-disrupting chemicals in wildlife and humans. *Environmental Health Perspectives, 101*(5), 378.

Collier, S. J., & Ong, A. (2007). "Global assemblages, anthropological problems." In A. Ong & S. J. Collier (Eds.), *Global assemblages* (pp. 3–21). Malden, MA: Blackwell.

Dàhé Jiànkāng Bào. (2008, 1 December). National emergency in sperm banks in China—Only 37 qualified sperm out of 328 sperm donors in Henan. Retrieved from http://tech.icxo.com/htmlnews/2008/12/01/1322076_0.htm.

Daniels, C. R., and Golden, J. (2004). Procreative compounds: Popular eugenics, artificial insemination, and the rise of the American sperm banking industry. *Journal of Social History, 38*(1), 5–27.

Daniels, C. R., & Heidt-Forsythe, E. (2012). Gendered eugenics and the problematic of free market reproductive technologies: Sperm and egg donation in the United States. *Signs, 37*(3), 719–47.

Daniels, K. R., & Taylor, K. (1993). Secrecy and openness in donor insemination. *Politics and the Life Sciences, 12*(2), 155–70.

Dikötter, F. (1998). *Imperfect conceptions: Medical knowledge, birth defects, and eugenics in China*. New York: Columbia University Press.

Dow, K. (2016). *Making a good life: An ethnography of nature, ethics, and reproduction*. Princeton, NJ: Princeton University Press.

Edwards, R. (1983). The current clinical and ethical situation of human conception (The Galton Lecture of 1982). In C. O. Carter (Ed.), *Developments in human reproduction and their eugenic and ethical implications* (1st Ed.) (pp. 53–116). London: Academic Press.

Ehrenskjöld, C. (2011, 16 September). Vi drukner i sæd. *Ekstrabladet*. Retrieved from http://ekstrabladet.dk/kup/sundhed/article4077152.ece.

Erwin, K. (2006). The circulatory system: Blood procurement, AIDS, and the social body in China. *Medical Anthropology Quarterly, 20*(2), 139–59.

Evens, E. McD. (2004). *A global perspective on infertility: An under recognized public health issue*. Carolina Papers International Health. Chapel Hill: University of North Carolina.

Farquhar, J. (1991). Objects, processes, and female infertility in Chinese medicine. *Medical Anthropology Quarterly, 5*(4), 370–99.

Fay, P. W. (1997). *The Opium War, 1840-1842*. Chapel Hill: University of North Carolina Press.

Feldman, G. (2011). If ethnography is more than participant-observation, then relations are more than connections: The case for nonlocal ethnography in a world of apparatuses. *Anthropological Theory, 11*(4): 375–95.

Ferguson, J. (1990). *The anti-politics machine: "Development," depoliticization, and bureaucratic power in Lesotho.* Minneapolis: University of Minnesota Press.

Fleck, L. (1979). *Genesis and development of a scientific fact.* Chicago: University of Chicago Press.

Fong, V. (2006). *Only hope: Coming of age under China's one-child policy.* (1st Ed.). Stanford, CA: Stanford University Press.

———. (2007). Morality, cosmopolitanism, or academic attainment? Discourses on "quality" and urban Chinese-only-children's claims to ideal personhood. *City & Society, 19*(1): 86–113.

Fortun, K. (2009). *Advocacy after Bhopal: Environmentalism, disaster, new global orders.* Chicago: University of Chicago Press.

Foucault, M. (1977). *The order of things: An archaeology of the human sciences.* London: Tavistock.

———. (1980). *Power/knowledge: Selected interviews and other writings, 1972-1977.* (C. Gordon, L. Marshall, J. Mepham, & K. Soper, Trans.). New York: Pantheon Books.

———. (1991). Questions of method. In G. Burchell, C. Gordon, P. Miller, & M. Foucault (Eds.), *The Foucault effect: Studies in governmentality: With two lectures by Michel Foucault* (pp. 73-86). London: Harvester Wheatsheaf.

Franklin, S. (1997). *Embodied progress: A cultural account of assisted conception.* London: Routledge.

Franklin, S., & Roberts, C. 2006. *Born and made: An ethnography of preimplantation genetic diagnosis.* Princeton, NJ: Princeton University Press.

Gammeltoft, T. M. (2014). *Haunting images: A cultural account of selective reproduction in Vietnam.* Berkeley: University of California Press.

Gammeltoft, T. M., & Wahlberg, A. (2014). Selective reproductive technologies. *Annual Review of Anthropology, 43,* 201–16.

Goodarzi, M. O., Dumesic, D. A., Chazenbalk, G., & Azziz, R., 2011. Polycystic ovary syndrome: Etiology, pathogenesis, and diagnosis. *Nature Reviews Endocrinology, 7*(4), 219–31.

Graham, S., Mohr, S., & Bourne, K. (2016). Regulating the "good" donor. In S. Golombok, R. Scott, J. B. Appleby, M. Richards, & S. Wilkinson (Eds.), *Regulating reproductive donation* (pp. 207–31). Cambridge: Cambridge University Press.

Greenhalgh, S. (2008). *Just one child: Science and policy in Deng's China.* (1st Ed.). Berkeley: University of California Press.

———. (2010). *Cultivating global citizens: Population in the rise of China.* Cambridge, MA: Harvard University Press.

Greenhalgh, S., & Winckler, E. (2005). *Governing China's population: From Leninist to neoliberal biopolitics.* (1st Ed.). Stanford, CA: Stanford University Press.

Guo, Y., Ma, Y., Chen, G., & Cheng, J. (2016). The effects of occupational exposure of carbon disulfide on sexual hormones and semen quality of male workers from a chemical fiber factory. *Journal of Occupational and Environmental Medicine, 58*(8): e294–e300.

Gürtin, Z. (2012). "Practitioners as interface agents between the local and the global: The localization of IVF in Turkey." In M. Knecht, S. Beck, & M. Klotz (Eds.), *Reproductive technologies as global form: Ethnographies of knowledge, practices, and transnational encounters* (pp. 81–110). Frankfurt: Campus Verlag.

Handwerker, L. (1995a). The hen that can't lay an egg (*bu xia dan de mu ji*): Conceptions of female infertility in modern China. In J. Urla & J. Terry (Eds.), *Deviant bodies* (pp. 358–86). Bloomington: Indiana University Press.

———. (1995b). Social and ethical implications of in vitro fertilization in contemporary China. *Cambridge Quarterly of Healthcare Ethics, 4* (03): 355–63.

———. (1998). The consequences of modernity for childless women in China: Medicalization and resistance. In M. Lock & P. A. Kaufert (Eds.), *Pragmatic women and body politics* (pp. 178–205). New York: Cambridge University Press.

———. (1999). Health commodification and the body politic: The example of female infertility in modern China. In A. Donchin & L. M. Purdy (Eds.), *Embodying bioethics: Recent feminist advances* (pp. 141–57). Lanham, MD: Rowman & Littlefield.

———. (2002). The politics of making modern babies in China: Reproductive technologies and the " new" eugenics. In M. C. Inhorn & F. van Bale (Eds.), *Infertility around the globe: New thinking on childlessness, gender, and reproductive technologies* (pp. 298–314). Berkley: University of California Press.

Hanson, F. A. (2001). Donor insemination: Eugenic and feminist implications. *Medical Anthropology Quarterly, 15*(3), 287–311.

Hochschild, A. R. (2012). *The managed heart: Commercialization of human feeling*. Berkley: University of California Press.

Hoeyer, K. (2007). Person, patent, and property: A critique of the commodification hypothesis. *BioSocieties, 2*(3), 327–48.

———. (2010). After novelty: The mundane practices of ensuring a safe and stable supply of bone. *Science as Culture, 19*(2), s. 123–50.

———. (2013). *Exchanging human bodily material: Rethinking bodies and markets*. Berlin: Springer Science & Business Media.

Hörbst, V. (2012). Assisted reproductive technologies in Mali: Asymmetries and frictions. In M. Knecht, S. Beck, & M. Klotz (Eds.), *Reproductive technologies as global form: Ethnographies of knowledge, practices, and transnational encounters* (pp. 161–96). Frankfurt: Campus Verlag.

Hu, F. B., Liu, Y., & Willett, W. C. (2011). Preventing chronic diseases by promoting healthy diet and lifestyle: public policy implications for China. *Obesity Reviews*, *12*(7): 552–59.

Hu, S. (2001, 3 May). Where there's sperm, there's demand. *Shanghai Star*. Retrieved from http://app1.chinadaily.com.cn/star/2001/0503/fo6-1.html.

Huang, C., Li, B., Xu, K., Liu, D., Hu, J., Yang, Y., Nie, H., Fan, L., & Zhu, W. (2017). Decline in semen quality among 30,636 young Chinese men from 2001 to 2015. *Fertility and Sterility*, *107*(1): 83–88.

Inhorn, M. C. (1994). *Quest for conception: Gender, infertility, and Egyptian medical traditions*. Philadelphia: University of Pennsylvania Press.

———. (1996). *Infertility and patriarchy: The cultural politics of gender and family life in Egypt*. Philadelphia: University of Pennsylvania Press.

———. (2003). Global infertility and the globalization of new reproductive technologies: Illustrations from Egypt. *Social Science & Medicine*, *56* (9): 1837–51.

———. (2004). Middle Eastern masculinities in the age of new reproductive technologies: Male infertility and stigma in Egypt and Lebanon. *Medical Anthropology Quarterly*, *18*(2), 162–82.

———. (2006a). He won't be my son. *Medical Anthropology Quarterly*, *20*(1), 94–120.

———. (2006b). Making Muslim babies: IVF and gamete donation in Sunni versus Shi'a Islam. *Culture, Medicine, and Psychiatry*, *30*(4), 427–50.

———. (2011). Globalization and gametes: Reproductive "tourism," Islamic bioethics, and Middle Eastern modernity. *Anthropology & Medicine*, *18*(1): 87–103.

———. (2013). Why me? Male infertility and responsibility in the Middle East. *Men and Masculinities*, *16*(1), 49–70.

———. (2015). *Cosmopolitan conceptions: IVF sojourns in global Dubai*. Durham, NC: Duke University Press.

———. (2017). Medical cosmopolitanism in global Dubai: A twenty-first-century transnational intracytoplasmic sperm injection (ICSI) depot. *Medical Anthropology Quarterly*, *31*(1), 5-22.

Inhorn, M. C., & van Balen, F. (Eds.) (2002). *Infertility around the globe: New thinking on childlessness, gender, and reproductive technologies*. Berkeley: University of California Press.

Inhorn, M. C., & Wentzell, E. A. (2011). Embodying emergent masculinities: Men engaging with reproductive and sexual health technologies in the Middle East and Mexico. *American Ethnologist*, *38*(4), 801–15.

Inhorn, M. C., la Cour Mosegaard, M., Tjornhoj-Thomsen, T., & Goldberg, H. (Eds.). (2009). *Reconceiving the second sex: Men, masculinity, and reproduction*. New York: Berghahn Books.

Ivry, T. (2009). *Embodying culture: Pregnancy in Japan and Israel*. New Brunswick, NJ: Rutgers University Press.

Jia, X.-H. (2001, 24 December). The choice of life and life choices. *Science and Technology Daily*. Retrieved from http://www.people.com.cn/GB /kejiao/42/155/20011224/633758.html.

Jiang, L. (2015). IVF the Chinese way: Zhang Lizhu and post-Mao human in vitro fertilization research. *East Asian Science, Technology, and Society*, *9*(1), 23–45.

Jiang, M., Chen, X., Yue, H., Xu, W., Lin, L., Wu, Y., & Liu, B. (2014). Semen quality evaluation in a cohort of 28,213 adult males from Sichuan area of south-west China. *Andrologia*, *46*(8), 842–47.

Johnson, M. H. (2011). Robert Edwards: The path to IVF. *Reproductive Bio-Medicine Online*, *23*(2): 245–62.

Johnson, M. H., Franklin, S. B., Cottingham, M., & Hopwood, N. (2010). Why the Medical Research Council refused Robert Edwards and Patrick Steptoe support for research on human conception in 1971. *Human Reproduction*, *25*(9): 2157–74.

Kaufman, S. R. (2015). *Ordinary medicine: Extraordinary treatments, longer lives, and where to draw the line*. Durham, NC: Duke University Press.

King, D. E., & Stone, L. (2010). Lineal masculinity: Gendered memory within patriliny. *American Ethnologist*, *37*(2), 323–36.

Kipnis, A. (2006). Suzhi: A keyword approach. *China Quarterly*, *186*, 295–313.

———. (2007). Neoliberalism reified: Suzhi discourse and tropes of neoliberalism in the People's Republic of China. *Journal of the Royal Anthropological Institute*, *13*(2), 383–400.

———. (2011). *Governing educational desire: Culture, politics, and schooling in China*. Chicago: University of Chicago Press.

Kleinman, A., Yan, Y., Jun, J., Lee, S. Zhang, E., Tianshu, P., Fei, W., & Guo, J. (2011). *Deep China: The moral life of the person*. Berkeley: University of California Press.

Knecht, M., Beck, S., & Klotz, M. (Eds.). (2012). *Reproductive technologies as global form: Ethnographies of knowledge, practices, and transnational encounters*. Frankfurt: Campus Verlag.

Koch, L., & Svendsen, M. N. (2005). Providing solutions—defining problems: The imperative of disease prevention in genetic counselling. *Social Science & Medicine*, *60*(4): 823–32.

Koenig, B. A. (1988). The technological imperative in medical practice: The social creation of a "routine" treatment. In M. Lock & D. Gordon (Eds.), *Biomedicine examined* (pp. 465–96). Culture, Illness, and Healing 13. Dordrecht : Springer Netherlands.

Kohrman, M. (2005) *Bodies of difference: Experiences of disability and institutional advocacy in the making of modern China*. Berkley: University of California Press.

Kristof, N. D. (1991, 15 August). Some Chinese provinces forcing sterilization of retarded couples. *New York Times.*

Kr'løkke, C. (2009). Click a donor: Viking masculinity on the line. *Journal of Consumer Culture, 9*(1): 7–30.

Kr'løkke, C. H., & Adrian, S. W. (2013). Sperm on ice: Fatherhood and life after death. *Australian Feminist Studies, 28*(77), 263–78.

Kyung-Sup, C. (1999). Compressed modernity and its discontents: South Korean society in transition. *Economy and Society, 28*(1), 30–55.

Lamoreaux, J. (2016). What if the environment is a person? Lineages of epigenetic science in a toxic China. *Cultural Anthropology, 31*(2), 188–214.

Landecker, H. (2011). Food as exposure: Nutritional epigenetics and the new metabolism. *BioSocieties, 6*(2), 167–94.

Larkin, B. (2013). The politics and poetics of infrastructure. *Annual Review of Anthropology, 42*(1), 327–43.

Latour, B. (2014). Agency at the time of the Anthropocene. *New Literary History, 45*, 1–18.

Lau, J. T. F., Wang, Q., Cheng, Y., Kim, J. H., Yang, X., & Tsui, H. Y. (2008). Infertility-related perceptions and responses and their associations with quality of life among rural Chinese infertile couples. *Journal of Sex & Marital Therapy, 34*, 248–67.

Lave, J., & Wenger, E. (1991). *Situated learning: Legitimate peripheral participation.* Cambridge: Cambridge University Press.

Law and Society. (2011, 8 November) "Stolen" baby girl found by police: Suspects are a pair of mother and daughter. Retrieved from http://www.8a6a.com/?p=314.

Legg, S. (2011). Assemblage/apparatus: Using Deleuze and Foucault. *Area, 43*(2), 128–33.

Li, J. (2005, 6 January). Reproductive human cloning. *People's Daily.*

Liu, L. [1] (2006). Quality of life as a social representation in China: A qualitative study. *Social Indicators Research, 75*, 217–40.

Liu, L. [2] (2010). Made in China: Cancer villages. *Environment: Science and Policy for Sustainable Development, 52*(2), 8–21.

Lock, M. (1993). *Encounters with aging: Mythologies of menopause in Japan and North America.* Berkley: University of California Press

Lock, M., and Kaufert, P. (2001). Menopause, local biologies, and cultures of aging. *American Journal of Human Biology, 13*(4): 494–504.

Lora-Wainwright, A. (2010). An anthropology of "cancer villages": Villagers' perspectives and the politics of responsibility. *Journal of Contemporary China, 19*(63), 79–99.

Mamo, L. (2005). Biomedicalizing kinship: Sperm banks and the creation of affinity-ties. *Science as Culture, 14*(3), 237–64.

Marcus, G. E. (1995). Ethnography in/of the world system: The emergence of multi-sited ethnography. *Annual Review of Anthropology, 24*(1), 95–117.

Marques-Pinto, A., & Carvalho, D. (2013). Human infertility: Are endocrine disruptors to blame? *Endocrine Connections, 2*(3), R15–R29.

Martin, L. J. (2010). Anticipating infertility: Egg freezing, genetic preservation, and risk. *Gender & Society, 24*(4): 526–45.

———. (2017). They don't just take a random egg: Egg selection in the United States. In A. Wahlberg & T. Gammeltoft (Eds.), *Selective reproduction in the 21st century* (pp. 151–70). Basingstoke, UK: Palgrave Macmillan.

Meng, Q., Ren, A., Zhang, L., Liu, J., Li, Z., Yang, Y., Li, R., & Ma, L. (2015). Incidence of infertility and risk factors of impaired fecundity among newly married couples in a Chinese population. *Reproductive Biomedicine Online, 30*(1): 92–100.

Mertes, H., & Pennings, G. (2011). Social egg freezing: For better, not for worse. *Reproductive Biomedicine Online, 23*(7), 824–29.

Mohr, S. (2014). Beyond motivation: On what it means to be a sperm donor in Denmark. *Anthropology & Medicine, 21*(2), 162–73.

———. (2015). Living kinship trouble: Danish sperm donors' narratives of relatedness. *Medical Anthropology, 34*(5), 470–84.

———. (2016). Containing sperm—managing legitimacy. *Journal of Contemporary Ethnography, 45*(3): 319–42.

Mohr, S., & Hoeyer, K. (2012). Den gode sædcelle . . .: En antropologisk analyse af arbejdet med sædkvalitet. *K&K: Kultur & Klasse, 40*, 113–45.

Moore, L. J. (2008). *Sperm counts: Overcome by man's most precious fluid.* New York: NYU Press.

Moore, L. J., & Schmidt, M. A. (1999). On the construction of male differences: Marketing variations in technosemen. *Men and Masculinities, 1*(4): 331–51.

Morgan, L. M., & Roberts, E. F. (2012). Reproductive governance in Latin America. *Anthropology & Medicine, 19*(2), 241–54.

Morgan, T. H. (1924). Human inheritance. *American Naturalist, 58*(658): 385–409.

———. (1925). *Evolution and genetics.* (2nd Ed.). Vol. 9. Princeton, NJ: Princeton University Press.

Murphy, M. (2008). Chemical regimes of living. *Environmental History, 13*(4), 695–703.

———. (2011). Distributed reproduction. In P. Currah & M. Casper (Eds.), *Corpus: Bodies of knowledge* (pp. 21–38). New York: Palgrave Macmillan.

———. (2013). Chemical infrastructures of the St Clair River. In S. Boudia and N. Jas (Eds.), *Toxicants, health, and regulation since 1945* (pp. 103–15). London, Pickering and Chatto.

Murphy, R. (2004). Turning peasants into modern Chinese citizens: "Population quality" discourse, demographic transition, and primary education. *China Quarterly, 177,* 1–20.

Nature. (1994). China's misconception of eugenics. *Nature 367* (6458), 1-2.

Peking University Third Hospital. (2003). Reproductive medicine and assisted reproductive technology international seminar report. http://www.bysy.edu .cn/bysy/dept/fu/meeting1.htm.

People's Daily. (2011, 9 May). Couples who were born in 1980s become main force in infertile group and they are seeking medical treatment urgently as unwilling "to be DINK." Retrieved from http://health.people.com.cn /GB/14585103.html.

Petryna, A. (2002). *Life exposed: Biological citizens after Chernobyl.* Princeton, NJ: Princeton University Press.

Polge, C. (2007). The work of the Animal Research Station, Cambridge. *Studies in the History and Philosophy of Biology & Biomedical Science, 38:* 511–20.

Politiken. (2007, 1 June). Forsker advarer: Som art er vi i fare. Retrieved from http://politiken.dk/tjek/sundhedogmotion/familieliv/ECE316044 /forsker-advarer-som-art-er-vi-i-fare/.

Power, M. (1999). *The audit society: Rituals of verification.* Oxford: Oxford University Press.

Prainsack, B., & Wahlberg, A. (2013). Situated bio-regulation: Ethnographic sensibility at the interface of STS, policy studies, and the social studies of medicine. *BioSocieties, 8* (3): 336–59. doi:10.1057/biosoc.2013.14.

Qingdao News. (2005, 3 June). The data shows that sperm crisis era has come—Sperm quality declines of 1% per year. Retrieved from http://www .qingdaonews.com/content/2005-06/03/content_4822001.htm.

Qiu, R. Z. (2003). Does eugenics exist in China? Ethical issues in China's Law on Maternal and Infant Care. In R. Z. Qiu (Ed.), *Bioethics: Asian perspectives* (pp. 185–96). Dordrecht: Springer Netherlands.

———. (2007). Philosophical concept of reproduction and its cultural transformation with technology advancement. Workshop on informed consent in reproductive genetics and stem cell technology and the role of Ethical Review Boards, Beijing, 1-5 April.

Rao, M., Meng, T. Q., Hu, S. H., Guan, H. T., Wei, Q. Y., Xia, W., Zhu, C. H., & Xiong, C. L. (2015). Evaluation of semen quality in 1,808 university students, from Wuhan, Central China. *Asian Journal of Andrology, 17*(1): 111.

Rapp, R. (2000). *Testing women, testing the fetus: The social impact of amniocentesis in America.* New York: Routledge.

———. (2017). The egg imaginary. In A. Wahlberg & T. Gammeltoft (Eds.), *Selective reproduction in the 21st century* (pp. v–viii). Basingstoke, UK: Palgrave Macmillan.

Relman, A. S. (1980). The new medical-industrial complex. *New England Journal of Medicine, 303*(17), 963–70.

Reuters. (2007, 9 April). Pollution, stress blamed for poor China sperm count. Retrieved from http://www.reuters.com/article/us-china-health-fertility -idUSPEK29006120070409.

Riggs, D., & Scholz, B. (2011). The value and meaning attached to genetic relatedness among Australian sperm donors. *New Genetics and Society, 30*(1), 41–58.

Roberts, E. F. S. (2012). *God's laboratory: Assisted reproduction in the Andes.* Berkeley: University of California Press.

Rose, N. (2006). *The politics of life itself: Biomedicine, power, and subjectivity in the twenty-first century.* Princeton, NJ: Princeton University Press.

Rose, N., & Miller, P. (1992). Political power beyond the state: Problematics of government. *British Journal of Sociology, 43*(2): 173–205.

Rothman, B. K. 1993. *The tentative pregnancy: How amniocentesis changes the experience of motherhood.* New York: W. W. Norton.

Sazua. (2011, 8 November). A rare case of stolen baby at night was solved in Jiangsu Province, the suspect is a 23 year-old woman. Retrieved from http://forum.sazua.com/about2237.html#2182.

Scheper-Hughes, N. (2000). The global traffic in human organs. *Current Anthropology, 41*(2): 191–224.

Scott, R. (2005). Prenatal testing, reproductive autonomy, and disability interests. *Cambridge Quarterly of Healthcare Ethics, 14*(1), 65–82.

Shao, J. (2006). Fluid labor and blood money: The economy of HIV/AIDS in rural central China. *Cultural Anthropology, 21*(4), 535–69.

Shapiro, H. (1998). The puzzle of spermatorrhea in Republican China. *positions, 6*(3): 551–95.

Shapiro, N. (2015). Attuning to the chemosphere: Domestic formaldehyde, bodily reasoning, and the chemical sublime. *Cultural Anthropology, 30*(3): 368–93.

Sherman, J. K., & Bunge, R. G. (1953). Observations on preservation of human spermatozoa at low temperatures. *Experimental Biology and Medicine, 82*: 686–88.

Shanghai Daily. (2011, 7 November). Nurses vanish as baby is stolen from hospital. Retrieved from http://english.people.com.cn/90882/7637444 .html.

Shanghai News Channel. (2008). Shanghai sperm bank urgent situation; sperm crisis era begins. Retrieved from http://www.315rencai.cn/play. php?id=XMTM3MTQzNDMy.

Shih, L. (2017). Moral bearing: The paradox of choice, anxiety, and responsibility in Taiwan. In A. Wahlberg & T. Gammeltoft (Eds.), *Selective reproduction in the 21st century* (pp. 97–122). Basingstoke, UK: Palgrave Macmillan.

Silva, S., & Machado, H. (2009). Trust, morality, and altruism in the donation of biological material: The case of Portugal. *New Genetics and Society, 28*(2), 103–18.

Sina News. (2008, 25 September). Sperm quality is declining and male infertility is rising. Retrieved from http://baby.sina.com.cn/health/08/2509/1008121546.shtml.

———. (2011a, 9 March). Focus on university students keen on sperm donation—some people worry about the ethical risks. Retrieved from http://news.sina.com.cn/s/2011-03-09/033522077898.shtml.

———. (2011b, 6 June). The "the sperm crisis" in the world. Retrieved from http://news.sina.com.cn/c/2011-01-06/093321769340.shtml.

Skakkebaek, N. E., Rajpert-De Meyts, E., & Main, K. M. (2001). Testicular dysgenesis syndrome: An increasingly common developmental disorder with environmental aspects: Opinion. *Human Reproduction, 16*(5): 972–78.

Sleeboom-Faulkner, M. (2010a). Eugenic birth and fetal education: The friction between lineage enhancement and premarital testing among rural households in Mainland China. *China Journal*, no. 64 (July): 121–41.

———. (2010b). Reproductive technologies and the quality of offspring in Asia: Reproductive pioneering and moral pragmatism? *Culture, Health & Sexuality, 12*(2), 139–52.

Sohu News. (2011, 25 February). Sperm is affected by environment: Various kinds of pollutions make sperm quality decline. Retrieved from http://green.sohu.com/20110225/n279524333.shtml.

Song, P. (2016). Medical violence as a technology of care: Responding to the biomedicalization of death in Chinese hospitals. Paper presented at the American Anthropological Association Annual Meeting, Minneapolis, MN, November.

South China Morning Post. (2013, 11 December). Smog crisis in China leads to increased research into effect of pollution on fertility. Retrieved from http://www.scmp.com/news/china/article/1378103/china-boosts-research-effect-pollution-fertility-amid-smog-crisis.

Stafford, C. (2000). Chinese patriliny and the cycles of Yang and Laiwang. In J. Carsten, (Ed.), *Cultures of relatedness: New approaches to the study of kinship* (pp. 35–54). Cambridge: Cambridge University Press.

Steptoe, P. (1968). Laparoscopy and ovulation. (Letters to the editor). *The Lancet, 292*(7574) (26 October), 913

Sturgeon, J. C. 2010. Governing minorities and development in Xishuangbanna, China: Akha and Dai rubber farmers as entrepreneurs. *Geoforum, 41*(2): 318–28.

Sung, W. K., Brown, K.-E. & Fong, V. L. (2017). How flexible gender identities give young women advantages in China's new economy. *Gender and Education*. doi: 10.1080/09540253.2016.1274380.

Svendsen, M. N., & Koch, L. (2011). In the mood for science: A discussion of emotion management in a pharmacogenomics research encounter in Denmark. *Social Science & Medicine, 72*(5): 781–88.

Swanson, K. W. (2011). Body banks: A history of milk banks, blood banks, and sperm banks in the United States. *Enterprise & Society, 12*(4): 749–60.

———. (2012). The birth of the sperm bank. *Annals of Iowa, 71*(3): 241–76.

Taylor, K. (2005). *Chinese medicine in early Communist China, 1945–63: A medicine of revolution.* London: Routledge.

Throsby, K. (2004). *When IVF fails: Feminism, infertility, and the negotiation of normality.* Basingstoke, UK: Palgrave Macmillan.

Timmermans, S., & Almeling, R. (2009). Objectification, standardization, and commodification in health care: A conceptual readjustment. *Social Science & Medicine, 69*(1), 21–27.

Tjørnhøj-Thomsen, T. (2009). "It's a bit unmanly in a way": Men and infertility in Denmark. In M. C. Inhorn, T. Tjørnhøj-Thomsen, H. Goldberg, & M. la Cour Mosegaard (Eds.), *Reconceiving the second sex: Men, masculinity and reproduction* (pp. 226–52). Oxford: Berghahn Books.

Tsing, A., Bubandt, N. O., Gan, E. and Swanson, H. A. (2017). *Arts of living on a damaged planet: Ghosts and monsters of the Anthropocene.* Minneapolis: University of Minnesota Press.

Turnbull, D. (1989). The push for a malaria vaccine. *Social Studies of Science, 19*(2): 283–300.

UNEP & WHO. (2013). *State of the science of endocrine disrupting chemicals—2012: An assessment of the state of the science of endocrine disruptors prepared by a group of experts for the United Nations Environment Programme (UNEP) and WHO.* Geneva: WHO.

Vertommen, S. (2016). From the pergonal project to Kadimastem: A genealogy of Israel's reproductive-industrial complex. *BioSocieties, 11*(1), 1–25.

Villadsen, K., & Wahlberg, A. (2015). The government of life: Managing populations, health, and scarcity. *Economy and Society, 44*(1), 1–17.

Wahlberg. A. (2008). Reproductive medicine and the concept of "quality." *Clinical Ethics, 3*(4): 189–93.

———. (2009). Serious disease as kinds of living. In S. Bauer & A. Wahlberg (Eds.), *Contested categories: Life sciences in society* (pp. 89–112). Surrey, UK: Ashgate.

———. (2010). Assessing vitality: Infertility and good life in urban China. In J. Yorke (Ed.), *The right to life and the value of life: Orientations in law, politics, and ethics* (pp. 371–98). Surrey, UK: Ashgate.

———. (2014a). Human activity between nature and society: The negotiation of infertility in China. In K. Hastrup (Ed.), *Anthropology and nature* (pp. 184–95). London: Routledge Falmer.

———. (2014b). Herbs, laboratories, and revolution: On the making of a national medicine in Vietnam. *East Asian Science, Technology, and Society, 8*(1): 43–56.

———. (2015). Making CAM auditable: Technologies of assurance in CAM practice today. In N. Gale & J. McHale (Eds.), *Routledge handbook of complementary and alternative medicine: Perspectives from social science and law* (pp. 129–43). London: Routledge.

Wahlberg, A., & Gammeltoft, T. (Eds.) (2017). *Selective reproduction in the 21st century.* London: Palgrave Macmillan.

Wahlberg, A., Rehmann-Sutter, C., Sleeboom-Faulkner, M., Lu, G., Döring, O., Cong, Y., Laska-Formejster A., He J., Chen H., Gottweis H. & Rose, N. (2013). From global bioethics to ethical governance of biomedical research collaborations. *Social Science & Medicine, 98*: 293–300.

Wahlberg, A., & Rose, N. (2015). The governmentalization of living: Calculating global health. *Economy and Society, 44*(1), 60–90.

Waldby, C., Kerridge, I., Boulous, M., Carroll, K. (2013). From altruism to monetisation: Australian women's ideas about money, ethics and research eggs. *Social Science and Medicine 94*: 34-42.

Wang, F., & Yang, Q. (1996). Age at marriage and the first birth interval: The emerging change in sexual behavior among young couples in China. *Population and Development Review, 22*(2): 299–320.

Wang, L., Zhang, L., Song, X. H., Zhang, H. B., Xu, C. Y., & Chen, Z. J. (2016). Decline of semen quality among Chinese sperm bank donors within 7 years (2008–2014). *Asian Journal of Andrology 19*(5), 521–25.

Washington Post. (2010, 28 October). Study: BPA has effect on sperm. Retrieved from http://www.washingtonpost.com/wp-dyn/content/article/2010/10/27 /AR2010102707803.html.

WHO. (2010). *WHO laboratory manual for the examination and processing of human semen.* Geneva: WHO.

Whyte, M. (2013). Episodic fieldwork, updating, and sociability. *Social Analysis, 57*(1): 110–21.

Wu, C. (2011). Managing multiple masculinities in donor insemination: Doctors configuring infertile men and sperm donors in Taiwan. *Sociology of Health and Illness, 33*(1), 96–113.

Wu, L., Jin, L., Shi, T., Zhang, B., Zhou, Y., Zhou, T., Bao, W., Xiang, H., Zuo, Y., Li, G., & Wang, C. (2017). Association between ambient particulate matter exposure and semen quality in Wuhan, China. *Environment International, 98*, 219–28.

Xiao, S. (2008) Suffering with assisted reproduction: Clinical and ethical concerns. Paper presented to the BIONET Conference on Ethical Governance of Reproductive Technologies, Therapeutic Stem Cells, and Stem Cell Banks, Changsha, 1–3 April.

Xinhua News Agency. (1999, 24 June). China's 1st notables' sperm bank opens. Retrieved from http://www.people.com.cn/english/199906/25/chnmedia .html.

———. (2011, 14 May). Sperm bank: 95% of donors are college students. Retrieved from http://www.zgnt.net/content/2011-05/14/content_1828811.htm.

Xtata (2010, 5 June). The prevalence of male infertility in Guangzhou is increasing dramatically. Retrieved from http://gz.xtata.com/g/20100605/58536796 .shtml.

Yang, J. (2015). Informal surrogacy in China: Embodiment and biopower. *Body & Society*, *21*(1), 90–117.

Zalasiewicz, J., Williams, M., Smith, A.G., Barry, T.L., Coe, A.L., Bown, P.R., Brenchley, P., Cantrill, D., Gale, A., Gibbard, P., Gregory, F.J., Hounslow, M.W., Kerr, A.C., Pearson, P., Knox, R., Powell, J., Waters, C., Marshall, J., Oates, M., Rawson, P., & Stone, P. (2008). Are we now living in the Anthropocene? *GSA Today*, *18*(2), 4–8.

Zalasiewicz, J., Williams, M. Steffen, W., & Crutzne, P. (2010). The new world of the Anthropocene. *Environmental Science and Technology*, *44*, 2228–31.

Zeng, Y., & Hesketh, T. (2016). The effects of China's universal two-child policy. *The Lancet*, *388*(10054), 1930–38.

Zhang, C. (2016, 30 August). Chinese women head overseas to freeze their eggs. *New York Times*. Retrieved from https://www.nytimes.com/2016/08/31 /world/asia/china-us-women-fertility.html.

Zhang, E. (2007). The birth of nanke (men's medicine) in China: The making of the subject of desire. *American Ethnologist*, *34* (3), 491–508.

———. (2011) Introduction: Governmentality in China. In Zhang, E., Kleinman, A., and Tu, W. (Eds.). *Governance of life in Chinese moral experience: The quest for an adequate life* (pp. 1–24). New York: Routledge.

———. (2015). *The impotence epidemic: Men's medicine and sexual desire in contemporary China*. Durham, NC: Duke University Press.

Zhang, E., Kleinman, A., and Tu, W. (Eds.) (2011). *Governance of life in Chinese moral experience: The quest for an adequate life*. New York: Routledge.

Zhang, S.C., Wang, H.Y., & Wang, J.D. (1999). Analysis of change in sperm quality of Chinese fertile men during 1981–1996 [in Chinese]. *Reproduction & Contraception*, *10*: 33–39.

Zhao, Z. (2008, 29 July). Experts say: serious sperm problem, in 60 years, 62% decline. *Global Times—Life Times*. Retrieved from http://health.sohu .com/20080729/n258448484.shtml.

Zhou, X., & Hou, L. (1999). Children of the Cultural Revolution: The state and the life course in the People's Republic of China. *American Sociological Review*, *64*(1): 12–36.

Zhu, J. (2013). Projecting potentiality: Understanding maternal serum screening in contemporary China. *Current Anthropology*, *54*(S7): S36–44.

Zigon, J. (2015). What is a situation?: An assemblic ethnography of the drug war. *Cultural Anthropology*, *30*(3), 501–24.

INTERVIEWS

Zhang, L. (2008, February 25). Interview 1: Interview with Professor Zhang Lizhu: 20th anniversary of China's first test tube baby. China Obgyn.net. Retrieved from http://www.china-obgyn.net/news/0008342344.html.
———. (2009, September 15). Interview 2: Zhang Lizhu: Creating new life.) Chinese Association of Science and Technology website Retrieved from http://zt.cast.org.cn/n435777/n435799/n1130428/n1131288/11834696.html.
———. (2009, 12 October). Interview 3: Great love is boundless—Child-granting Guanyin. Tencent News Channel interview. Retrieved from http://news.qq .com/a/20091012/000671.htm.
———. (2011, 26 August). Interview 4: Zhang Lizhu: Reproductive medical science expert from Peking Medical College Third Hospital. *Fendou*, CCTV. Retrieved from www.cctvfendou.com/html/shilu_20130113_1588.html..

LAWS AND REGULATIONS

Hunan Province. (1989). Family Planning Regulations in Hunan Province. Issued at the twelfth meeting of the Seventh People's Congress Standing Committee of Hunan Province on December 3.
———. (1999). Hunan Province Family Planning Regulations (Amended). Issued by the Standing Committee of Hunan Province on August 3.
Ministry of Health (MoH). (2003a). Regulation on Assisted Reproductive Technology. Issued and Revised by Ministry of Health, P. R. China, July.
———. (2003b). Ethical Principles for Human Assisted Reproductive Technology and Sperm Banks. Issued and revised by the Ministry of Health, People's Republic of China, July.
———. (2003c). The Basic Requirements and Technical Specifications of Human Sperm Banks. Issued by the Ministry of Health, People's Republic of China, July.
P. R. China. (1994). Law on Maternal and Infant Health Care. Issued by the 10th Meeting of the Standing Committee of the Eighth National People's Congress. 27 October.
———. (2001). Marriage Law. 1980 law amended according to the Decision on Amending the Marriage Law of the People's Republic of China made at the 21st Meeting of the Standing Committee of the Ninth National People's Congress, 28 April.

Index